KITCHEN
guide to
Brews and Potions

PATRICIA TELESCO

New Page Books
A division of The Career Press, Inc.
Franklin Lakes, NJ

Copyright© 2005 by Patricia Telesco

All rights reserved under the Pan-American and International Copyright Conventions. This book may not be reproduced, in whole or in part, in any form or by any means electronic or mechanical, including photocopying, recording, or by any information storage and retrieval system now known or hereafter invented, without written permission from the publisher, The Career Press.

KITCHEN WITCH'S GUIDE TO BREWS AND POTIONS

EDITED BY GINA TALUCCI

TYPESET BY KATE HENCHES

Cover Design by Cheryl Cohan Finbow
Cover Illustration by Fiona Preston
Interior Illustrations by Colleen Koziara
Printed in the U.S.A. by Book-mart Press

To order this title, please call toll-free 1-800-CAREER-1 (NJ and Canada: 201-848-0310) to order using VISA or MasterCard, or for further information on books from Career Press.

The Career Press, Inc., 3 Tice Road, PO Box 687,
Franklin Lakes, NJ 07417
www.careerpress.com
www.newpagebooks.com

Library of Congress Cataloging-in-Publication Data
Telesco, Patricia, 1960-
Kitchen witch's guide to brews and potions / by Patricia Telesco.
    p. cm.
Includes bibliographical references and index.
ISBN 1-56414-790-8 (pbk.)
    1. Witchcraft. 2. Beverages—Miscellanea. 3. Brewing—Miscellanea. I. Title.
BF1572.R4T44 2005
133.4'3--dc22

                                    2005049136

Contents

Introduction

"I rejoice with the land, when it rains, and all that dwells drinks from one common cup of sky."

—Marian Singer

In magick, the cup is a symbol of the Goddess, that ever-fruitful fountain from which the nectars of originality, wisdom, and blessings flow. Like the Horn of Plenty or Cauldron of Cerridwen, there is always enough of this vibrant liquid to quench the driest of spirits. This wellspring metes out to each of us exactly what we need: one person gets a chalice of compassion, another goblet of gladness, another still, a tumbler of tolerance.

Upon altars across the world, cups adorn holy places. Sometimes this tool holds water, sometimes wine. Be it a Shaman's bowl or a Catholic's communion chalice, their presence is a strong reminder that beverages are a significant part of many religious traditions.

This book comes to you with that heritage in mind, offering options for an assortment of enchanted drinkables. Some are presented for health, some to help celebrate the Wheel of the Year, some to encourage specific positive attributes, and others, for simple pleasure. All of these have immense potential from a magickal perspective to enrich your life.

Beyond the recipes presented herein, I have included several chapters on the history of refreshments, specifically those used for worship, medicine, and magick. Beverages played a key role in each of these areas, one application frequently overlapping another. For example, a medieval monk may have prepared angelica tea to help a sickly patient. His reason for doing so was probably the folklore that said angels gifted humanity with angelica specifically for this purpose.

These types of narratives contribute to an appreciation of the possible metaphysical applications for beverages. In the aforementioned illustration, angelica wine or tea can be used in rituals for overall well-being. Additionally, when wishing for better understanding of or communion with guardian spirits, either choice would be an excellent addition to your altar. In both cases, history provided an informed foundation from which to build your magickal construct.

I find brewing to be a tremendously satisfying activity. It has become a household tradition to share samples of homemade wines with my guests. We also make special mixtures for holiday gift-giving much as other people bake cookies! This activity developed into a family hobby in which everyone participates by adding an ingredient, taste-testing, and weaving in their magick.

Similarly, brewing can give your imagination and creativity another outlet to explore, and an alternative means to express your Path. Each new creation presents an opportunity to stir in a spell to meet prevalent needs. By adding elements of ceremony to your preparation process, these beverages become part of the same Divine source that permeates New Age ideals.

Let's take the example of apple mead. This beverage finds its roots growing in ancient Rome, where it surfaced in everything from celebrations to healing wounded soldiers. So, magickally speaking, mead symbolizes joy and health. To these ends, you would stir clockwise around the brew pot while chanting, "Health to me, joy be free!" Apples are also tokens of beauty and wisdom, giving you an alternative focus. Additionally, apples are a large part of harvest festivals such as Halloween, making mead a perfect addition to any fall table.

The greatest beauty of beverage creation is that its magick doesn't have to be complicated. Even the simplest drinks have spiritual implications hidden in their folklore, myths, and correspondences. Water is a perfect example.

Magickally, water is an emblem of purification, healing, insight, and the lunar nature. Because of its primordial importance to humankind, there are a myriad of Divine figures dedicated to spring and fresh water. Included in this list are Ahurani, the Persian Water goddess and Baldur, the Norse god of wells. Either of these visages could be called upon to bless your drink, or another of your own choosing (see Appendix B).

Putting this illustrative information together takes only a little resourcefulness. For example, to create a drink that will improve spiritual perception, invoke Luned (from Arthurian traditions) to sanctify the water. Visualize bright, inspirational light filling the cup. Finally, sip the water to internalize the magick.

Another good illustration is fruit juice. Nearly all fruits have positive correlations with love, joy, or health (if not all three). So, the next time you need an emotional lift, visualize bright blue light (the color of peace or happiness) filling your juice before you drink it. For romance, create a distinctive love potion for yourself and your mate with specially chosen fruit juices as a base. Here, strawberry and passion fruit are good choices (see Appendix A).

Alcoholic beverages, especially wine, present a different set of variables to consider. In magick, for awareness, consuming too much alcohol would induce the opposite desired result. On the other hand, wine is important to religious ceremonies, especially those concerning transmutation (Catholicism) and libation (Pagan/Wiccan). Positive kitchen witchery discovers the balance necessary to make these diverse factors work together harmoniously.

Wine has been an appropriate and a proper presentation to Gods and Goddesses (see Chapter 2). This puts the art of brewing into a slightly different and Divinely inspired light. Various orders of monks, including those at Notre Dame and St. Gall, created and tended the most widely acclaimed liquors, beers, and wines. It was as if the preparation of sacred drinks could not be left to the hands of commoners. Instead, the trust lay with holy people who used their knowledge to improve their orders' finances.

Part of New Age ideology is the belief that everyone has a Divine vocation, not just select individuals. This is something we can all discover through a diversity of mediums, techniques, and paths. Thus, I tender these recipes as a sensitive and enjoyable exploration of beverages as a potential medium for magick.

Some portions of the metaphysical and New Age community do not approve of any use of alcohol. Nonetheless, the history of beverages indicates that spirituous drinks can assume an honored place in our rituals, should we desire. To truly honor something means that it is not abused, but added as appropriate to the occasion.

Just as with magickal cooking (see *Kitchen Witch's Cookbook*), preparing metaphysically enhanced beverages for yourself or a group should be a well-considered endeavor. Ask yourself simple questions such as: Are your guests driving? Are any members of your circle allergic to alcohol or pregnant? Are any A.A. members going to be present? If any of the answers are yes, then having well-marked alternatives to alcoholic libations is a thoughtful courtesy you can extend.

This book offers options and variations to personalize each recipe to reflect your needs, or those of family and guests. History is one part of this picture, providing cultural richness and a variety of traditions to accentuate your Path and spiritual goals. The remainder of the portrait comes from your own capable hands and creative spirit.

The Appendices list possible brewing Gods and Goddesses and include an inventory of additives and ingredients with their magickal correspondences. Additionally there is a glossary of terms, mail order suppliers, and folklore examples that can furnish ideas for, or themes in, your brewing efforts. Also, blank, lined pages appear at the back of the book for personal notes, successful variations, and recipes, keeping all your treasures neatly in one place.

By making our own ritual brews, we partake in an honored heritage. Whether for an offering, libation, or pure enjoyment, let's begin reclaiming this legacy! Blend your talent with innovation, vision, love, and discretion to make tasty, magickal blessings for yourself, friends, family, and visitors. Stir up your Witch's brew today!

* In no instance are any ingredients to be used as a substitute for proper modern medical attention. Additionally, readers are encouraged to check the correct genus, species, and parts of all flowers used in brewing as some species and parts are toxic (while others are not).

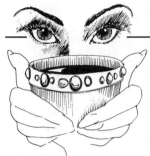

Part I

Myths, Magick, and Religion

"The thirsty earth soaks up the rain and drinks, and gapes for drink again the plants suck in the earth and are with constant drinking lush and fair.
Fill all the glasses then, for why should every creature drink, but I?"

—Abraham Cowley

Chapter 1

Brewing in History and Religion

"As he brews, so shall he drink."
—Ben Johnson

To understand the place of beverages in human affairs better, first roll back the pages of time—past the advent of pasteurization, before chlorinated water, even before indoor plumbing! In those days, fermented drinks could be found in almost any home. Throughout ancient civilization, fermented or boiled beverages afforded one means of thwarting the plague, consumption, and many other communicable diseases. People believed in the healthful nature of these drinks, extolling some as having life-prolonging attributes. During centuries when many children did not live to see their first birthdays, such a wonder was worth trying. This is also the main reason why contemporary children in Europe are familiar with wine as part of the dining ritual. It, along with beer, became regarded as a necessary part of the food groups.

Today, we do not have to look far to observe other remnants of these and similar practices. There is the traditional toast at weddings or honorary gatherings. When people come to our homes, we offer coffee, tea, or wine by way of hospitality. We still call items with an alcoholic content "spirits," a designation that comes from when we still believed that a plant's inherent energies went into the final product (and so one could become possessed of it). Champagne bottles christen boats, and, in some rural settings, folks still brew by the waxing of the full moon to insure the success of their endeavors. Truth be told, you can find such a person in these pages!

As you read, you'll quickly see how the history of beverages isn't easily separated from religion, because many of the first brewers were clergy. This implies a certain sacredness about beverages that's well worth pondering in terms of how to apply this concept in our own sacred spaces by way of libations, asperging, and cups upon our altars.

History

There is some type of magickal mystique to fermented beverages that is powerful and effecting. So much so that it was sometimes hard to distinguish exactly what type of beverage certain ancient writers were speaking about. For continuity and clarity's sake, I will consistently use the term *beer* in the remainder of this book for those drinks whose major alcohol content is formed by grain, *wines* by fruits and sugar, and *meads* by honey. *Melomel* is mead with fruit flavoring and *metheglin* is a mead with herb flavoring to which "spirits" may or may not be added. So, let's take a little closer look at the chronicles that built the reputations of these bewitching beverages.

Beer

"The hoary sage replied, 'come my lad and drink some beer.'"

—Samuel Johnson

Somewhere in the Euphrates Valley a Sumerian farmer, peasant, or, perhaps, a cook, stumbled on the notion of soaking barley in water, and grinding those grains into flour for bread. Eventually this led to using bread as an agent for brewing. When floated in another substance, bread unwittingly provided yeast for fermentation.

Exactly how this application came about is a mystery. One possibility is that dry journey cakes soaked in water for consumption were neglected for some reason. When their owner discovered the error later, he noticed small bubbles in the liquid and an aroma that did not indicate souring. Once tasted, the world would never be the same.

History accounts for brewing techniques as far back as 6000 B.C., but this date is ambiguous at best. Even at this early juncture, farmers dedicated about 30 to 40 percent of harvested grain crops in Babylon and Egypt to brewing efforts. This leads to the supposition that beer is far older than expected. Beer may be close to 10,000 years old, with beer-like substances appearing in China around the 23rd century B.C.

When Egyptians discovered beer, they attributed the success of the drink to Osiris, and offered him libations of the same at many festivals (see Chapter 2). By 2300 B.C., cuneiform writing and Theban tomb depictions demonstrate a diversity of beers being circulated in the Southern Egyptian region, including light and dark classes. There were also those set aside for ritual use.

During this era and several that followed, beer was not as refined as that which we now enjoy. It tended to be thicker, had remnants of the brewing process at the bottom of the cup, and a questionable flavor. Hops was but one source of flavoring until about 8 A.D., except in the region of Bavaria. As the preferred source of taste, Hops did not catch on until around 1400. This did not lessen the popularity of beer in the least though, as an English book of lists from the 1100s shows at least 40 breweries. Not surprisingly, this was also the period when King Henry II taxed Ale for the first time.

By the time we move from ancient civilization to Medieval Europe brewing and malting became an art, frequently practiced by at least one member of every good sized household. This group was predominantly female, known by the semiofficial title of Malster or Brewster. And when the settlers went to Plymouth, they didn't leave their beer behind. The Pilgrims regarded beer as a Divine, wholesome blessing that held a place of honor alongside bread.

By the late 1800s there were thousands of small brewing companies established in the United States. This number slowly diminished as the public decided what they liked best. By 1930, a few regional brewers began considering the dilemma of national distribution. Low calorie beers appeared during WWII, and resurfaced around 1960 with growing awareness of health and physical fitness. Today, imported beers and microbrews are most popular in the United States, offering a variety of tastes and colors to the American consumer.

Wine

> "Wile wine and friendship crown the
> board, we'll sing the joys they both afford."
> —John Dryer

Grapes were discovered around 3000 B.C. in the region now known as Russia. The Bible, Edda, Memorial tablets from Ramses IV (1166 B.C.), and Euripides all speak of various uses for wine, among other notable texts. Thus, we can safely conclude that wine is nearly as old as beer.

In its earliest stages, only the wealthy enjoyed wine. Its preparation was long, arduous, and costly. First it was pressed carefully by foot, poured into jugs, and then stopped up with leaves and mud. The remaining residue created poorer qualities of wine for the commoners. Because of this prevalent tendency toward social elitism, one contemporary symbolism for wine in magick could be prosperity.

Egyptians had a special panache for wine making, equal only to their adoration of this substance. They believed that the goddess Isis gave the knowledge for brewing to humankind as a representation of deeper life principles. In this region the favorite ingredients for wine included dates, pomegranates, and palm sap. If tasty, the resulting drink was given to kings with pride or placed before altars to implore God's blessings. For anyone who has Isis as a patron goddess, wine is a perfect offering.

In Greece, wine became a major source of income and eventual wealth. Like the Egyptians, the Greek brewers had a Divine inspiration in Dionysus. As the story goes, when being held captive on a ship, with true flamboyance, Dionysus tossed his prized goblet into the sea. This turned the water into wine. It gives us pause to wonder if early Biblical writers drew from this story for a type of Christ.

Of all cultures and peoples, however, France made the greatest impact on the history of wine making. The Rhine Valley proved a rich harvesting ground for grapes of fine quality. Following suit, the wines of France quickly gained acclaim throughout the Roman Empire. Thousands of casks moved down river on barges to merchants, who, in turn, carried the beverage to eager consumers.

The Celts had a passion for beer and wine along with accompanying bawdy festivals. Of all the drinkers in history, the Celts are remembered for their appetite for the "vine," and consumption to drunkenness. When visiting Scotland, I heard more than one story where a robust party erupted into battle, the alcohol acting on the warrior clans like fire in a potbellied stove! There was another, less violent, side to Celtic drinking traditions, though. Clan ties, and the larger ties to the entire Celtic community, were a serious matter. Here, wine was mostly for nobility, consumed from a communal cup to show mutual trust and kinship.

Apples and grapes became the main ingredients for most early wines. Slowly, as people refined their techniques, other fruits started appearing. Of these, berries were most popular because of their profuseness. Citrus was not widely used in Europe because of prohibitive import costs. Instead, brewers added small portions of rind for light flavoring. As we now know, citric acid also aids the fermenting process. Additionally, fresh herbs, such as ginger root, seasoned the wine, introducing tannin, which yields smoother, well-balanced aromatic beverages.

Mead, Melomel, and Metheglin

"I, in these flowery meads would be; these
crystal springs should solace me."

—Thomas Carew

Mead was a honey wine popular in Europe, Africa, Central America, and Australia. In the Middle Ages, it warranted a special drinking vessel known as the Mather Cup. This vessel, which had several handles and a squared off top, exclusively held this fermented honey nectar.

Wines or beers flavored with honey owe at least part of their beginnings to Rome, where a fermented honey water called *mulsum* was used as a dessert. Two alternatives to this were concoctions flavored with myrtle berry (*myritis*) or fruit juices (*melomel*). Romans loved using honey as a base for medicinal liquors and just about anything else they could think of.

The great Greek healer Hippocrates also employed honey in his prescriptions, especially those pertaining to colds and wounds. This led to broader acceptance of honey drinks in Greece, the closest to mead being called hydromel. Like the Romans, Greeks varied this base by adding rose petals (*omphacomel*) and even wine and cheese (*kykeon*). The latter was a ritual beverage exclusively used during harvest festivals.

About the only difference between a mead and melomel is the addition of fruit (or fruit juice) to the base. From here, the next logical step for early brewers was adding other flavorings from their own pantries. This practice developed into the beverage known as metheglin, being lauded by Sir Kenelm Digby (fourteenth century culinary writer) as one of the best, all-purpose tonics. Metheglin is from two Welsh words *meddyg* and *llyn*, meaning medicinal liquor. It is a heavily spiced mead favored by the people of Wales and Northern climes. When sugar became popular, this drink was called "hippocras" or more simply, "spiced wine."

Distilled Drinks

> *"Brandy must be a decoction of hearts*
> *and tongues, because after drinking it I*
> *fear nothing and I talk wonderfully."*
> —James G. Frazer, *The Golden Bough*

Many countries and individuals try to credit themselves with inventing distillation. We know that Aristotle discussed distillation of water to make it drinkable, and that Pliny the Elder discusses flammable wine, but even this is inconclusive to prove a specific origin for distillation. As an alternative, we could try looking to China, where brewers took to freezing instead of boiling. This led to the development of certain rice liquors as observed by Marco Polo. In 800 A.D., a mixture similar to those he described traveled through Japan (*Sake*) to the Mediterranean where Arab alchemists employed their traditional approaches to try and recreate similar beverages.

Arabs distilled herbs and flowers for perfume and cosmetics. One powder used in makeup was Al-Kohl. This was actually a byproduct of distillation to which we owe the modern word *alcohol*. So it was that an Arab writer, living in Spain, described the distillation of wine around the 10th century. Even so, the technique itself did not make a strong appearance on the European continent until around 1100 A.D. in Italy.

By the 16th century, whiskey, gin, vodka, and rum were available. They quickly became the base for other drinkables, vodka (which originated in Poland) being most popular because of its neutral taste. Come the 18th century, merchants throughout Europe distributed a wide assortment of flavored liqueurs.

In reviewing the restaurant menus of France from that period, I discerned the following selections from an astonishingly intricate list: A Grand Chartreuse, a "fine" Orange, Absinthe, a ginger flavored drink, Cacao with Vanilla, Brandy, Armagnac, and Rose. Among them, the recipe for Chartreuse, which incorporates 130 plants and herbs, was still a secret to all but three friars at a time!

In a contemporary setting, distilled beverages, in small amounts, have the unique advantage of being flammable (if used with care). Thus, they can act as an alternative symbol of the Fire Element on our altars.

Drinking Vessels

> *"Sparkling and bright in liquid light, does*
> *the wine our goblets gleam in!"*
> —Charles Fenno Hoffman

Just as eating off fine china makes a meal more sumptuous, people of early civilizations appreciated both the vessels and containers that held wines, meads, and beers. Egyptian tomb paintings from 1600 B.C. depict silver and gold drinking bowls. In Genesis 44:2, we even find Joseph requesting that his servant pack a special drinking bowl for a journey.

Besides the human hand, a seashell, or gourds, one of the first drinking vessels used for imbibing was animal horn. Some with traces of silver etchings surfaced in Greece, dating 2000 B.C. (pre Minoan). At first the horns were simply cleaned, soaked with water several times, and then soaked again with alcohol. Later, crafts people decorated them with precious metals or emblematic carvings. The only problem with the drinking horn, until a clever artisan came up with a stand, was that it had to be emptied before setting it down!

Bowls were another frequently employed drinking tool, having a broader range of application in Asia and Africa. At first made of wood or metal, later ones could be found encrusted with gems or precious metals. These bowls received the title of *mazer* in some areas, which in Old English refers to maple wood. This is the chief timber product used in bowl construction on the European continent.

Bowls sometimes got placed on small stands, giving yet another astute artisan something to think about in the development of the goblet or chalice. Every culture had unique ways of forming a goblet to personal tastes. Normans preferred round-bottomed cups, and the Gothic motif had feet and toes below conical cups rather like their gargoyles. In Tudor England, they sculpted six-part flowing bases balanced with hemispheric bowls. Of the lot, the Scandinavians were probably the most stubborn crew, preferring silver tankards to goblets right up until the 1700s.

Religion

> *"We've quaffed the Soma bright*
> *and are immortal grown;*
> *we've entered into light*
> *and all the Gods have known."*
>
> —Rig-Veda

> *"There is naught, no doubt, so much the*
> *spirit calms as rum and true religion."*
>
> —Lord Byron

Alongside scholarly, political, or personal pursuits, people offered bountiful quantities of beverages publicly as the perfect gift of nature. Anything admired by commoners and kings alike will eventually find its way into religious lore, observances and ritual. The question remains, why? What inspired such reverence?

One interesting angle on this query comes from the Native American traditions. Here, when a person fashions something, a little part of their spirit (essence) enters that creation. So, if one makes wine and drinks it, are we then drinking of our own inherent Divine power? It is worth considering, especially in a ritualized setting. In any case it's but one possibility. To discover the roots of our own religious drinking traditions, we first have to explore the archaic uses and their meanings in diverse settings.

For example, Egyptian tombs reveal that portions of food, drink, money, and even beloved pets were placed in tombs to help the spirit exist happily in his or her new reality. This was based on the belief that if the human spirit could not die, then the living should supply it with the things of enjoyment—among them of course, wine! Mind you, good heartedness was not the only motivation for these gifts. People also believed that offerings kept an angry or restless spirit from wandering about.

Offerings

> *"In the days of festivals of the Gods, who*
> *gave men wine for Their banquets?"*
>
> —Plato

We have already seen that the ancients started a long tradition of leaving offerings before the Gods. The earliest offerings were very simple ones: water as a life-giving force, and milk, the juice of motherhood, accompanied first fruits, grains, and sometimes livestock. As the rudimentary knowledge for making beer and wine spread, these beverages became popular for sacrifice.

Whether in thankfulness, to plead for aid, as part of ritual, or as a remembrance, wine in particular filled special vessels upon the altars of Gods and Goddesses including Gestin of Sumeria, Pagat of Ugarit, Ishtar of Mesopotamia, Horus of Egypt, Poseidon of Greece, and Liber of Rome. The Hebrews had two offerings that included liquid libation. The first was a monthly donation to God that included bread, a ram, seven lambs, and two bullocks along with a beverage. The other was strictly an offering of drink, usually meaning wine.

Germans called those who brewed beer for Pagan offerings *Dasture* until Christianity became more prevalent. The Dasture office was sacred, and always chosen on New Years Day. The holder of this office received a few aids to cut firewood and tend to other chores so the Dasture could be fully mindful of his or her duties. One brew of the Dasture, created solely for offerings, was a mead called Sinnreger. This roughly translates as meaning "kettle stirrer" because of its invigorating effect. Priests offered *Sinnreger* to the Gods of the Sacred Grove then shared it among celebrants during festivals such as Winter Solstice.

Central Asian and Sanskrit writings record the oldest forms of beverage offerings. Here we learn of the Soma, a mountain plant that devout Hindus gathered by moonlight in a sacred area. Priests or faithful followers of Indra crushed Soma using stones to extract juice, then kept it to ferment for future offerings.

Soma was usually placed on rustic altars made from turf, stones, and kindling. Aryans threw it into the fires by the ladle full and distributed it among the priests. So powerful was the acclaim of this beverage that the Rig Veda claimed it as a "master of a thousand songs" and "leader of sages." It even gave power to the Gods. In later years, Soma shared during any gathering became the symbol of devout friendship.

Another intoxicant read about in Sanskrit is Sura. This is millet, water, curds, butter, and barley fermented together. Sura was as popular as Soma, but gained some negative implications because of its potency. From this, it is but one short step to the Persian sacred drink known as *haomas*. White haomas was the drink of immortality, given by Ormuzd. Accordingly, priests presented haomas to Ormuzd alongside meat and holy water.

Chinese sacred writings from 3,000 to 4,000 years ago, known as the Shoo King and the Shi King, intricately describe the spirituous offerings of these people. The priests of the region only made sacred beverages when heaven bid them to, and then it was only consumed on sacrificial days. Stern warnings about the dangers of abusing Divine gifts accompanied the creation of, and partaking in, such drinks.

Tablets from the time of Ramses III in Egypt indicate that similar practices occurred there as well. "Proper" offerings were so abundant that wine flowed through the Nile. In fact, at one point, the populace acclaimed the House of Ramses for its generous contributions to the temples. By the end of his reign these offerings totaled more than 500 oxen, 5 million sacks of corn, 6 million loaves of bread, 250,000 jugs of wine, and 460,000 gallons of beer.

Finally, in Alexandria there was the curious custom of placing a glass of honeyed wine on the table on the last day of the month, as an offering and devotional to the Goddess (probably Isis). This is a lovely and subtle offering, which I see no reason not to "borrow." It reminds me a bit of the Old Testament custom of leaving one seat at the table open for the prophet. Small gestures such as these let the Divine powers know that we remember them, and welcome them in our sacred space of home.

Legends, Lore, Customs, and Tales

"If ancient tales say true, nor wrong these holy men."

—Lord Byron

It is difficult to separate the legends of beverages from actual application in a religious or cultural setting. This occurs because the stories themselves were often the basis for analogous liturgical or domestic actions. Thankfully, there are surviving allegorical tales that help us understand early civilization's indigenous and ritual employment of drinkables with greater clarity. These same stories provide marvelous symbols and ideas to adapt into the contemporary magickal settings.

We begin with Norse peoples who claim that before entering Valhalla one must first consume all the beer, wine, and so on, spilled in this life. This belief acts as a gentle chastisement towards care with such precious liquids, and a reminder to offer all spilled beverages to the gods. For those passing this vigorous test, there is a feasting hall prepared.

Spirits pass a special drinking horn at their welcoming banquet, filled with mead from the base of the Yggdrasil tree. This insures the horn will never run dry. Additionally the mead heals any wound sustained in life. Happy Norsemen share Divine liquids here (specifically ale) while keeping company with Odin and Frigg as they pass their time in the netherworld.

We also can turn our Norse books to another page and read of Bragi. Bragi was the son of Odin, and a god of muse. In his keeping was the mead of poets, captured from the giants. This mead granted ardor to any who could snitch a sip. As such, Bragi becomes a good choice to call on for Divine aid in brewing efforts. Alternatively, we read of Oegir whose sacred duty was to tend beer production in Asgard. At every harvest festival (most likely Lammas), it was the duty of the Gods to drink with Oegir in memory of his service. So, a small offering to Oegir from your first batch of wine should encourage continued success!

Another good story comes from Euripides. In *Bacchae*, Euripides writes of Dionysus saying, "he, born a God, is poured out in libations to the Gods." In other words, the God and the substance were one in the same. Each time the Greeks poured wine, Dionysus was there sharing

Divine energy. Thus, when the Gods drank of this beverage, they could almost incestuously reclaim part of their own power; when humans enjoyed it, Dionysus was there encouraging revelry! Therefore, if you follow a Greek-style magickal path use wine as a libation for your Gods.

The knowledge of Dionysus, coupled with the writings of Aristotle (circa 300 B.C.) in the *Book of Drunkenness*, makes it apparent that Greeks preferred wine over beer both personally and religiously. Romans of high birth shared the Greek distaste for beer, probably considering it a drink for barbarians and peasants. Yet despite themselves, the Latin term for beer (*Cerevisia*) may owe its origins to the Roman Goddess of agriculture, Ceres. Literally translated in this context, the word *Cerevisia* could mean "strength (or life) of Ceres." While some Roman philosophers would groan at the connection, this definition makes beer a marvelous beverage to choose for any altar honoring Ceres.

In China, ancestor worship played a key role in the way people utilized alcoholic beverages. Folk legends of this culture taught that when one leaves fermented beverages for the deceased, the ancestors partake of it, and are made happy by the drink. For the Chinese, this was a way of blessing their family, even in the hereafter.

Moving from China to Hindu lands, an Indic legend claims that Indra drank Soma from three mighty bowls to absorb life-giving essence (considered lunar and feminine in nature). Most powerful in this state, Indra continues to receive Soma at any celebration honoring him. In this instance, the extraction of Soma became a ritual, taking place in stages at morning, noon, and night. This procedure magickally improved potency for both the worshiper and the gods.

The Persians honored their version of Soma (see page 23) in a very special way. The spirit of anger (Aeshma) attended most spirituous beverages in this region, or other malignant spirits. Haomas, however, was protected by, and filled with, the Goddess Ashi who presides over fortune and wealth. Thus, this drink provided victory in battle, and the golden version of haomas nurtured one's soul.

Persians regarded another drink called *Banga* saturated with Aeshma until Zoroaster (the founder of the Magi) came on the scene. As the leader of a religious sect, Zoroaster elevated Banga to a Divine level. He claimed it transported the drinker to a heavenly plain. This may very well have been true, since the primary ingredient of Banga was hemp seed that produced hallucinations! The resulting astral visions inspired Zoroaster. So, he taught the value of Banga to his priests, thus rewriting Banga's negative reputation for all history to see.

Egyptian myths recount a wonderful story about Ra, who called upon Hathor, to destroy the human race when he wearied of them. At one point he reconsidered his hasty judgment. Hathor, however, was not easily dissuaded. To soften her heart, he made 7,000 jugs of beer and poured them on the fields. When Hathor reached those regions, instead of people she found her reflection glimmering off the brew.

Hathor drank of the beverage, was satisfied and calmed. Ra's quick thinking saved humankind. Thus, the modern magician might choose beer to asperge a Circle in any ritual for protection. Beer also makes a good spell component for astute decisions, safety, and calming anger. Finally, it would be suitable in a cup to venerate Ra and Hathor upon the altar.

No matter the land or legend, however, one truth comes through clearly in all my research. Most early peoples considered intoxicants as a wonderful boon from heaven; a birth right, if you will. This gift allowed humankind to see or experience the Divine being more clearly. As such, they became part of religious mysteries, remnants of which we still see today.

The liquid was not evil, except when human weakness misused the treasure. Should this happen, be you peasant or king, fables warn that you will certainly feel the full wrath of the gods. I'm sure anyone who has ever had a bad hangover vehemently agrees with this bit of folk wisdom!

Other Applications

> *"There is at the surface, infinite variety of things; at the center there is simplicity of unity, of cause."*
> —Ralph Waldo Emerson

Experience and inspiration though a material boost was not unknown to the religious realms. The ancients believed that the body and mind, in communion with Divine power, could act as a beautiful expression of that power. To help them achieve this state, they looked toward substances that already contained part of that Great Spirit, or a demi-Spirit all their own. By quaffing the intoxicant, people symbolically took a Godly aspect into themselves. In other words, they allowed it to possess them.

One good illustration is from ancient Greece and Rome, where Sibyls often prophesied in a state of frenzy, sometimes aided by alcohol. Of these, the prophetesses in Cumae (lower Italy) and Erythrea (Ionia) were most celebrated. The idea was to achieve an altered awareness where possession by Apollo could occur. It is interesting to note that our modern word *enthusiasm*, meaning intense, rapturous feelings, takes its origins from Greece. *En-theos* literally means united with God.

Another group of cunning women from ancient Peru used a drink called *Chica* mixed with herbs to help them obtain a suitable state of mind to answer questions. While I doubt the contemporary magician would desire intoxication for divinatory attempts, the symbolism still has its uses. For example, have a glass of wine nearby to anoint divination tools. Alternatively, trace protective symbols with wine on your fingertips in place of an athame or wand.

Beyond their use for religious inspiration, certain beverages of notable reputation also improved trade, marketing, and even motivated some explorations. We know this partially due to linguistical links between cultures shown by a word such as wine:

> Gwin: Welsh
> Fin: Irish
> Foinos: Greek
> Vinum: Latin
> Vin: French

Another confirmation comes from the Chinese philosophers and priests. These men faithfully sent out ships searching for the elixir of immortality known as *Tze Mai*. While sailors investigated age-old stories recounted by sacred texts (and made maps), the alchemists at home tried to discover the elusive formula. In the process, the Chinese enjoyed advancement in the areas of medicine, science, and geography...oh, yes, and brewing, too!

Comparable events occurred in Babylon where caravans transported plum and date wines to neighboring lands. These items fetched a handsome price in cash, barter, or trade. Cities under the control of Alexander were favorite spots to stop and sell, increasing the coffers of Babylon and clever merchants.

As they, the Chinese, and other peoples, traveled the fame of certain beverages and their Divine origins spread. These hearty souls transported an assortment of folklore, recipes, customs, and religions from their respective cultures to each region visited. This exchange helped to broaden the vision of the "known world" to the common populace. It also provided increased knowledge and proficiency in a variety of arts and sciences, some techniques of which remain with us today.

Let's move out of the ancient realms for a moment now, and into the Middle Ages. In the castle of a king or lord, beverages pleased both guests and nobles. At any gathering, the king must have the best libations available as he gained his position through "Divine right." The nobles and lords also received better wines than the remaining company. So, in this setting, the ruling authority accepted "offerings" in lieu of the gods.

From this point forward, brewing practices in religion and the social realms intermixed, then slowly separated again. Wine and beer was far more available, and more people made it themselves. Popularization and growing understanding of brewing processes displaced much of the attractive mystery surrounding alcohol. The country villager might periodically offer wine to the land, the well, or to the gods in thankfulness. The church maintained communion. Even so, most people lost sight of brewing as a religious expression, its origins, and importance through their history.

Today

> "And the vine said unto them, should I
> leave my vine which cheereth both God
> and man?"
>
> —Judges 9:12

A little of the romantic beauty has gone out of many practices today. Science has given us so much that old mysteries are now commonplace knowledge. How can we reclaim the wonderment and appreciation for things that we can buy readily almost anywhere?

Thankfully, in some homes and countries people cherish their traditions. In Japan, for example, tea and Saki are still venerable drinks, carrying with them many customs that defy understanding by Western minds. Voodoo sects use rum in certain rituals, and followers of Hawaiian Huna employ gin for some spells.

In China, rice wine continues to appear at harvest festivals where everyone raises pledge cups to the ancestors in thankfulness. This action symbolizes unity. Similar actions, by way of a toast, can be seen in modern marriage ceremonies. Additionally, communion continues to be taken by Christians. But what of the remainder? What of the gods?

Neo-Pagans and Wiccans have an opportunity to revitalize the ancient reverence for beverages as a Divine gift. Consider while we serve cakes and wines at our rituals, are we truly aware of their significance to us? If a lack of knowledge is the problem, we need to return to square one: learning. With history, heritage, and related symbolism as a foundation, we can then instruct others in this abundance. Then, at least in the religious magickal realms, beverages will reclaim their honor for future generations.

Chapter 2

Medicinal and Magickal Uses for Beverages

*"Gentle Healer,
Lady of the Shamans bowl
pour out your touch from Gods of old
and make this world whole."*
—Marian Singer

*"Here stands mead, for Baldur brewed,
over the bright potion, a shield is laid."*
—The Younger Edda

Folk remedials included beverages as an effective base for thousands of years. For proof, we need look no further than the Roman battlefield, Polish soldiers, and the Celtic warriors. In all three cases, physicians used liqueurs laced with herbs to ease the pain of wounds and begin the healing process. Many of those physicians were also clergy, having been entrusted with literally the physickal and spiritual well-being of those in danger. More interesting still is the overlapping of metaphysickal symbolism with Christian words in some remedies. This wasn't the only arena in which beverage medicines, magick, and religion overlapped, however, as you'll soon see.

Medicinal

On the home front, teas and tonics, physicks and tinctures took care of family maladies. Women were both wives and physicians to a household, usually trained in folk remedies by their mothers. While they could not read or write, many of them could put the contemporary herbal hobbyist to shame with their field knowledge of plants, preparations, and applications. Except for the occasional traveling priest, monk, physician, or wise person, this familial knowledge was the backbone of healthcare well into the 1900s.

One essential component for home medicines was alcohol. Liqueur effectively covered up the taste of a disagreeable herbal mixture. It also provided a practical way to get a stubborn person to rest. The amount prescribed was not large, only necessary.

From a magickal perspective, it is important to recognize that many of these concoctions also had symbolic value. Red wine, for example, became a healing drink for someone with blood problems (due to the color). Then, too, people believed many alcoholic beverages were inherently healthy. With Persian haomas, for example, the sacred text of *Zend Avesta* says, *"of all the healing virtues, haomas, whereby thou art a healer, grant me some."* It should additionally be noted that medicinal liqueurs are only one part of the folk medicine cabinet. This repository regularly included non alcoholic substances as well.

Beer

> *"Oh, many a peer of England brews, livelier liquor than the muse, and malt does more than Milton can, to justify God's ways to man."*
>
> —Alfred E. Houseman

It is important to acknowledge the social implications and foundations for certain alcoholic beverages as healthful. In German society, for example, people appraised drinking large commodities of beer as a sign of strength. Before the advent of Christianity, family priests might decree that the populace should drink until supplies were exhausted to honor the Gods and insure ongoing health.

Plinius in *Natural History* (XXI, 50) noted that hops were a good nutrient. Being commonly known, herbalists recommended hops (or beer brewed with hops) to relieve sleeplessness, dizziness, nausea, headaches, and twitching muscles. Similarly, oat or oat-based beer appears as a fine addition to tonics, easing nervous exhaustion and improving concentration. Egyptian texts from 1500 B.C.E. recommend beer dregs for ischury (retention of urine), and an olive (or perhaps olive oil, depending on your translation) mixed with beer for colic.

Moving forward in history a little, one story of St. Brigit (450 A.D.) reveals positive religious connotations for beer in healing. According to legend, while nursing a group of lepers, St. Brigit changed water to beer by sheer faith. This story, combined with the fact that medieval churches allotted as much as three sections of land for cultivating beer ingredients, indicates that the church respected this substance. Its popularity commonly, religiously, magickally, and medicinally continued to grow.

During the Middle Ages, herbalists and healers recommended small amounts of beer to aid digestion. Because the Medieval apothecary was subject to whim, this was rarely a plain beer. Instead it often included healthful herbs and/or honey. Medicinal beers regularly contained yarrow (a stimulant frequently applied to wounds), rosemary, anise, caraway, ginger, and juniper berries.

One of the bestwritten examples of medicinal beer comes to us through *Physicka Sacra* by St. Hildegard, an

abbess of a Benedictine nunnery on the Rhine. In 1100
A.D. her writings portray hops as bearing preservative qualities that could decrease the instances of many sicknesses.
In one recipe, she claims that beer prepared with seven
ash leaves (a magickal number) and special herbs will
"purge the stomach and ease the chest" (*Physicka Sacra*,
Lib. III, Cap. XXVII). St. Hildegard also tells us that certain dishes prepared with beer instead of wine are more
healthful because of the boiling process that beer
incorporates.

This particular illustration also illuminates an important point about paganism and the church. Certain purported effects of herbs, and their uses by the clergy were
"technically" magickal in methodology. Because Christianity grew up in a Pagan world, many tried-and-true symbolic methods adapted to the new face of God very slowly.
Typically, the approach remained unchanged except for
altering the incantation so it venerated Jesus or Mary (a
type of the God and Goddess). The result was a pattern
familiar to the ailing individual, thereby giving them comfort.

Time did little to transform the original notions of beer
as healthful. It remained in popular use for folk medicine
until the prohibition (1920-1934). And when the ill effects
of alcohol began to take public notice beer all but disap-
peared from use as a medicinal beverage, except periodically in rural settings.

Cider

> "With all the Gallick wines are not so
> boone, as hearty Sider, y'strong drink of
> wood."
>
> —Vicar of Dilwyn, 1651

Depending on the period reviewed, sequentially, cider was either a wine (ancient Greece and Rome), a long drink (Middle Ages), or a fruit juice (modern). It became popularly accepted in 16th century England, where healers started using it almost immediately. On one hand, certain cautions had to be maintained, as cider-making equipment could cause lead poisoning. On the other hand, this marvelous beverage eliminated scurvy on sea voyages! In the sailing adventures of these years, sailors took cider on board, often in diluted form. It kept far better than fruit, and could replace any drinking water that got tainted on long journeys.

In English tradition, harvest was the best time to drink cider for health. Because cider was alchemically a "cold" drink, it was an excellent remedy for those with fevers. Even in the 1700s, fall was cold-and flu-season! Cider also helped cool farm hands who found themselves overheated from autumn's painstaking work. Today, cider still makes a marvelous choice for ritual cups in any harvest motif.

Distilled Beverages

> *"Aqua Vitae is the mistress of all medicines."*
>
> —H. Braunschweig

Hieronymus Braunschweig was a notable figure in medicine and pharmacology in 15th century Germany. He lauded the qualities of Aqua Vitae, and recommended it to cure headaches, renew color, stop baldness, and kill fleas! With acclaim such as this, it is easy to see why people of the Middle Ages revered distilled beverages for medicinal applications.

Over time, the capable hands of apothecaries and monks added herbs to liqueurs during preparation. Spices already played an important role in the medieval kitchen. Thus, many curative herbs were also found readily in the pantry. Prevalent superstition and knowledge helped decide which herbs to use for each sickness. For example, sage with brandy was a remarkable panacea, or so its creator's claimed. Sage takes its name from the term "alvia," meaning "I save."

The base of medicinal liqueurs changed according to what was popular at the time. A book from the early 1700s called *Secrets of Wines* (author unknown) discusses curative waters based in brandy. These included stomach water, plague water, maternity anise, and heart cordials. In the first two cases, we see the explicit medicinal application, but the later two definitely have roots in folklore and magick. This particular writing gives the contemporary magician pause to consider brandy in spells or rituals for love and fertility.

Metheglin and Mead

> *"This meathe is singularly good for consumption, stone, gravel, weak-sight and many more things."*
>
> —Sir Kenelm Digby

Finish lore says heaven is a storehouse for sacred honey that has the power to heal all wounds. Hippocrates (circa 400 B.C.) agreed with this philosophy, recommending honey in his medicinal writings for everything from coughs to skin wounds. From this vantage point, it is but a short jump to perceiving mead and mead related drinks as similarly healthy.

The Germans and Scottish equated the strength-imparting abilities of mead to that of eating meat. They also considered mead an aphrodisiac, which aided reproduction. These beliefs combined into the Northern tradition of celebrating marriage with a month of mead drinking. This insured the couple of joy and fertility. Our modern term *honeymoon* comes from this practice.

As early as the first century, the Greek philosopher Dioscorides praised the healing properties of mead. The best medicinal mead was a small brew, prepared and aged for about five days. This amount of fermentation yielded only sufficient amounts of alcohol to relax the patient, thus the term "small" refers to alcohol content.

A review of several historical figures improves our understanding of the popular use of mead and metheglin. Julius Caesar, for example, preserved his personal vigor and keenness of mind with metheglin. Another important figure to speak of the advantages of mead and metheglin was Sir Kenelm Digby, a great courtier in the middle ages who refers to metheglin as being "excellent for colds and consumption."

Looking forward in history, even toward the 1700s people did not loose sight of these notions. In a report from 1695, London, we read, "they have likewise metheglin compounded of milk and honey, and it is very wholesome" (*History of the Principality of Wales* by Nathaniel Church, London England, 1695) speaking in regard to the Welsh peoples.

Physicks

> *"Physick, for the most part, is nothing else*
> *but the substitute of exercise or temperance."*
> —Joseph Addison

The physick garden of the Middle Ages emulated natural science, including a special section for "simples," which were medicinal plants and herbs. Ultimately the physick garden celebrated Mother Natures' wisdom and talent to better the life of humankind. These gardens could often be found growing hand-in-hand with the local monastery or apothecary, for use by same. In this setting, the definition of a physick preparation was a food or drink made with plants or spices that have purgative qualities. Be aware, however, that historical writers often used the term "simple" or "physick" interchangeably.

What I like about the physick garden is that it reminds us of the value of growing our own herbs, especially when using them for health and spirituality. As they grow, you can saturate each plant with the energies for which you intend to use them after harvesting.

Tea

"I am glad I was not born before tea."
—Sidney Smith

In China, known as *Teha*; Malaysia, *Teh*, and in Middle English Tey, *tea* is an infusion or decoction of plants or herbs in water. A review of tea's uses in the medicinal realm is worthy of a book unto itself. I believe humankind tried every plant and spice on this planet at least once as part of a curative tea.

While ancient history sites numerous documented healthful applications for teas, the best available source comes from our Victorian ancestors who were enamored of the substance. Besides being a social contrivance, curative teas surfaced in almost all cookery books of the day. These recipe collections recommended beef tea as food for the sick room, sage and honey tea for throat infections, mint for stomach complaints, catnip for children's maladies, pennyroyal for colds, and strawberry leaf tea to disburse chancre sores, just to name a few. Some teas additionally blended in alcoholic beverages to improve the physickal effects, such as whiskey, honey, and lemon tea for a cough.

Tinctures

> *"Sweet herbs from all antiquity."*
> —Sidney Lanier

A *tincture* is an alcohol flavored scantly with spices or vegetable matter in solution. Generally the mixture consists of four ounces herb to eight ounces alcohol. This blend is warmed or allowed to soak for two weeks in sunlight, then strained. Tinctures acquire their name from the "tinge" in color afforded by the steeping process.

As late as 1919, books such as *Home Made Beverages* by Albet A. Hopkins appeared recommending tinctures like the following:

- Raspberry vinegar, clove, and honey for asthma.
- Cohosh, myrrh, skunk cabbage, and cayenne for spasms.
- Cayenne, myrrh, and brandy for fits.
- Angelica root, catnip, motherwort, sweetflag, aniseed, dill seed, fennel seed, and lady slipper for colic, restlessness, and flatulence.
- Lavender for cough or cold.
- Bloodroot and garlic for whooping cough.

Tinctures have the additional advantage of possessing a long shelf life if kept sealed and stored in a cool, dark area. They are simple to prepare, and can be easily applied in small commodities to accent magickal cooking and brewing efforts.

Tonics

> *"Genius, in truth, means little more than*
> *the faculty of perceiving in an unhabitual*
> *way."*
>
> —William James

A tonic is anything mixed with water to invigorate, re-vitalize, stimulate, strengthen, or give nutriment. These mixtures return the body and spirit to a normal tonal quality, thus the name *tone-ic*. Traditional herbs used in tonics include bay, bayberry, blackberry, agrimony, boneset, cat-nip, cayenne, century, chamomile, dandelion, golden seal, nettle, peppermint, sage, tansy, wormwood, and yarrow.

The most popular modern tonics are really nothing "newfangled." Ginseng mixed with water, used to reduce stress, improve recuperative powers, and enhance mental awareness, is a famous medicinal plant from China. In this region Ginseng had its beginnings at least 4,000 years ago with similar applications.

Another herb categorized as a tonic is angelica. Stu-dents of natural medicine, including Mary SummerRain and Michael Murray, tell us that angelica is good for PMS, allergies, menopause, and easing muscle spasms. In Asian lands, angelica was just as popular for remedial use as Gin-seng in the Orient. It gained its name because of its "an-gelic" qualities, as a gift from heaven.

Beyond the illnesses discussed in this chapter, I hap-pened upon one curative that left me with a smile. An an-cient English translator of Greek verse recounted a wonderful ditty from Athenaeus, revealing that the ancients knew more than their fair share about hangovers and ap-propriate tonics to cure them:

"Last evening you were drinking deep,
so now your head hurts, go to sleep;
take some boiled cabbage when you wake,
and there's an end of your headache"
—Translated from Athenaeus, Deipnos I, 62

I honestly can't say that I've tried this, but apparently it was revered much like contemporary society views a Bloody Mary! Some things never change.

Wine

"It's a wine of virtuous powers, my mother
made it of wild flowers."
—S.T. Coleridge

In 1500 B.C., priests evoked the Snake Goddess of Egypt before making wine. This seems to have nothing to do with medicinal wines until you realize that the snake itself is an ancient symbol for health, longevity, and resurrection. The Staff of Hermes is the most potent remaining example we have of this concept.

An interesting ancient tradition focused on health is that of Wassailing at the Yule celebration of Northern European peoples. Either spiced apple ale, apple cider or apple wine participated in the celebration to toast the Great Apple tree. Wassail comes from an Anglo Saxon term which means *whole*. All those who drink from the Wassail cup ensure themselves of good health and happiness. I cannot help but wonder if the origins of the age-old saying about "an apple a day" might owe its origins to this bit of history. Either way, the apple continues as a powerful emblem for good health available.

In the 1710 *Household Companion,* we see items such as borage wine recommended for hypochondria because it comforts the heart and relieves fainting spirits. Likewise, herbalists suggested balm wine for improving digestion and expelling melancholy. In other period texts, cowslip wine appears as a curative for jaundice, elderberry for colds, raspberry for throat infections, and barley wine for kidney trouble.

Continuing to the turn of the century, Edward Spenser in his book *The Flowering Bowl* (1903) praised wine as effective against the "stones." In his account, he recommends cutting the end of a birch branch in March and suspending it in bottles with one gallon of water, one pound of sugar, yeast, mace, and cinnamon. In truth, a kind of birch-beer wine! This attitude toward wine so late in history is not startling. As wine became more popular, many of the healthy attributes of mead were simply transferred to it, because the two were so closely related.

Magickal Beverages and Potions

"There is nothing so powerful as truth,
and often nothing so strange."

—D. Webster

We have seen beverages at the altar, at the sick bed, and upon our own table. So what of magick? Well, in part we've seen hints of magickal processes throughout our exploration. But perhaps the most enduring and widely-utilized example of beverages in magick is the ever-faithful love potion.

First made in far Eastern lands, almost every ingredient imaginable got mixed into the brew pot to improve romance, passion, or both. For a perfect example, look to the famous story of Tristan and Isolt. These star-crossed youths accidentally drank a magick love potion so powerful that it lasted beyond death. A tragedy yes, but also a shrewd reminder of just how much responsibility goes with mystical efforts, especially those treading on the territory of the frail human heart.

Another slightly dark mark on the history of love potions comes from the era of Louis XVI. The King's sorceress, Catherine LaVoisin, was an expert on herb preparations including poison. Mostly, however, her knowledge of magickal arts was employed for love potions even by the King's mistress. Some of the favored court herbs for arduous ends include dill, cinnamon, caraway, coriander, nutmeg, rose petals, fennel, and celery. All of these are perfectly safe to use today.

In other similar potions of that era, wine mixed with moonwort, daffodil flowers, ginseng, myrrh, parsley, yarrow, myrtle, leek, or jasmine effected the same results. Each magician based their compounds on mythical and magickal associations. These correlations came from the herb's inferred alchemical alignments, governing Deities, and so on. This is exactly what we hope to do later in the recipe section of this book!

Love isn't the only thing our ancestors treasured. We also see a lot of magickal concocting in the sick room. If a healer wanted an ailment to wane, he or she might prepare a potion during the waning moon, for example. Another illustration was that of placing toads in the Witches stewpot to make a heart elixir. The frog has long been regarded as a healer, and today, we know that the skin of a toad contains a chemical very similar to digitalis. So, it is likely that this magickal potion (as odd as it sounded) did, indeed, help the patient.

A third illustration comes from ancient China where children with convulsions received ground "dragon bone" (dinosaur bones). Contemporary physicians now administer calcium, the main substance bones are made of, under similar conditions today. So, while some early transcriptions for "Witches brews" were anything but appetizing, these writers unwittingly gave the Cunning Folk due honor in history as contributing to pharmacological studies and breakthroughs.

On the less pleasant side of this overview, many of the items used for magickal ends were not "safe" or terribly savory, let alone actually helpful. In some cases the "best guess" was all a country Wise person could offer. Again, they based that guess on all the knowledge and lore personally amassed. We see this evidenced in texts such as *The Magick of Kirani, King of Persia* (Cyranus, London 1650) where the author recommends satyrion seed, honey, and the liqueur of a roe's gall to aid conception. Such a mixture hardly ranks on my top 10 list of things I always wanted to try!

This point is very important to keep in mind. While there are many wonderful ideas for magickal aids presented herein, not all of them are feasible in our modern reality.

Protection

"Beneath the shadow of great protection, the soul sits, hushed and calm."
—James F. Clarke

A Norse legend recounted in *Nibelung Lay* tells us of the warrior Sigurd found by a Valkyria who was disowned by Odin. Sigurd implores the Valkyria to teach him wisdom, and she replies by giving him a horn of beer with runes carved into it. The runes were those for health, victory, protection, and winning favor.

During their conversation, she also instructs him very specifically on how to inscribe and bless the runes for his cup (Naud-need). Then, in the future, if he felt there was treachery or poison to worry about, he could cast garlic (also known as the magick leek) into his cup with any liqueur. If there was danger, his cup would shatter, or the drink turn a hideous color.

If no such tankard was immediately available, an alternative method found in Peru was claiming a beverage before the gods. In the Yasha liturgy, there is a psalm to the sacred haomas where the writer raises the cup to the sky saying "I claim to thee, O' yellow one for inspiration, for strength, for vigor" (*Zend Avesta*, Yasha liturgy Verse 17). The hope was that by blessing the drink, no ill effect could ensue, even as we pray before meals today.

Another interesting bit of protective sorcery comes through Apollonius who writes of Argonauts pouring mead on the waters before a ship sailed. I believe this action was a means to invoke and placate the gods of the sea, and thus insure a safe voyage. It is likely that our contemporary custom of launching ships with champagne or good wine has roots in this ancient custom.

Mead, wine, and beer were not the only substances used in rites for protection. On New Years Eve in West Country, people ritually burn the piece of hawthorn that hung in the kitchen throughout the previous year. They accompany this rite with a song "Auld Cider," a song praising cider! The words are repeated in a mantra like manner over a deep note. With each syllable, participants make a bow (totaling nine bows over three repetitions).

While cider does not play an active role in this rite, its name is an important pivotal point. The phrase "Auld Cider" is repeated three times, the number of body, mind, and spirit in symmetry. Bowing nine times equates to the number of inspiration and universal law! In this manner, people used the magickal symbolism of numbers combined with an age-old tradition to empower their observance and guard their lands.

It would be inappropriate to write any section on shielding magicks without also mentioning water. Water and religion have worked hand in hand for such a long time that we often don't recognize the connection, or take it for granted. The uses of holy water in Catholicism prove that Christianity maintained strong beliefs about water's ability to cleanse and heal. Additionally, a review of the sacred sites of Europe reveals hundreds of holy founts, wells, rivers, and so on. Time's passage has not diluted this element's symbolic power in any way.

If, at last, all these defensive approaches fail you, there are still more suggestions. Jet powdered in water will help keep snakes at bay, boneset tea repels evil spirits, and myrrh, white frankincense, and flaked jet stone in wine will cure you of elf magick. For the latter to work effectively, fast one night, and partake of the substance for three, nine, or 12 mornings to break the spell (*Anglo Saxon Charms*, 1909). Finally, angelica steeped in vinegar and drunk quickly turns away any negative magick that managed to sneak by your defenses.

Health/Curatives

> *"May what I see increase and what I suffer decrease."*
>
> —Jacob Grimm, 1883

As we saw earlier in this chapter, healers used a variety of symbols in the process of creating healing potions. A woman seeking aid for fertility received treatment during the waxing to full moon. In this example, the growing lunar sphere resembles the Mother Goddess with a full womb. She might also receive yellow potions, for creativity and productivity, and the number of ingredients could total seven, the traditional number of lunar influence. Here are two correspondence lists for your reference.

Common Color and Number Correspondences

- Red: vigor, fearlessness, endurance, Fire.
- Orange: force, outcomes, warmth, empathy.
- Yellow: intellect, prophesy, inventiveness, Air, activity.
- Green: development, abundance, confidence, well-being.
- Blue: Water, harmony, restoration, happiness, reflection.
- Purple: devotion, commitment, perception.
- White: safety, cleansing, purity.
- Black: banishing, the void, rest.
- Brown: Earth, Nature, groundwork, new undertakings.
- Pink: relationships, diversion, leisure, positive outlooks.

- 1: oneness, beginning, agreement, Sun Magick, energy.
- 2: symmetry, sanctification, alliance.
- 3: balance, objectives, body-mind-spirit trinity.
- 4: components, time, aspirations, triumph, Elements.

- 5: adaptability, perception, psychic endeavors.
- 6: protection, devotion, completion of tasks.
- 7: wisdom, variety, moon magick.
- 8: power, personal transformation, control.
- 9: universal law, service to others.
- 10: dependability, rationality.
- 12: productivity, longevity, a full year.
- 13: veneration, forbearance, belief.
- 21: respect, remembrance, excellence.
- 40: ascetic states, retreat, revitalizing self, communion.

The truly astute wise person also chose components according to their astrological significance, or picked them at special times to enhance potency. For example, herbs harvested when the moon is in Pisces or Virgo will improve the fertile energy. Such efforts also can amplify magickal beverages today, so keep this in mind as you're reading the recipes in Part II.

Blessing/Fertility/Weather Magick

"Good health and good sense are two of life's greatest blessings."

—Publilius Syrus

In reviewing magickal techniques, one appears again and again for a multitude of applications; that of sprinkling a beverage on an item or around an area. In the West Country, there is the Twelfth Night custom of taking cyder to an apple tree, encircling it, and pouring while chanting a poem for bounty. Interestingly enough, cyder was consumed up until the 18th century at Maypole dances in Britain in much the same manner. We can bring this tradition back to life by serving apple juice during these holidays, or placing a glass of apple wine upon our altars.

Other beverage sanctifications for trees occur in different regions. On St. Swithin Day (July 15 -Anglo Saxon), each tree is blessed, then anointed with cyder over the trunk, and tapped three times. If it rained on this day, it portended fertility and a long rainy season (continuing for 40 days thereafter). Rain or shine, however, the ritual continued and the trees graced with cyder to insure their health and fruitfulness.

Wine and water also both participate in rituals to help bring rain. Sprinkling water from a sacred well in ceremonial fashion was one way of coaxing the Gods toward opening heavens' vaults to save a dying crop. Rural people applied wine similarly when a well ran dry. Today, consider pouring out wine to the land and the Powers during times of drought or when you personally need refreshing.

In all cases, the meting out of the beverage becomes an offering that implores the favor of Nature or the Gods. In the process, a type of cleansing is also implied, such as during the dedication of a child. Even in non-Christian traditions, a priest or priestess introduces the young one to water by a drop on the lips, or a misting (Wiccan Blessing Ways). This action insures health, protection and bestows Divine favor.

This imagery finds a slightly different expression in modern magickal traditions. Here, an aspurger (a heather branch being one example) sprinkles the participants of a Circle to remove negative energy and invoke blessings.

Divination

"The course of nature is the art of god."
—Edward Young

Roman Sibyls used wine to encourage an altered state of awareness for the purpose of becoming a Divine Oracle. Euripides mirrors this notion when he writes about Dionysus. Euripides accounts of this God saying that, while enticing people to drink, Dionysus also provided inspiration, specifically foresight. We find the same theme repeated once again in Hindu tradition where drinking Soma equated to "taking in" the God Indra. The Divine being then could use the sacred vessel of a human worshiper as a channel for prophesy and wisdom. There is undeniable evidence that Christianity did not succeed in completely eradicating such beliefs or resulting magickal practices. In some regions the local Pagans seemed determined not to be forced totally underground as late as the Middle Ages. One bit of history confirming this originates in Slavic regions.

During the Middle Ages the worship of a Sun God named Swiatowit still occurred. Most popular on the island of Rugen, Swiatowit's depictions show him carrying a drinking horn! Each harvest, the faithful placed a cup of sacred mead in the hands of a figure honoring this Being. Some time later, the priest would take the cup, reading the quantity left as a forecast for the coming year. Then half the mead was poured out, the other half consumed by the priest, and the cup carefully refilled.

Finally, one of the most common ways of applying beverages in divination is through spattering or scrying the surface. In the former, after being appropriately offered and accepted by the Gods, the seer pours their liquid to the earth. Interpreting the images was much like reading tea leaves. In the latter, the seer gazes on the surface of the drink as if it were the veneer of a crystal ball. They then wait for literal or symbolic images for an answer.

Oath-Taking—Magickal Unity

> *"There is no bridge so difficult to cross as*
> *the bridge of a broken promise."*
> —Hosletters U.S. Almanac, 1897

Words have power. Our ancestors knew the truth of this, and they also knew that few individuals are honest or forthright 100 percent of the time. Therefore, to insure compliance with a promise or oath, mini-rituals with beverages developed. In this respect, the taking of a drink magickally sealed the agreement to ones lips. It also meant an acceptance of dire consequences from the gods should the pledge be broken. With this illustration as a basis, the contemporary magickal coven could begin using a special cup to welcome newly initiated members.

One depiction of this custom comes to us from Germany. Here, legend calls the cup used for love magick the *Minne Cup*. Originally, *minne* meant remembrance. It also was the name of early Goddess figure. People usually raised the Minne Cup filled with sacrificial beer in memory of a loved one. Later the meaning changed so that if two drank from the Minne Cup (first the man in honor of affection, then accepted by the woman) it bound them in love.

Here and in similar marriage observances around the globe, wine becomes the symbol for love's sweetness. A breakable glass is an emblem of the fragility of human devotion. Either way, once shared, the Gods, friends and family all witness and recognize the union. As such, the gift of a cup for handfastings could be a potent symbol of the couple's mutual pledge in the years to come.

Besides as a means to show unity or to link "destiny," partaking from one cup indicated trust. In Germany, for example, proper etiquette dictated that a host always offered a freshly filled goblet to honored guests first. To refuse the cup from ones host was an insult, akin to claiming their promise of hospitality and safety was untrue. Similarly, accepting it acknowledged welcome, and acted as an unspoken pledge on the guests' part to be thoughtful. Analogous customs appeared in Arabia as well.

So, when you begin brewing, remember to share some with special visitors, thereby extending your hospitality to them. This gives you the opportunity to impart a newly acquired skill, and lovingly created magick, with people who deserve it most: family and friends.

Chapter 3

From Cauldron to Cup—
Magickal Brewing Methods

"And now he saw with lifted eyes
The East like a great chancel rise
and deep through all his senses drawn
received the sacred wine of dawn."
—Sir Henry Newbolt

"There is a right and wrong handle to
everything."
—Rudolph E. Raspe

Certain approaches to magickal beverage creation need to be considered for the best, and tastiest metaphysical results. Initially, the most important part of the inventive process both spiritually and physically is having a clean work area. Take a few moments to remove any items that could become distracting. As you straighten up, visualize white, bubbly light pouring from your hands into the kitchen.

Burn a little incense or create a stovetop, simmering potpourri for cleansing and purification. A perfect choice of readily available pantry herbs for this are basil and sage. Blend 1 tsp. of each herb in 1 cup of water over a low flame. If you will be working in the kitchen for a while, add more herbs and water following those proportions so the pan doesn't burn.

Next, bring your tools and ingredients together and whisper a brief blessing over them. Your kitchen is about to become a sacred space, and your cooking utensils the magickal tools to blend ingredients into harmony and power. Use comfortable, meaningful words, and welcome your chosen Divine presence for sanctification. If you desire, set up a protective magickal Circle at this time.

Now you can start cooking! Keep your intentions firmly in mind all while you blend and stir. Visualize appropriately colored light filling the beverage. Chant and sing, or play uplifting music. Continue in this expectant mind set until the beverage is ready to be bottled, aged, or consumed, depending on the recipe.

Last, but not least, remember to mark your storage vessels with labels indicating the date of preparation and their functions. Good examples are abundant:

> *For love:* Raspberry Romancer, Passion fruit Fervor.
>
> *For joy:* Happiness Harbinger, Peachy-Keen.
>
> *For insight:* Prophetic Punch, Oracular Orange.

This is where you really get to have some fun with your metaphysical brewing, so enjoy!

Choosing Additives and Ingredients

> *"Observe moderation. In all, the fitting season is best."*
>
> —Hesiod

The painter decides among colors, textures, and backgrounds. A musician looks to notes and instruments for their Divine expressions. In similar manner, the ever-ingenious Kitchen Witch surveys the pantry to discover delectable, magickal potential.

In Appendix A there is a list of some common components for beverage making, their most customary magickal associations and a little data that I have learned about their uses in brewing. This serves as a quick reference guide. For additional information, I recommend investing in a detailed magickal herbal or food book (such as my *Kitchen Witch's Companion, Citadel Press, 2005* and *Herbal Arts, Citadel Press, 1998*). These resources help you decide which aromatics and flavors are best for achieving your magickal goals.

Combine those chosen gently with other ingredients so that the resulting energy is balanced, and the taste pleasant. A magickal brew for internal transitions will do little good if you can't stomach it. On the other hand, preparations specifically made for libations or symbolism can combine anything you like! In this case, clearly mark the bottle with a warning that states in bold lettering "NOT FOR CONSUMPTION" to avoid mishaps.

In deciding among compounds consider their color, the total number of items mixed together, the herbs, spices, and fruits, the final storage container, or whatever else you can think of to improve symbolic impact. This affords tremendous creative freedom because every ingredient has more than one metaphysical application! Add to that your own vision and you suddenly come up with a myriad of options that function well in a variety of settings.

This is the beauty of kitchen magick. It requires few tools, few expensive items, only a little time, and blends wonderfully with any tradition you happen to follow.

Throughout this book recipes have been compiled so they convey specific magickal energies. These are guideposts only. Use them as they are, or change them to suit more personal goals. Remember, what is meaningful about an ingredient to me may be quite different for you. Always use what is most pleasurable in taste and personally significant for best results.

Magickal Concocting

"When the wine goes in, strange things come out."
—Johann Christoph Friedrich Von Schiller

Time, temperament, and technique; these are the three words to keep in mind for magickal beverage formulation. First, let's look at timing. We have already seen that certain phases of the moon were used historically to help mystical efforts. So, when making a drink to help encourage weight loss, begin the process by a waning moon for the "shrinking" symbolism. Conversely, if preparing something to help conception, the waxing and full moon are best.

In magick pertaining to physical strength, mental faculties, leadership, logic, education, reason and legal matters, work during the daylight hours. The golden rays of the sun are strongly aligned with these energies. Conversely, night and lunar influences bear energies for insight, fertility, mysteries, emotions, and so on. Additionally, days of the week and every hour of the day has certain planetary aspects that can figure into your magickal "formula." To discover what these traits are, consult a reliable astrological calendar, moonsign, or sunsign book.

Another dimension to timing is the aging process necessary to most fermented beverages. It is very easy to adjust the making of a wine or beer, and the aging period to create something more meaningful. Some examples include:

- Making wine with Fire related fruits and herbs on the night of Beltane over a gas stove (for fire), and storing it for next year's celebration.

- Starting a brew early enough to present it as a special birthday gift to a friend (including a list of ingredients and their meanings).

- Aging wine to share at a handfasting or initiation for a year and a day.

- Preparing a beverage on the day of a couple's marriage and presenting it on their anniversary to celebrate and renew love.

Holidays, festivals, and observances present a third consideration in timing. Some festivals are centered around beverages, beverage Deities, or use beverages as a central element to the celebration. Depending on your viewpoint, these dates can be applied in one of two ways. First, you could prepare an appropriate beverage for the observance ahead of time. Second, you can make the beverage on the day of the celebration to honor the occasion. Here are some examples:

- **Rosalia** (June 4—Ancient Greece). The Greeks celebrated this date in many ways. Primarily it was an opportunity to litter the temples of Aphrodite with rose petals. Additionally, women bathed in rose water to increase their attractiveness and burning rose incense improved luck.

  Try making rose water today to use in cooking. Or make a sparkling rose wine to celebrate the spirit of beauty and love. Leave water with fresh rose petals on the altar to welcome Aphrodite and encourage romantic energies in your home.

   Winegrower's Fete (August 29—Old France). In the 16th century a guild formed among the winegrowers of Vevey France. Each year until 1889 they held a special festival that had many similarities to Cerealia in Roman times.

Attended by thousands, people donned Louis XV costumes. Next came a parade guided by a depiction of Pales, the Goddess of flocks, wearing a robe of blue. She is followed by white oxen, and children dressed as shepherds and yodelers. Next came Ceres in a flowing red gown accompanied by harvesters and bakers. All around this, fauns and satyrs danced merrily wearing appropriate garb. Afterwards everyone retired to a night of feasting and drinking in the company of friends and local leaders.

Today, you can place a cup of any grain beverage (beer) on your altar honoring Ceres, and a grape wine to remember Bacchus. This is also an appropriate day to begin any brewing effort.

   Allan Apple Day (October 27—Cornwall England). The unmarried men and women of this town purchase an Allan Apple on this day. At nightfall, they place the apple under their pillow until morning. Before dawn the fruit must be eaten without a sound. The participant then goes outside, dressed just as he or she is, to sit beneath a tree. The first person to pass is believed to be his or her future spouse! Also, if the participant feels no cold while waiting, he or she will remain warm all winter (possibly thanks to a new mate)!

Come October 27, consider pouring yourself a fresh glass of apple juice or making another beverage using apples as a base. This will help bring love into your life.

∽ **Hodening** (Wales). Taking place sometime during the Yule season, Hodening is an odd custom also known in parts of England. Part of this celebration includes young men going to various households, improvising poems that demand they be let in. The person at the door also replied with a rhyme. This competition of bardic skill went on until one party ran out of ideas. If the Hodener's won, they came in for Yule ale, cakes, and a gift. Otherwise, they had to go on their way.

This is a fun tradition that could be enacted with friends and family. Be sure to have ale and snacks prepared, as you will probably want to lose this competition!

Next comes temperament. I do not recommend doing any magickal brewing if you are tired, out of sorts, harried, sick or otherwise ill-disposed. It is difficult to concentrate when you aren't feeling well. Also, sometimes excess negative energy can accidentally flow into your beverage instead of the positive magick you intend. Treat the creation of ritual beverages as any other spiritual endeavor—with compassion, insight, and sensitivity—and you can't go wrong.

Finally, technique considers the whole of your approach from what kind of spoon(s) you use, the cooking pot and even the direction of stirring. For growing, positive, encouraging energies, mix your brew in a sunward motion (clockwise). For banishing bad habits, negative energy or to reverse ill fortune, stir the liquid counterclockwise (widdershins).

Stoneware or seasoned iron pots and wooden spoons are highly recommended over plastic and aluminum. These are more natural and yield a betterflavored drink. Consider keeping these items set apart just for your magickal brewing efforts. This is not necessary, but it helps to encourage the exact sympathy desired in your magickal beverages to slowly become part of the pot and spoon. Just as any magickal tools, the more you work with them the more they absorb personal energy.

Another neat twist to consider in techniques is the order in which you add the base ingredients. While yeast *cannot* be added until very specific points in your cooking process, other ingredients aren't so limited. Waiting to add components at a particularly potent planetary hour, or adding them in a unique progression are two ideas along these lines.

To illustrate, let's assemble a beverage to encourage love, then have that romance blossom into something more permanent. First add pink rose petals to the cauldron to stimulate feelings of excitement and friendship in the "right person." Follow this with cinnamon, sacred to Aphrodite, for growing love. Here, the progression of your additives follows the natural flow of relationships. The only difference is affixing magickal energy to encourage that flow.

Practical Considerations

"Practicality is common sense mingled
with frugality, humor, creative insight, and
a little fortitude for good measure."

—Marian Singer

This section acts as a foundation to any type of brewing effort. While some brewing instructions are recipe specific, or distinctive to a particular category, there are some sensible suggestions universal to this book. The more fastidious matters will be discussed in their appropriate sections later, however there's one point you should know at this juncture. The Alcohol, Drug, and Firearms commission allows home brewers to make 100 gallons per year legally as head of household; families can produce 200 gallons. None of this may be sold without a license, however. Brew responsibly.

In terms of necessary items, I suggest that you collect lots of glass bottles in many shapes and sizes. Do not, unless absolutely necessary, use plastic. Plastic retains scents and flavors that can ruin your beverages. Additionally, it is more difficult to sterilize. If you must use plastic, throw away the container after the second fermentation to alleviate increased chances of bacteria.

As you collect containers, keep in mind that screw tops and corks are valuable to the brewer. Both of these can be loosened during the initial stages of fermentation to bleed off excess pressure. I call this "burping" the bottles. Also, you can secure both type of lids with wax once the beverage reaches maturity.

Keep decorative containers set aside for distinguished finished products. Employ simpler vessels for fermentation or transportation to social events. Small airline bottles are great sizes for holiday "sampler" packs. Give these to new acquaintances, friends, or family to see which blends they like best before endowing them with larger supplies.

Suggested Alcoholic Beverage Tools

- ↷ Gallon sized screw top or cork bottles.
- ↷ Balloons and rubber bands which make excellent make-shift fermentation locks.
- ↷ A cool, dark storage area.
- ↷ Strainers, cheesecloth, or gauze to filter out sediments.

- Large cooking pans which are not aluminum.
- Funnels in various sizes.
- Large wooden spoon or other stirring utensil; a slotted spoon to remove large brewing components (fruit, and so on).
- Sharp knife for cutting herbs and fruits.
- Mortar and pestle to macerate root herbs such as ginger.
- Active bread, wine or beer yeast.
- Accurate measuring tools.
- A clean, tight woven, cotton cloth to cover beverages during the first fermentation. Clean dish towels work.
- A must jar—this is a type of plastic or glass container where brewing leftovers (fruit, spices, bits of wine) go.
- A large plastic storage container with top (or a cooler).

Non Essential Alcoholic Beverage Tools (But Fun Ones)

- A hydrometer—this measures the alcohol content of your finished wines, meads, and so on. (see resources in the back of this book).
- Fermentation locks—these come in various sizes to keep your bottles from accidentally exploding when pressure builds. They are inexpensive (usually under $1 each) and keep you from having to clean up a very sticky mess.
- Camden tablets—these help the pace of fermentation to be steady. Also sometimes called "nutrients."

 ࣶ Fermentation casks—beautiful wooden casks
    that make your cellar look like the brewing
    closets of olde. These also give a distinctive
    flavor to wines and beers often peculiar to
    the type of wood from which the barrel is
    made. An alternative is a glass Carboy (price
    about $15) with cap and stopper.

 ࣶ Clarifying tools—these usually consist of a
    glass jar and special tubing that allows only
    the clear wine to be siphoned off your fer-
    menting container.

 ࣶ Corn sugar—makes beverages that ferment
    more quickly and have clearer flavors.

 ࣶ Sparkaloid—helps to clarify beers.

 ࣶ Citric acid—may be used in place of citrus
    fruit when you want the content but not the
    flavor.

 ࣶ Sorbistat—prevents refermentation once a
    beverage has been boiled to stop the process.

Nonalcoholic Beverage Suggested Tools

For the most part, items found in most home pantries
encompass all the tools for this job. Besides bottles for
storage and ingredients, you need:

 ࣶ A good set of measuring cups and spoons.

 ࣶ Mixing bowls; preferably stoneware or pottery.

 ࣶ A blender or food processor; wire whisks.

 ࣶ A harp knife and wooden spoon; if you don't
    mind, you can certainly use your athame for
    magickal cooking efforts. Wooden spoons

aren't "essential," but they absorb personal energy better than plastic or metal.

∽ Strainers, sieve, or cheese cloth; the later is best when filtering beverages with fine particles.

∽ Various sized funnels (so they fit in different width bottle necks).

∽ Non aluminum pots and pans

∽ Freezer safe pans or glasses for chilled beverages.

After collecting your bottles, boil them in soapy water and rinse thoroughly. Certain types of fruits attract marvelous insects and molds, and this is *not* a petri dish experiment. Cleanliness is essential to successful, safe beverages. This goes for all of your pots, pans, spoons, and funnels too. Don't skimp on this step!

If you are planning to make fermented beverages, it is worth checking for brewing supply stores in your area. Look under hobbies, crafts, brewing, and malting in the Yellow Pages. The alternative to this is mail order. Dependable sources for this appear in the back of this book. Also check with a few nearby bartenders about local brewing clubs. These groups provide hands-on, in-person advice for continuing problems or fresh ideas.

When you first begin brewing, try to stick to one category of beverages until perfecting that technique. You will have greater success this way, leading to improved personal satisfaction, and the confidence to continue. The brewing process has similarities that carry over from one category to another, so your learning time is not wasted.

Also, there are little idiosyncrasies in fruit and spice combination that surface in practice sessions. For example, knowing that strawberries ferment very quickly and actively changes the entire approach for making strawberry wine, specifically in the quantities of fruit used.

Such discoveries are part of the magick of brewing. They teach us much about nature's chemistry lab, so take your time and enjoy them! It is for this reason that I recommend storing all your fermenting beverages initially (during the most active stage of fermentation) in a plastic container. That way if something really takes off and accidentally explodes from pressure, you have a sealed situation that's easy to clean up.

In choosing recipes, initially find ones that are simple and inexpensive. Simplicity encourages early success in your attempts. However, if you do fail, being cost-effective from the beginning eases the pain and honest frustration that occurs in figuring out what went wrong. Don't be overly critical with yourself in this scenario, even the renowned European monk-brewers had their "off days"!

For a while, brew for yourself or family members, choosing recipes that include ingredients you personally like. If you don't enjoy fresh peaches or allspice, it's unlikely that peach-allspice wine will please you. It will also be difficult to tell if this blend is well-balanced after brewing. By working with pleasurable components, you get honest, valid opinions on quantities of fruit, spices, and so on until finding the perfect harmony.

If you have difficulty discovering recipes with personally appealing ingredients, you can substitute. Cinnamon is an option for allspice, for example. Do be careful, though, not to eliminate any necessary ingredients. A friend of mine did this once and couldn't figure out why his wine didn't start fermenting. The answer was simple. He'd altered the recipe and decreased the sugar content.

In my friend's case, the yeast didn't have enough food to survive. In other situations, spices such as ginger root provide essential nutrients (such as tannin) that help the fermentation process. So, read your recipes carefully, heeding any cautions the author gives for advice.

Don't be afraid to cross reference sources either. One author may have a superior strategy for wine making, but lousy directions for beer. Then, too, most authors write about things according to personal taste, which may not thrill your pallet in the least. Once you become adept at beverage making, you will know which items work best together for desired results. Cross referencing aids this process by illustrating the most consistent, successful approaches that have all the elements you enjoy.

Once in a while it is fun to have brewing parties. Gather together all your curious friends, advise them of the basics they need to bring, and watch to see what unique combinations they come up with. No matter how long I have been brewing, it seems my students have this knack for creative one-upmanship. Further, the exchange is very beneficial. Like home cooking, sometimes you can get into a brewing "rut," which parties like this redirect and inspire.

Along the same lines, take a periodic trip to your local library for books on beverage making. I personally think the public library is a terribly neglected resource. On those shelves are hundreds of books, some remaining unopened, and many of which can be incredibly helpful to both brewing and metaphysical topics. I should warn you, however, that after one or two visits it becomes quite addictive!

Additionally, don't overlook local secondhand bookshops and antique stores. Locally we have booksellers with bargain basements full of treasures for under $5. Here, the browsing brewer discovers herb and spice books, old cookbooks, bartender guides, and even a few health tomes with recipes for tonics. Periodically, the serious brewer should invest in a few of the more costly texts such stores carry, but this isn't necessary to the success of early efforts.

Date everything! Some wines and meads safely age for years, and are better for the time. Others are considered "short" liqueurs and need to be consumed immediately, within two weeks, or a few months from preparation. After that period what you have left is something akin to vinegar. If a recipe includes shelf-life information, be sure to mark it clearly on the bottle. This will keep you from accidentally serving an embarrassingly unpalatable beverage (usually after bragging about your home-brewing) to dinner guests.

It is also considerate to place a list of ingredients on your labels when serving to friends. Many people exhibit odd allergic reactions they may not have told you about. A designation placed prominently on bottles may save your guest a bad set of hives, or in worse case scenarios, it may even preserve their lives.

Finally, when preparing beverages for magickal effects or rites, please give people the courtesy of knowing if it's alcoholic, and if it's already energized. This neatly honors free will and also allows those with a taboo against drinking alcohol to politely decline.

Serving Vessels

*"Come friends and companions, let's take
a full glass."*

—Berg

Once prepared, the next thing to think about is presentation of the beverage. Just like layingout a meal, decanters and glasses can be symbolically potent and visually lovely. Many times it is the finishing touches on any project that really sets it apart.

In reviewing the opulence of medieval and Renaissance table settings, we see that our ancestors agreed with this notion. Gold and silver, precious gems, and fine cups carved from whole pieces of jade embellished many banquets. This was a way of flaunting one's means, but I also feel these exhibits were remnants from earlier times. Precious substances deserved appropriate containers to honor their sacred function.

Many people can't consider gold due to exorbitant prices. Instead, substitute silver plate, stoneware, and hand made pottery. Similarly, I enjoy cut glass and treated brass decanters over more costly options. They have an antique flavor befitting the age-old processes I use.

As far as actually finding vessels, some local bars will save bottles for you if you ask nicely. Good Will and second hand shops are spectacular places to unearth beautiful decanters and bottles inexpensively. As you formulate your collection, keep in mind the final use for each item.

Consider their colors, shapes, and sizes to equate them to a magickal scenario or goal. For example, blue bottles might house beverages encouraging peace or improved meditative states. Use round flouted carafes for fertility or Goddess energy, and gold colored goblets to empower beverages for strength, leadership, and so on.

When fortune really smiles on you, decanters and decorative cups can be found bearing scenes. One might relate nicely to the Wheel of the Year such as fall leaves; another, have the visage of a particular deity such as Athena with her owl; another yet carry depictions of specific circumstances such as animal images for rituals pertaining to totems and familiars. For that matter, and more simply, the container might be made in the country where your tradition originated.

The beauty of this approach is that from the first musing about a beverage until the time it is meted out, everything has deep meaning in a magickal realm. The pleasure of your guests, the magickal energy created and the end results are truly marvelous to watch. Here your extra efforts manifest in personal satisfaction and enjoyment by all.

Creative Toasts

*"Now fill your glass ane an a', and drink
the toast I gie ye."*

—D. Henderson

If you didn't already have enough options, here is yet one more! Toasting over beverages is a venerable tradition comparable to an art form. Some people in history had bouts of toast-duels to see who had the better talent for crowd-pleasing and flowery flattery.

The term toast came into usage around the 1600s in England and neighboring countries when it was customary to float bits of dry bread in the Wassail Bowl. Hosts offered this bread to the most honored guest at the table because it gave the Wassail savor and zest. More than likely, this really dates back to when bread was the main constituent in brewing for yeast, and thus inspired fermentation. Alternatively, this practice may originate with feelings about bread and grain as an emblem of providence.

The idea of a "toast" is far older than the Wassail tradition. In Chapter 2, we looked at the religious uses of beverages. Here, drink offerings were held to the sky to salute the Divine, then poured on the ground, honoring and appeasing that God or Goddess. When created for special observance, participants raised their glasses in tribute to that occasion. Eventually, the practice translated itself into toasting achievements, friends, celebrations, and so on.

In researching this book, I found a wonderful old text called *Waes Hale* (By Edithe Lea Chase and Captain W.E.P. French. Grafton Press, 2003). This is a collection of literature appropriate for toasts, or actual quoted toasts handed down through family lines. This, combined with other texts, helped me assemble a few possibilities to consider for future toasting occasions. Some are amusing, some honor a Pagan visage, and others yet are thematic. What's important here isn't so much the words, but the feeling you put behind them.

In terms of magick, the toast equates to a brief spell, incantation, benediction or invocation. The words can be simple, rhyming, a quote from a book, or whatever seems appropriate. As you raise your glass, envision the energy being raised. As you speak, release the intentions of that toast with your words to bless all in attendance.

One nice tradition from Medieval times serves as an example. A loving cup (a large goblet filled with mead) was present at every notable feast. The host took the first sip, then passed the cup to each guest in order of rank and honor. The chalice always went around the table completely once to signify fellowship. When someone finally drained the last drop, their duty was to toast the guests and host in some befitting manner.

If you adopt a similar custom after a study group meeting, beseech the gods to impart wisdom and discernment to the assembly. When at a handfasting, the passing of the cup denotes support from those gathered to witness the event. Here a fitting toast for is one for joy, peace, and prosperity to the couple. At an initiation, give the new coven member a cup to signal an official welcome. The individual can then present a toast for unity.

No matter the occasion, it is not difficult to find a way to express your feelings in a positive manner. If you are not good at public speaking, draw on the marvelous resource of classical authors for aid. Look to parts of your traditional invocations, prayers and songs. Find words that are comfortable on your lips and mirror the emotion of your heart, and everyone will be touched by the effort.

Friendship

> *"Friendship is the wine of life, let's drink of it and to it."*
>
> —G.F. Handel

> *"Here's to mine, and here's to thine; now's the time to clink it.*
> *Here's a flagon of old wine, and here we are to drink it."*
>
> —Richard Hovry

> *"Bread to feed our friendship, salt to keep it true, water that's for welcome, wine to drink for you."*
>
> —W. French

> *"Friendship, mysterious cement of the soul! Sweetener of life and solder of society."*
>
> —Blair

Pagan Tones

> *"Bacchus, God of joys divine, be thy pleasures ever mine."*
>
> —Anonymous

> *"Great spirit of the grape—delirious kiss of lips immortal from the sky, rare nectar of Olympus born of bliss, bright spark of Aphrodite eye."*
>
> —Madge Merton

*"Now then the songs, but first more wine,
the Gods be with you, friend of mine."*

—Eugene Field

*"Here's to the nine muses—they must have
been a ball team."*

—S. Stoppe

*"Come thou monarch of the vine, Plumply
Bacchus with pink eyne, in thy vats our
cares are drown, with thy grapes our hairs
be crowned, cup us till the world goes
round."*

—Shakespeare

Just for Fun

*"Here is a riddle most abstruse, canst read
the answer right?*
*Why is it that my tongue grows loose only
when I grow tight?"*

—De Beers

*"There are five good reasons why I drink,
good wine, a friend, because I'm dry...or
lest I should be, by and by, or any other
reason why!"*

—John Simmond

*"And wine can, of their wits beguile, make
the sage frolic and the serious smile."*

—Homer

"You raised the grapes, you raised the vine, and later you raised, well, a high-old shine!"

—W. French

"Since natures' holy law is drinking, I'll make the law of nature mine and pledge the universe in wine."

—Tom Moore

Religion

"What makes doctrine plain and clear, about two hundred pounds a year, and that which was proved before, proved false again...two hundred more!"

—Butler

Love

> *"God made man frail as a bubble, God made love and love made trouble!"*
>
> —Dryden

Summary

You now have all the tools you need to start successful brewing, the three most important of which are two good hands and one keen wit! Inevitably during the process of creating magickal beverages you will come across "snags," new ideas, and down right genius periodically. Invention is the mother of all these things, including the occasional obstruction.

Try to be patient with yourself and look upon setbacks as an opportunity to learn something valuable. Throughout the refinement process, not only will your beverages improve, but so should your vision of magick especially as it pertains to the sacred space of home. Approach your artistic endeavor as if you were walking between worlds with an empty bucket, soon to be filled with the elixir of magick itself, then drink your fill!

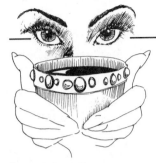

Part II

The Recipes

Introduction

I would like to stress, at this juncture, that my approach to brewing is very simple. There are certainly far more complex approaches that you can use, some of which are found in books such as those listed in the bibliography. What you see here is the way I learned to brew, and thus far have been very happy with the results. I've also found that starting out simple makes the learning process much easier. Everything you do here can be applied to fancier methods very easily.

For simplicity, this part of the book is set up alphabetically starting with beer and ending in wine. Any chapters that have both alcoholic and non alcoholic beverages are separated mid-way so you can easily locate a recipe of your preference, and one suited to your goals. You'll also notice that each recipe includes magickal associations, and bits of myth or lore that could potentially influence the overall energies in the recipe. Read these over and determine if the recipe can be used as it stands for your goals. If it doesn't or if it has a totally different meaning to you, you have two options: Either refine it to meet current needs by changing some of the components, or find another recipe more closely related to your current intentions.

Chapter 4

Beer

"Beer is liquid Bread."

—Liebig

Known to the Anglo Saxons as *Breowan*, Germans as *Briuwan*, Norse as *Brugga*, French as *Brasser*, and Irish as Brach, by any name beer is beverage of "every man." In one writers' account we read, *"Beer is in use with a number of peoples, and each one brews it somewhat differently"*(Strabo XVII 2.5). No matter the process employed or base ingredients, because of its commonality beer became symbolic of the simple pleasures enjoyed with friends, especially celebrations and sports events.

An interesting note in the history of beer making comes from Northern regions. One of the few places where legal transactions could take place besides church was the beer hall. This area was especially designed to serve various social functions, including indicating the levels of importance among guests. Here, beer was passed over a central fire by the daughter of the house when serving a special visitor. Symbolically this represented honor and purity. Similar rituals and esteemed halls venerated this "common" beverage throughout Norse districts from the era of the Vikings to well past the Middle Ages.

Sometimes held in disregard by upper classes, who seemed to prefer their wines and meads, laborers, servants, monks, and housewives predominately made beer, keeping its heritage alive. The legacy of common folk is one for the magickal brewer to remember and honor. This spirit of enterprise, among a group considered otherwise inconspicuous, reminds us how meaningful our own creative energy can be.

One final note in the contemporary history of beer— at least one German company is considering putting brewing into orbit! At the time of this writing, experiments were underway in the Columbia Space Shuttle to determine if cosmic rays and the lack of gravity can alter yeast to produce a tastier beer.

Helpful Hints for Beer Making:

    If possible, always use dry beer yeast versus a bread yeast. Beer yeast is always labeled for top or bottom fermentation and yields a much clearer beverage with no lingering "yeasty" flavor. Note that the brewer's yeast sold at health food stores is not suitable for brewing (it's actually inactive).

ೞ Of hops readily available through brewing stores, Cluster, Cascade, Hallertau and Saaz are some of the best.

ೞ Irish moss, if added to the boiling process for the last few minutes helps clarify your beer.

ೞ Whenever possible use spring water as a base for your beer. This is especially important for people who live in cities with poorer quality water. Any sediments in the tap water can drastically change the flavor of your finished product.

ೞ When you notice that the bottom of your fermenting jars look as if they are covered with film, it is time to rack off the clear liquid. Leaving sediment in the bottom of the jar makes for bitter beers. Racking may be done either by carefully pouring off the top portion of the beer and rinsing the bottle or by siphoning.

Cherry-Clove Ale

1 lb. sweet cherries

4 cups sugar

10 whole cloves

3 qts. strong ale

Directions: Prick cherries with a toothpick on all sides then place them in a 4-quart container with a lid. An excellent choice is a container made of wood or earthenware. Sprinkle the sugar over top of these then fill with the ale. Cover loosely as fermentation should begin within

48 hours. When the rapid bubbling has ceased, strain, cork, and store for six months to a year before drinking. The remaining cherries make marvelous pies and conserves.

Magickal Associations: Clear vision, unhindered joys.

History/Lore: Cloves appeared in Europe between 4 and 6 A.D. There, they remained mostly a culinary herb, but modern magickal practitioners often view them as protective, cleansing and an aid to psychic sight. Cherries always engender thoughts of clear spring days and contemplation. Japan holds cherry blossom festivals where the major activity is simply enjoying the beauty of the flowers.

Alternatives: This is a very simple brew which has the advantage of being very easily changed to suit a wide variety of tastes and magickal goals. One very tasty alternative is strawberries mixed with a stout beer to strengthen love.

DANDELION BEER

1/2 qt. dandelion flowers

1/2 inch ginger root, bruised

1/2 lemon diced finely

2 qts. water

1 cup brown sugar

1/4 cup white sugar

1/8 cup cream of tartar

1/8 oz. beer yeast (top fermenting)

Directions: Wash your dandelion flowers then place them in a large pot along with the ginger, lemon, and water. Boil this together for 15 minutes. In another large container, mix the sugars and cream of tartar together, slowly pouring in the hot liquid to dissolve. Strain and allow to cool to lukewarm.

Meanwhile, suspense the yeast in 1/4 cup warm water. Add this to the cooled liquid to begin fermentation. Keep in a warm place with a heavy cloth over the top for three days before straining and bottling. Age for one week, then enjoy. Shelf life on this is short—about six weeks before it gets very bitter.

Magickal Association: Prophesy, psychic visions, dream oracles.

History/Lore: The most loved and hated plant of all time, dandelions are rich in vitamins and minerals. They are also known to mark the sun by closing their petals when it is dark. They are symbolic of ancient prognostication, and were often used for love augury.

Alternative: Strawberries are, again, a good choice in this recipe, but as an additive. Add about 1/2 quart during the initial boiling process for a sweeter, slightly pink beer which is magickally good for health and happiness. If you plan to eliminate the dandelions, use the juice of two large citron instead to maintain magickal significance.

LEMON BEER

4 qts. boiling water

1 lemon sliced and seeded

1 cup sugar

1/8 oz. beer yeast

raisins (optional)

Directions: Turn the flame off below the boiling water and add sliced lemons and sugar. Cover to let cool until lukewarm. Meanwhile, dissolve the yeast in 1/4 cup warm water and let it stand. Pour this into the pot, stirring once then allow to age overnight (a full 24 hours) until bubbles form on the surface. Strain this into your bottles. If desired, add a raisin to each bottle. Chill before serving. This is a short shelf-life recipe which is ready to consume immediately. After two to three weeks it will become too bitter to drink, but can instead be mixed with brown sugar to make a sweet and sour glaze for poultry.

Magickal Associations: Purification, cleansing, refreshed love, and ideas.

History/Lore: Lemon brings zest and active energy to any beverage. Because it has a natural purgative quality it is mostly associated with magick for refinement. Lemon rind has also been frequently used in love sachets and potions.

Alternative: Substitute 1 1/2 pounds of currents for the lemons in this recipe and reduce your sugar by 1 cup for a beer empowered for protection and Fire Magick.

SMALL BEER #1

3 cups bran hops
3 gal. water
1 Tbs. malt extract
1 gal. molasses
2 tsp. beer yeast

Directions: Boil the bran hops in water for three full hours, then strain. To the hot liquid, stir in molasses until well incorporated. Cool to lukewarm. Meanwhile suspense your yeast in warm water, adding it to the molasses mixture when properly cooled. Cover with heavy cloth for one full day, then strain again while pouring into a cask or bung. Leave your fermenting container open slightly until fermentation has all but ceased (about one week). Bottle and store. This keeps well for about two months.

Magickal Associations: Swift decisions and movement, keen sense of timing.

History/Lore: This was very popular on the frontier, being that it was only mildly alcoholic and fermented very quickly for use. A recipe similar to this one was penned by George Washington.

SMALL BEER #2

4 qts. water

1 1/2 cups sugar

1/4 cup nettle leaves

1/2 cup brown sugar

1 inch bruised ginger root

1 pkg. beer yeast

1/2 tsp. grated lemon peel

sugar cubes

1/2 tsp. grated orange peel

Directions: Place the nettle leaves with ginger, lemon peel, and orange peel in water. Bring to a boil, then lower heat to simmer for a half hour. Strain. To this add sugars, stirring until totally dissolved. Cool the liquid until luke-warm. While you are waiting, suspense the beer yeast in 1/4 cup warm water. Add this to the spiced water and let it sit in a warm area with a cloth over it until all signs of bubbling seem to stop. Strain again while bottling, adding two sugar cubes to each quart bottle. Let this sit closed securely for seven days before drinking. Shelf life is another two to three weeks.

Magickal Associations: Grace, peace of mind, seclusion.

History/Lore: Versions of spiced small beers appear in many lands—specifically to this recipe, Wales, a country known for its beauty and solitude.

Alternatives: For a beer with more cleansing qualities, try adding 1 tsp. full of freshly ground grapefruit rind and two fruit slices during the boiling. For fuller flavor, substitute honey for sugar in the same proportions. Taste test this, as sometimes more sweetness may be desired to offset the grapefruit.

RHUBARB BEER

2 handfuls dandelion leaves and roots, freshly picked and washed

4 sticks rhubarb

1 gal. water

2 lbs. cane sugar

1 tsp. ground ginger root

1/2 oz. beer yeast

Directions: All the ingredients for this, except the yeast should be placed in a large pan and boiled for one hour. When this is finished, allow to cool to lukewarm, adding the yeast which has been suspended in warm water. Bottle after 24 hours, sealed tightly. Drink in three to 40 days without spoilage.

Magickal Associations: Natures abundance, providence, the harvest.

History/Lore: A favorite farmers beer, prepared from items readily given from a bountiful land. Sometimes nettles were also added for nutritional value.

Alternatives: Interesting flavors can be accomplished by adding bits of other common farm fruits or vegetables which you personally enjoy the taste of.

QUICK GINGER BEER

3 inch piece fresh ginger root

1 lemon, peeled (retain) and juiced (retain)

1/4 cup Northern Brewer Hops (if available)

1 1/2 cups sugar

4 qts. hot water

1/4 oz. suspended beer yeast

Directions: Mince and crush the ginger with the back of a spoon or with mortar and pestle. Put this in a large bowl with sugar and lemon peel, pouring the boiling water over top. Stir in hops and allow to steep until lukewarm. Now add lemon juice and yeast mixture. Cover the entire bowl and allow to sit for at least 12 hours before straining and bottling. Ready within five days, retains good flavor for about a month.

Magickal Associations: Power, success, and victory.

History/Lore: Ginger was a widely known spice to the ancient world, being written about by Confucius and being eaten readily in cookies as early as the Egyptians in Cheops. A version of this particular recipe owes its origins to the American frontier.

Alternatives: Try adding various fruits to this mixture at the point where the boiling water is blended in as they pertain to your goal. Strawberries might be included for love or peaches for wisdom.

OUTBACK BEER

2 lbs. sugar

1 1/2 oz. hops

1 tsp. beer yeast

1 gal. water

5 lbs. brown sugar

1 lb. malt extract

Directions: Boil one half (2 quarts) of your water, adding the hops in a cheesecloth container or tea ball to steep. Allow the low, rolling boil to continue for 15 minutes. Remove the bag, then add all other ingredients except yeast, making sure everything dissolves. Turn down heat, add remaining water, and return the hops bag to the pot, leaving the out yeast until the entire mixture is lukewarm.

Leave the pan in a warm area for seven days, skimming off any froth. You will know its ready to bottle when the top clears and sediments fall to the bottom. Remove only the clear liquid, pouring carefully into another pan to settle for 24 hours again. Repeat the following day, only this time pour off clear liquid into bottles, filled 3/4 way full, adding fresh water to the top. Cap securely allowing to age one month before drinking. Best enjoyed cold.

Magickal Associations: Ingenuity, adeptness, quick-mindedness.

History/Lore: Recipes similar to this were very popular for home brewers who had little access to bars due to their remote proximity to villages, and so on, in Australia.

Alternatives: It was not uncommon for other native herbs, roots, flowers, and so on to be added to such basic mixtures to vary their flavor. Similarly, you might want to try blending in accessible kitchen spices such as cinnamon for prosperity or keen insight for job hunting. Another good choice is nutmeg which is considered an aphrodisiac by the Arabs, and which often found itself whole in ale as described by Chaucer.

HIGHLAND BITTER ALE

2 chamomile tea bags

3 tsp. chopped gentian root

3 Tbs. coriander seeds

2 tsp. orange peel

5 whole cloves

1 1/2 qts. Scottish ale

2 small cinnamon sticks

Directions: Place the tea bags, root, seeds, orange, and cloves in a large bowl to crush and mix. Pour this into a large-mouthed jar with secure lid and add ale. It is very important that the jar is covered tightly so the froth of the ale is not lost to this process. Let it sit for seven days, then

strain and rebottle securely. May be enjoyed at room temperature, hot, or cold.

Magickal Associations: Vitality, well-being, wholeness.

History/Lore: Various bitter liquors are served at the
Scottish table before meals to strengthen the stomach and
encourage good health. Gentian is an herb that was considered medicinal in quality and was known by the folk
name of "bitter root."

Alternatives: For the ale, try substituting in equal portions any scotch, other distilled beverages, wine or even
apple cider for those who prefer non alcoholic drinks.

Apple Beer

8 cups hot ale

1 1/2 tsp. nutmeg

1 1/2 tsp. ginger root, ground

brown sugar to taste

8 baked apples, peeled and cored

Directions: Pulp the apple pith and brown sugar together
until you like the flavor which results. Add to this nutmeg
and ginger. Now, slowly add the warmed ale, stirring until
well blended. If desired, float some sweet cakes on top.

Magickal Associations: Earth magicks, the harvest,
wisdom.

History/Lore: Known sometimes by English country-
men as Lambs Wool, this drink was often prepared on
August 1st to honor the angel who protects fruits, seeds,
and all that grows from the land. One cannot help but
notice the similarity of this term to *Lamas* or *La mas ubal*
which literally translates to "day of the apple." Eight apples
are used in this recipe as a number for personal change
and improved control.

TRADITIONAL MULLED ALE

2 cups ale
2 whole cloves
2 tsp. crushed fresh ginger root
2 Tbs. butter
2 Tbs. sugar
2 eggs beaten

Directions: Place ale, clove, ginger, butter, and sugar into a large sauce pan and bring to a slight boil. Slowly pour this mixture into the beaten eggs, then transfer into a large bottle. Pour this into another jug, repeating this several times to build up froth, then return to the pan to re-heat. Remove ginger and cloves before serving hot.

Magickal Associations: Partnership, love, and romance.

History/Lore: A favorite Victorian treat, mulled ale is a warm, welcoming beverage for cold winter nights in front of a romantic fire. The number 2 is employed throughout this recipe to encourage positive emotions and communications between two people.

MAPLE BEER

2 lbs. dark malt extract (dried)
1/2 qt. real maple syrup
2 1/2 gal. water
1 oz. hops pellets
1 pkg. yeast

Directions: Place malt, syrup, water, and hops together in a large pot over medium flame and bring to a boil. Continue to boil for 20 minutes, scooping off any froth. Cool to lukewarm, then add yeast which has been mixed with 1/ 4 cup warm water and allowed to sit for at least 15 minutes. Cover and allow the entire beverage to sit in a warm place for three days, then bottle securely for two weeks before drinking.

Magickal Associations: Long life, sweet pleasures, guided mystical energies.

History/Lore: This recipe appeared in Colonial America where sap was used as a basic sweetening ingredient for beers, yielding a tasty smoky flavor. Maple tree branches have been used for magickal wands, or to insure the health of children.

Alternatives: Adding a piece of vanilla bean to this recipe during the boiling process makes for a wonderfully unique blend.

SUNSET ALE

1 1/2 lbs. malt extract

1/2 oz. Bullion hops

4 oz. crystal malt

1/8 oz. Cascade pellets

1/2 tsp. gypsum

1 gal. water

1/4 tsp. salt

1/2 pkg. top fermenting

1/4 cup dextrose beer yeast

Directions: Bring your water to a low rolling boil adding gypsum and salt. Now add malts and boil for 20 minutes. Remove 1/4 cup of the liquid and cool to lukewarm to suspense the yeast in. Meanwhile, add the aromatic hops, simmering for 15 minutes (cascade) and cool. In a large container place 1/2 gallon cold water with yeast. Pour the beer liquid into this and cover loosely. Watch for all signs of fermentation to cease, then add dextrose and age for 4 to 6 weeks using a fermentation lock before bottling.

Magickal Associations: Fire and sun magick, courage, vitality.

History/Lore: This ale, when properly made, has a color similar to amber, which was once thought by Egyptians to be the solidified essence of the setting sun's tears.

Alternatives: For a less bitter ale, eliminate Bullion hops.

Chapter 5

Charming Cordials, Amultetic Aperitifs, Luscious Liqueurs

> *"From fumes of wine grown heady, my friends gave hope last eve."*
>
> —Hafiz

An old legend recounted by St. Simon (a French chronicler of the late 1600s) claims that cordials were originally invented to bring consolation to King Louis XIV in his elder years. Even as the name might imply, cordials are drinks which, when properly prepared, inspire a friendly, favorable atmosphere for conversation. They most frequently appear for sharing after dinner.

Historically speaking, if an aperitif was poured out before dinner, it had a medicinal application versus a moral benefit. Flavored brandy, for example, preceded meals to aid digestion and whet the appetite. This was especially true for brandies made with anise, orange water and lemon water. In Scotland, Whiskey blended carefully with chamomile, orange peel, and juniper berries was an honored stomach strengthener. This basic significance in service time should be kept in mind for your own magickal preparations.

Further, cordials are fruit-flavored drinks that encourage joy. Liquors are similarly so, except they can also be flavored with spices. However, there are many variations on this concept that work well in a social setting, some of which will be covered below.

ELDERBERRY-BLACKBERRY BETTERMENT

2 qts. elderberries

2 cups brown sugar

2 qts. blackberries

2 qts. water

2 cups brandy

ginger and clove (opt)

Directions: Place the cleaned blackberries and elderberries together in a large pot with water. Simmer over a low flame to extract the juice, crushing and stirring regularly for 30 minutes. Strain off juice into another pot. Rewarm the liquid so that sugar can be dissolved. Add any personally desired spices at this point and boil for 15 minutes. Cool and add brandy before bottling.

Magickal Associations: Any rite for Pan, connection to nature, health, and well-being.

History/Lore: Elderberries and blackberries figure heavily into folk remedials, the tree of the Elder itself being boasted as the only wood acceptable for Pan's Pipes.

Alternatives: The spices you choose to add to this recipe can aid magickal applications. Nutmeg is one option for luck, or allspice to accentuate the healthful aspects of this beverage.

APRICOT NECTAR

1 lb. ripe apricots, blanched
1 lb. dried apricots
1 cup apricot nectar
1 tsp. vanilla extract
1 qt. vodka
1 1/2 cups sugar

Directions: Slice and prick your whole apricots into eight pieces. Likewise, slice and prick the dried apricots. Disperse these equally into 1-quart jars with half the vanilla in each. Next, warm the vodka only slightly so that the sugar can be dissolved in it. Pour half of this mixture into each jar, cover and seal. This mixture should age three months for greatest success, the liquid being served as a cordial and the fruits as a dessert with whipped cream.

Magickal Associations: The spirit of Amour!

History/Lore: Apricot is considered a love food being sacred to, and ruled by, Venus. It was a favored fruit on Elizabethan tables and thought to owe its origins to Western Asia.

Alternatives: To add a little fervor to this beverage, reduce apricot juice by half, then blend in 1/2 cup passion fruit juice.

CRANBERRY-ORANGE COCKTAIL

1 lb. cranberries, ground
2 whole oranges, ground (seedless)
3 1/2 cups sugar
2 cups rum

Directions: Place all your ingredients, including any juice from the grinding process into a 2-quart jar with a secure lid. Keep in a cool area, shaking thoroughly once a day for the next six weeks. Strain into bottles and seal for use over the holidays.

Magickal Associations: The harvest, thankfulness, bounty.

History/Lore: This beverage is excellent to make with leftovers from the Thanksgiving table, which are already blessed with the energies of gratitude for Divine providence.

Alternatives: Reduce orange by one, adding two peeled, ground apples in its place. Magickally this encourages improved wisdom with one's resources.

FRUIT RATAFIA

1/2 lb. dried figs

6 ripe peaches, pitted

6 pomegranates, juiced

1 cup sugar (or more to taste)

1 qt. distilled spirits (your choice)

Directions: Place your ingredients in equal proportions split between two 1-quart jars. Make sure that peaches and figs are pierced first (use a fork or toothpick). Cover securely, shaking daily for one month then strain and bottle for use.

Magickal Associations: Commitment, approval, verification.

History/Lore: Ratafia comes from a tradition of the Middle Ages where parties accepting any legal transaction or agreement would share a drink to celebrate its "ratification." Figs here are used for insight, peaches for wisdom, and pomegranate for luck.

Helpful Hint: One of the easiest ways to juice pomegranate seeds is to place them inside cheesecloth, and press with the back side of a spoon in a bowl. Remove the white seeds when expressed, then twist the cloth to release the remaining juice. This is a little time consuming, but well worth the effort for the flavor it produces.

CITRUS TONIC

1 cup water

2 cups sugar

3 cups whiskey

2 cups mixed orange, lemon, and grapefruit peels

Directions: Warm the water in a small saucepan with sugar until dissolved. Add this to the whiskey and fruit peels. Please note that you should remove as much of the white lining from the peels as possible to alleviate tartness in this cordial. Leave the ingredients to set together in a sealed container for three months. Strain and serve warm with a touch of honey and cinnamon sticks.

Magickal Associations: Good health, revitalization, refreshed perspectives.

History/Lore: Being high in vitamin C, with a full bodied aroma, this beverage is wonderful during the winter months to ease the discomforts of colds. For this application, have a small portion before bed.

Alternatives: For fruitier flavor and increased vitamin benefit, decrease whiskey by 1 cup, adding 1/2 cup each orange and grapefruit juice, plus 1 tsp. lemon juice. Sugar content may need to be increased for personal taste.

PLUM DANDY

1 qt. brandy or vodka

1 lb. ripe plums

2 cups sugar

Directions: Place all your ingredients together in a large crock, well sealed. Shake daily for eight weeks. Strain the liquid off into bottles which should be sealed and aged six months before consumption. The fruit may be used for tarts, pies, or a spiked dessert with cream garnish after straining.

Magickal Associations: Safety of and open discourse among family and friends; kinship.

History/Lore: This cordial comes to us from the Ukraine where it is a favored beverage on cold nights with family or friends. Bits of the plum tree were sometimes used as protection to rural homes, by hanging the branches on the entryway so no avarice could come between those within.

Alternatives: This particular recipe works very well with peaches or pears, too, with similar magickal outcomes.

FOUR QUARTER HARMONY

1 cup diced quince (Earth)

1 cup mulberries (Air)

1 orange, peeled and sectioned (Fire)

1 large apple, diced (Water)

1 qt. vodka

2/3 cup honey

1/8 tsp. cinnamon and ginger

Directions: Place the fruits in a large oven-proof crock with vodka and allow to soak for four to five hours. Mix in the honey and spices next, covering the crock securely.

A flour and water paste over the edges helps to keep flavor, aroma and alcohol content at a good level. Place the entire mixture in the oven at 200 degrees Fahrenheit for 10 hours. Cool and strain, serving either hot or cold.

Magickal Associations: Balance, symmetry, accord.

History/Lore: Each of the four fruits chosen in this recipe correspond with one Quarter of the magick Circle (one Element). Just as in magick, combining each element in harmony produces some powerful and, in this instance tasty, results! This particular recipe comes from the Ukraine.

Alternatives: If you can not readily find quince, feel free to substitute fresh or canned pears (in juice, not syrup).

CHOCOLATE CRÉME DU MINT

2 oz. semi-sweet chocolate

1/2 cup cold water

1/2 cup sugar

1 cup heavy cream, whipped

1/2 qt. milk

1/2 L Rumple Mints (or other mint liquor)

Directions: Place the chocolate in a sauce pan with water and stir over low heat until totally melted and mixed. Add to this the sugar, cooking about ten minutes until thickened. Let this cool, folding in the whipped cream. Set aside. Next heat the milk over a low flame until lukewarm. Add your Rumple Mints and cream mixture, stirring until all is well incorporated. Enjoy hot, or store in the refrigerator, shaking before serving.

Magickal Associations: Pleasure, warmth, fanciful diversions.

History/Lore: Pre-Columbian civilizations in South America were known to cultivate chocolate. Later, Mexican chocolate was imported to the new world first as a delicacy, and later as an important baking staple.

Alternatives: For a beverage to encourage "sun" energies and health alongside enjoyment, use orange flavored liquor in this recipe in place of the mint. If the mint liquor is too expensive, use 1/2 liter of vodka and add 1 tsp. of mint extract to the chocolate water mixture while it is melting.

HEATHER HONEY CORDIAL

1 cup water
1 Tbs. vanilla extract (not imitation)
1 whole clove (per person involved)
1 small cinnamon stick
1 cup heather honey
2 cups vodka

Directions: Place the water in a large saucepan and bring to a low rolling boil. Add spices, allowing to infuse like a tea while the water cools. If you don't like cloves that much, remove them before the water reaches lukewarm. Strain, then rewarm to dissolve the honey, removing any froth that comes to the surface. Add vodka, strain, and bottle securely allowing to age for two weeks before consumption.

Magickal Associations: Messages, rapport, opening the lines of discourse.

History/Lore: This beverage, with but minor changes, owes its origins to Prussia, where it is believed to aid smooth speech and effective communications. Cloves were a favorite Medieval breath freshener used between lovers who hoped to steal a kiss!

Alternatives: To further accentuate the power of speech in this recipe, try replacing the vanilla with either mint or almond extract. Both of these are aligned with the Element of Air, which helps move messages towards their proper destination.

CURRANT-RASBERRY DELIGHT

3 cups freshly picked currants (red or black)

1 lb. frozen or fresh raspberries (red)

3 cups water

1 1/2 cups sugar (or to taste)

6 cups Absolute Currant

Directions: Place raspberries and currants together in a pan with water. Simmer over a low flame for two hours, pressing frequently with the back of a spoon. Remove and strain, keeping the fruit for tarts, ice cream topping, and so on. Place the juice back on the stove, slowly adding sugar. Taste frequently, making sure to add a little more than you like because this sweetness will be toned down considerably when you next blend in the currant vodka. Bottle and age for one month.

Magickal Associations: Sun and fire magicks (note the deep red color achieved in the finished product). If it comes out pink, it might be more appropriate for friendship and improved attitudes.

History/Lore: Currants were sometimes imported to England via Portugal along with oranges to benefit the Elizabethan table where they quickly became favored for all manner of sweets including jellies, comfits, and sotelties.

Alternative: For a smooth, older version of this beverage use honey instead of sugar. This yields a cordial similar to Raspberry Horilka (recipe later this book). This particular beverage is also good with traditional "fire" herbs such as cinnamon and ginger added during the simmering process.

MIGHTY MILK

1 qt. milk
1 small cinnamon stick
1 1/2 cups sugar
4 egg whites
1 tsp. lemon juice
1 cup cinnamon liquor
2 inch piece lemon peel

Directions: Place your milk in a small pan with 1 cup of sugar. Add lemon peel and cinnamon stick while simmering over low flame for about three to five minutes. Cool, strain, and set in freezer. Meanwhile, beat your egg whites with 1/2 cup of sugar, adding lemon juice when peaks form. Beat this mixture into the chilled milk very slowly with equal portions of the cinnamon liquor. Return to the freezer until a slush-like consistency forms. Serve in chilled glasses.

Magickal Associations: Improved potency, passion, fervent energy.

History/Lore: In the 1500s Arabic camel caravans would arrive at European markets bearing many spices including cinnamon which they knew would fetch a handsome price. In Chinese mythology, cinnamon was the spice of immortality. Magickally, cinnamon is ruled by Venus and considered a fire herb, making it an excellent aphrodisiac.

Alternative: For success and prosperity, substitute 1 inch of bruised ginger root and ginger liquor for the cinnamon in this recipe.

GRAINS OF PARADISE

1 qt. distilled beverage (your choice)
1/2 Tbs. cumin seed
1/2 Tbs. aniseed
1/2 Tbs. sesame seed
1/2 Tbs. angelica seed
1/2 Tbs. caraway seed
1/2 Tbs. coriander seed
1/2 Tbs. fennel seed
1/4 cup hot water
3/4 cup sugar

Directions: Place your seeds together in a blender, food processor or mortar to grind them into a fine powder. Put these in a large covered container with your chosen beverage. This needs to age for 30 days. After aging, take the sugar and dissolve in hot water. Carefully strain your seeded liquid into a different bottle, adding the sugar mix. Shake well until incorporated. Rebottle and age for another month before consuming.

Magickal Associations: Thoroughness, finishing projects, celebrating variety.

History/Lore: The number 7 (the number of seeds used for this cordial) is one of completion. There are seven days in the week, seven wonders in the world, and in the Biblical account of creation, it took seven days to form the Earth. Seven is also a potent number for Moon magicks and improved insight.

Alternatives: Any seed herb (such as dill) can be substituted into this recipe for another seed which you may not enjoy or just for variety. Likewise, try changing the number of seeds to reflect different magickal goals, such as five seeds for versatility and awareness.

RUSSIAN VOSTORG

1 cup cognac
2 Tbs. cherry liquor
1 tsp. lemon juice
2 cherries (garnish)
3 to 4 ice cubes

Directions: Depending on personal preference, this cordial can be prepared one of two ways. The first way is to place all the ingredients except the cherries in a blender for a whipped, icy beverage topped with whole cherries. The second is to simply place the components in a shaker and serve over ice.

Magickal Associations: One world perspectives, pleasure, broadening outlooks.

History/Lore: Shortly after the advent of air freight, many nations found customs, specifically those pertaining to food and drink changing to meet the new global awareness. In Moscow, certain official groups took to enjoying this cocktail instead of straight vodka before dinner. It's name in Russian translates to mean "delight."

Alternatives: One especially nice touch with this drink is to add a fresh, white gardenia as garnish to encourage peace.

Orange-Vanilla Whip

3 whole oranges

3 whole vanilla beans

2 cups sugar

1/2 cup water

3 cups tequila

Directions: Cut three equidistant slits in each orange, inserting 1/3 of each vanilla bean within the crevice. Place these in a large crock and set aside. Next, in a small sauce-pan, warm the water and sugar together until a syrup is formed. Pour this over the oranges along with tequila. Store in airtight container for three months in the refrigerator, shaking daily, then strain. Put into blender for a few minutes until frothy, then serve in chilled glasses.

Magickal Associations: Health and well-being for the whole person.

History/Lore: Vanilla beans were often thought to be a kind of magickal charm to ward off weariness. Likewise, oranges are a kind of health panacea, being rich in vitamin C. The number three in this recipe is repeated to encourage the triune balance of body, mind, and soul.

Alternative: Much the same magickal effect can be achieved using three apples with three allspice berries each lodged within them.

Chapter 6

Dessert Drinks

*"Fame is the scentless sunflower
with gaudy crown of gold;
but friendship is the breathing rose
with sweets in every fold."*
—Oliver Wendell Holmes

*"As sweet and musical as bright Apollo's
lute, and a perpetual feast of nectared
sweets."*
—John Milton

I think that there is a little bit of child in all of us. Some of my dearest memories of my father are those moments when he snuck a bit of gourmet candy (especially jelly beans) or baked luscious holiday treats, swearing all the while that he would never bake again. Yet, every year I found him in the kitchen, working furiously over some new confection with which to surprise the family. It is this memory, combined with an honestly inherited sweet-tooth, that inspired this chapter.

How often during hot summer months have you longed for a homemade dessert, but hated the idea of turning on the oven or fussing? In the case of dessert beverages, you don't need to worry about either! Instead, a blender becomes the implement of choice, simple ingredients suffice nicely, and the movement within this marvel of technology literally "whips up" a little magick with your drinks!

BANANA SPILT SPRITZ

1 pt. of your favorite ice cream

1 cup soda water or ginger ale

1 banana, sliced

2 tsp. maraschino cherry juice

2 tsp. of your favorite topping

whipped cream (garnish)

1 cherry (garnish)

sprinkles (garnish)

Directions: Place ice cream and 1/2 cup of the ginger ale in the blender on low setting. Slowly add the remaining soda with the other ingredients except garnishes. You may need to add more ginger ale to achieve a smooth enough texture to drink. Don't forget to put it in a large glass with two straws! This is definitely a beverage for sharing.

Magickal Associations: Love towards self and others, spiritual compassion, courtship and romance.

History/Lore: Banana splits bring out the romantic idealist in almost everyone. In India, the banana leaf was a predominant part of marriage rites. In Polynesia, the banana plant figures heavily into legends, and in some areas banana plants are thought to encourage luck. The cherry on top of this creation also encourages love, being ruled by Venus.

Alternatives: Consider changing the base ice cream to relate more directly to your magickal goals. Good examples include Neapolitan to build tolerance among "different" peoples, or cookies n' cream to encourage the innocent love of children to be born in your heart.

TURTLE TENACITY

1 pt. butter-toffee ice cream

1 1/2 cups milk

1 Tbs. hot fudge sauce

1 Tbs. hot caramel sauce

nuts (garnish)

Directions: Since self images are usually a function of the conscious mind, allow the ice cream to get soft in the light of the sun. Pour this into a blender with the milk and sauce on medium speed, beating until frothy. Garnish with nuts of your choice.

Magickal Associations: Boldness, assertive speech, self-assurance, building confidence.

History/Lore: While I am playing on a pun for a popular candy here, the symbolism of the turtle is no less important to this beverage. Visualize yourself like a great sea tortoise, slowly but powerfully emerging from your shell while drinking.

Alternatives: The types of nuts placed on top of your drink can enhance more specific magickal ends. Use almonds for healing self images, cashew or peanut to improve prospects for personal prosperity, coconut to help you feel secure in your Path or walnut to provide protection from negative thoughts about yourself.

APPLE-GRAPE GURU

1/2 cup grape juice

1/2 cup apple juice

1/2 cup apple yogurt

3 crushed ice cubes

Directions: Thoroughly mix all ingredients together until a full head of foam is achieved. Serve cold with a slice of apple or grapes as garnish.

Magickal Associations: Dream divination, spiritual insight.

History/Lore: An old superstition claims that eating grapes helps encourage prophetic dreams. This combined with the "healthy" wisdom of apples should allow you to interpret your visions sagaciously!

Alternatives: For peace in a relationship, delete the grape juice, increasing apple to 1 cup and adding a slice of fresh, peeled apple to the mixture, or as a garnish. Apples are ruled by Venus and have long been used in love divinations.

ORANGE JOY JUICE

juice of one orange
1 tsp. sugar
1 slice of lemon squeezed
1 tsp. maraschino cherry juice
1 cherry (garnish)

Directions: The best part about this beverage is the simplicity of preparation. You can literally pour your ingredients in a glass, swirl with a spoon, and enjoy.

Magickal Associations: Happiness, pleasure, satisfaction.

History/Lore: Lemons are thought to encourage pure-hearted feelings among people. In Voodoo traditions, the empty lemon is often used as a magickal container or cup. Oranges keep us happy through sound bodies and spirits. In the orient, oranges are sometimes given as a token of joyful wishes.

Alternatives: Substitute lime for lemon if you feel your happiness is being impeded by negative energies from others. Some traditions use lime twigs to protect from the "evil eye."

CACAO PROSPERITY

2 oz. sweet bakers chocolate
1 oz. unsweetened chocolate
2 Tbs. milk
1/2 stick cinnamon
1 Tbs. sugar
1/2 tsp. vanilla
1 beaten egg
nutmeg and heavy cream (garnish)

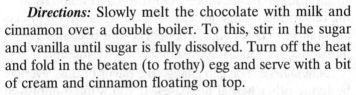

Directions: Slowly melt the chocolate with milk and cinnamon over a double boiler. To this, stir in the sugar and vanilla until sugar is fully dissolved. Turn off the heat and fold in the beaten (to frothy) egg and serve with a bit of cream and cinnamon floating on top.

Magickal Associations: Improving finances, abundance, getting your "money's worth."

History/Lore: In Mexico, the beans of the Cacao tree were used as currency, and only the rich could afford to drink beverages made from them, quite literally drinking wealth! Apparently this idea was not unique to Mexico as it has similar versions in ancient Mesopotamia, and even the Aztecs.

Alternatives: Try orange chocolate in place of the bakers for similar magickal effects, or mint chocolate to help heal a financially stressful situation.

SPARKLING VITAMIN C

1 cup orange pekoe tea
1 Tbs. honey

1 cup orange juice

1 cup ginger ale

3 strawberries (garnish)

1 slice of orange (garnish)

Directions: Pre prepare the orange tea (or orange spice). While it is still warm, stir in honey to dissolve. Cool, then blend together with orange juice and ginger ale. Serve chilled or over crushed ice with sliced strawberries and oranges for a bright, invigorating drink.

Magickal Associations: Energy, health, vitality, strength, rejuvenation.

History/Lore: Tea has long been considered not only a social drink, but one which helps calm and relax. By adding this to the orange juice, noted for its healthful effects and a little soda for energy "bubbles" this becomes a wonderful magick tonic when you need a pick-me-up.

Alternatives: You can change the flavor of this beverage by trying other herbal tea bases. If you wanted improved energy for health, for example, use apple-cinnamon tea.

RASPBERRY ROMANCE

1 cup fresh raspberries

1 cup pineapple juice

1/4 cup grapefruit juice

1 slice of lemon

Directions: Blend or mash the raspberries until very fine. Slowly add the other juices and a touch of sugar if needed to offset any tartness. Garnish with a slice of lemon.

Magickal Associations: Faithfulness, loyalty and commitment especially in relationships.

History/Lore: Pineapple juice thought to hinder stray passions, while berries in general are "love" foods. In some lands, ancient brides carried lemon flowers as a symbol of purity and tenderness.

Alternative: For a more erotic drink, substitute passion fruit juice for the pineapple. This particular mixture is a nice choice to try before conception rites.

PINA-COLADA IMPOSTER

1 cup coconut (or coconut milk)

1 cup pineapple juice

3 tsp. sugar

1 tsp rum extract

crushed ice

Directions: Canned coconut cream seems to work best for this beverage, having an already smooth texture. To this thoroughly mix in unsweetened pineapple juice, sugar and rum extract. Serve over crushed ice.

Magickal Associations: Protection from falsehood, improved awareness of deceptive images.

History/Lore: Both the pineapple and coconut are associated with protective magick; the coconut because of its strong, resilient shell and the pineapple because of the prickly outer spine. Since both these fruits magickal association comes from "without," this energy of this beverage is best suited for situations where external information seems misleading.

Alternative: Add a few strawberries to this drink to help you remove your rose-colored glasses pertaining to a romantic partner. In this instance, honey might be a better choice over sugar.

GIRL SCOUT STYLE COOKIE-CREAM

1/2 cup plain yogurt

1 tsp. sugar

1/2 cup chocolate milk

1 tsp. mint extract

Directions: This is a wonderful beverage which tastes akin to the Girl Scout Thin Mints. Place the first four ingredients in a blender (or use a hand beater) to mix thoroughly. Garnish with a girl scout cookie of your choice.

Magickal Associations: Resilience, stability, security. energy for "good deeds."

History/Lore: Minthe was once a nymph changed into an indestructible ground plant by Persephone. Mint is sacred to Aphrodite, and is also considered a good herb for protection and prosperity.

Alternatives: For more flexibility in relationships, add a sprinkle of coconut to the top of this beverage. Coconut trees have a reputation for being incredibly adaptable, their parts being applied to literally hundreds of uses.

DEATH BY CHOCOLATE

1 scoop chocolate fudge ice cream

1 cup chocolate yogurt

1/4 cup chocolate chips

1 cup chocolate milk

swirl chocolate syrup (garnish)

Directions: Place all ingredients except syrup into a blender on low speed for about 2 to 3 minutes. Add more milk if it is too thick. Beat on medium for another two minutes. Pour into a large glass, swirling a little chocolate syrup on top. Sit down and pat yourself on the back for just being a unique person, and enjoy!

Magickal Associations: Self love and pampering, sweet things in life, simple luxuries.

History/Lore: There is very strong scientific evidence to suggest that chocoholics actually do receive a kind of unique pleasure from eating this substance. Being that I am among this group, I like this drink as an alternative for those moments when I would otherwise want hot-fudge sundaes!

Alternatives: Thanks to the booming gourmet ice cream business, there are quite a few themes this beverage could reflect. You could try butterscotch with plain milk, butterscotch chips, and so on for golden sun energy or perhaps strawberry ingredients all around for joy and love.

STRAWBERRY-BANANA STIMULATION

1 banana

1 cup plain yogurt

1 cup milk

5 strawberries

1 tsp. honey

pinch of ginger or cinnamon (optional)

Directions: Blend together the first five ingredients until well incorporated. Ladies pour this into a brandy style glass, men into a long, champagne style one. As you drink, envision the energy moving to 'pleasure' centers to help encourage sexual enjoyment.

Magickal Associations: Sexual potency, stamina, fertility, fecundity, physical pleasure.

History/Lore: This is an especially nice beverage to try just before conception rites, or for people who are having problems enjoying physical contact. Plain yogurt encourages the spiritual nature while the banana is the male energies and strawberry, female.

Alternative: After drinking, nibble on a spearmint leaf to further encourage sexual interest and cleanse the breath for romantic encounters.

ORANGE-PINEAPPLE PURIFIER

5 cups orange juice

3 cups pineapple juice

1 slice of lemon, squeezed

1 vanilla cookie stick

orange whipped cream (garnish)

Directions: Pour orange, pineapple and squeezed lemon juice into a large covered container and shake well. For simple purification rites nothing else should be added. For dessert, however, I recommend one teaspoon of sugar, a gourmet vanilla cookie and some orange whipped cream to garnish it.

Magickal Associations: Cleansing, health, psychic and physical purification, change.

History/Lore: This drink is an excellent prelude to a ritual fast or bath, both of which have purgative qualities. In the case of the latter, I even suggest adding lemon, orange, and pineapple rind to the water. The reason these three fruits have been magickally linked to cleansing is fairly easy to observe when their juice touches any dirty or sticky area!

Alternatives: Lime, mint, and guava juice can be substituted for lemon, orange, and vanilla cookie. In this case, the mint leaf is used for garnish, the magickal effect being much the same.

BUTTERSCOTCH BREEZE

2 1/2 cups milk

2 egg beaten frothy

1 pt. butterscotch ice cream

2 tsp. brandy extract

dash nutmeg

Directions: Place milk and eggs together in blender, mixing until foamy. Next add the remaining ingredients and serve in a mug.

Magickal Associations: New beginnings, renewed health, the energy of spring and rebirth, the God and Goddess within.

History/Lore: The symbolism for this beverage comes to us from the ever versatile egg. The egg has been so important to human foods and trade that literally hundreds of superstitions have evolved around it. The first egg laid by a hen is thought very lucky to the point of encouraging wish-fulfillment, eggs are only to be brought into a house during day light, and broken eggs have often been used for scrying forms of divination. Magickally the egg is considered the sign of fertility as is seen so readily in Eostre celebrations. Many of the ancient creation stories and Deities have some type of egg figure into them.

Alternatives: If this particular beverage is being combined with an effort to conceive a child, appropriate ingredients to add include a banana, nuts or peaches. In the instance of a "health" beverage, use only one egg in the drink, visualizing your sickness being poured into the other which can later be buried.

THANKSGIVING DAY DELIGHT

2 cups cranberry juice

2 Tbs. brown sugar

2 slices ginger root

1/4 tsp. nutmeg

1/4 tsp. cinnamon

1 to 2 whole cloves

2 cups orange juice

Directions: If you are using whole cranberries for this, they must be ground very finely to extract the juice. Otherwise, a frozen concentrate is best. Warm the cranberry juice just enough to incorporate the brown sugar completely. Add spices and allow to cool. Blend this together with orange juice and two ice cubes for a refreshing holiday drink.

Magickal Associations: Joyous gatherings, kinship appreciation, gratitude for blessings.

History/Lore: I purposefully designed this drink to be close to traditional cranberry-orange relish, that is so predominant at Thanksgiving in our home. This is a marvelously healthful drink with rejuvenating qualities. To keep to the theme of the beverage, before drinking any yourself pour a little on Earth in thankfulness for Nature's providence, and that of the Divine.

Alternatives: Any fruit which is traditionally considered part of a "harvest" is a good option here, particularly apples which will also bring peace and love to your celebration, no matter when it takes place.

Chapter 7

Blossoming Beverages

> *"Such epithets, like pepper*
> *give zest to what you write,*
> *And if you use them sparely,*
> *they whet the appetite*
> *but if you lay them on too thick*
> *you spoil the matter quite!"*
> —Benjamin H. Hill

> *"She be fairer than the day, or the flowery*
> *meads in May."*
> —George Wither

Of all civilizations, three groups stand out among the rest as flower fanciers; the ancient Chinese, Medieval Europeans, and American Victorians. In the first instance, artisans fashioned transparent cups to highlight the beauty of the beverage within, often flavored by, and accented with, Chrysanthemums. Marco Polo noted in his travels that the Chinese also loved roses, jasmine, and orange blossom, the last two flavoring and scenting teas.

In the Middle Ages, the Nobles adored flowers, roses again finding notoriety above all other petals. Cookbooks from the period reveal hundreds of uses for roses including as a base for wines, beer, facial waters, conserves, pottage, meat and poultry flavorings, candies, perfumes, and literally a myriad of other applications to tantalize the imagination. Two examples are *The Closet Opened* and *Delights for Ladies*.

It should be noted, however, that roses were not the only blossoms to shine upon the Medieval table. The Alchemists, herbalists, and cunning folk of this period knew every edible bloom, and made practical use of that knowledge.

Moving forward into our own century, the Victorians, being a romantic lot, actually used an entire floral language to express their feelings. While a few flowers remained in culinary or medicinal use, slowly petals became objects for self-care and pampering. The perfume industry was well established, and potpourri and scented water adorned nearly every boudoir.

So it is for that reason, for the most part, that we must search older sources for flower beverages. Thankfully, herbalists today are reawakening the public to many of the healthy benefits flowers provide. Additionally, their flavors are akin to many common herbs and vegetables. This chapter celebrates flowers as part of our bountiful, magickal beverage table.

Nonalcoholic Recipes

SOLITARY MAY BOWL

1/2 handful of fresh woodruff

3 cups cider or apple juice

1 slice of orange

2 to 3 whole strawberries

2 tsp. sugar

Directions: Rinse the woodruff and strawberries thoroughly. Place your ingredients together in a bowl and mix well. To increase the flavor, warm the cider or juice first. Chill the bowl for a minimum of one hour before straining and pouring into a large glass to enjoy. Garnish with the berries. A great spring-time refresher!

Magickal Associations: Success, prosperity, protection, especially in "battles."

History/Lore: The beautiful white woodruff blossoms are considered sacred to the Goddess. In pre Christian times, the bouquet of this flower was used predominantly to scent a variety of drinks. In the Middle Ages, woodruff was thought a good tonic for sickness, fever, and to purge the blood.

Alternative: For a drink with greater cleansing quality, add a slice of lemon in place of the orange and add one to two whole cloves. Both versions of this may be served hot with a stick of cinnamon.

> In 1897 there were listed over 6,000 kinds of flowers in Europe alone, of them 10 percent are odiferous.

DANDELION DELIGHT

1 gal. orange juice

1 lemon, juiced

3 cups dandelion petals

1/4 cup of sugar

ginger ale (optional)

Directions: Clean off the dandelion petals with cool water. In the mean time, warm the orange juice and lemon together, then add dandelions. Make certain you only have petals (no green parts). Add the sugar, stirring constantly until dissolved, strain, and chill. For a light, bubbly body, measure 3/4 glass and 1/4 glass of ginger ale.

Magickal Associations: Divination, wind magick, wishes and goals, communicating with the Spirit world.

History/Lore: This lovely spring tonic makes good use of pesky weeds to rejuvenate the body with Earth's reawakening. Dandelions are high in vitamins and legends claim that Hecate once entertained Theseus with dandelion water.

Alternative: Try preparing the same recipe only using 100 percent lemonade as the base, and the juice of one orange instead. This has a refreshing, purifying quality and is wonderful on a hot summer day over crushed ice.

HONEYED HONEYSUCKLE

1 gal. grape juice
2 cups honeysuckle blossoms
1 1/2 cups orange juice
1 jasmine tea bag
1/4 cup honey

Directions: Place all your ingredients together in a large pot for simmering. Warm very slowly over low flame until honey is fully dissolved. If your petals turn translucent before the honey is mixed, remove them and continue warming. Cool to room temperature, strain, and chill. Shake well before serving.

Magickal Associations: Awareness (especially psychic), good fortune, financial stability, protection of health, friendship.

History/Lore: Known also as Woodbine, in the language of flowers honeysuckle symbolizes brotherly affection. It is featured in the Old Testament as the third flower in the Song of Solomon. In the Middle Ages, a syrup of honeysuckle was used to fight fever.

Alternative: I like this prepared simply with warm water or apple juice in place of the grape. With apple, this beverage is magickally appropriate for wisdom in relationships or with regard to personal resources.

VIOLET LIAISON

1 lemon sliced

1 orange sliced

1 qt. spring water

2 whole cloves

1/2 cup packed violet petals

Directions: Place the first four ingredients in your simmering pan first. Heat the liquid until tepid, but not hot. Add the violets and simmer until they are almost see-through. Strain and serve hot or cold in one glass with two straws!

Magickal Associations: Romance, love, keeping a cool head. and warm heart, protection in relationships.

History/Lore: Both Violets and cloves are strongly associated with human passions, thus in this recipe two singular cloves are used to symbolize a couple. When carried, cloves are thought to encourage romantic interest. Violets are under the zodiacal domain of Venus, symbolizing enchantment in the language of flowers.

Alternative: Try adding two chamomile tea bags to the simmering liquid to bring peace in a home where tensions have discouraged the spirit of romance.

BOUNCING BORAGE

1 1/4 cups water
1 Tbs. borage flowers
pinch vanilla bean
1 allspice berry
1 cup mulberry juice
1 tsp. honey

Directions: In a small pan or crock, warm your juice to boiling. Pour this over all other ingredients except the honey. Let steep for 15 minutes, strain, and add honey. Enjoy hot or chilled.

Magickal Associations: Energy in abundance, vitality, endurance, spunk.

History/Lore: Francis, Lord Bacon wrote that the Borage leaf has "excellent spirits" to repress "dusky melancholy and so cure madness." For health, borage is high in both potassium and calcium, and as such it is regarded as one of the four principal flowers among ancient civilizations.

Alternative: Replace vanilla with juice of 1/4 lemon and 1/4 orange for allspice, adding a slice of ginger root for energy in love, or purification before magick. The additional bonus to the latter is that borage is thought to aid psychic insight.

CHAMOMILE-HOP COMFORT

1 cup chamomile flowers
1 cup passion fruit juice
1 cup spearmint leaves
1/2 cup hop flowers
dash fennel

Directions: Use 1 tsp. of this mixture to 1 cup of warmed Passion fruit juice, steeped for 10 minutesand strained. Chill, then if desired, add a bit of heavy cream, plain or whipped. and strained.

Magickal Associations: Solace, serenity, peacefulness

History/Lore: This is actually a very practical preparation that helps ease tension and stress. Hops helps to bring drowsiness. Once sleep is obtained, spearmint is thought to help protect against nightmares and negativity. The Greeks referred to chamomile as "Apple of the Earth."

Alternative: Lavender can be substitute for spearmint in the proportion of 3/4 cup. This is strongly recommended for people experiencing spiritual depression or discouragement.

Black Currant Compassion

1 qt. raspberry juice

1/3 lb. budding black currant shoots

sugar to taste

Directions: Warm raspberry juice over low flame, allowing currant buds to simmer for about 20 minutes. Remove from heat and cool. Strain, tasting for personally desired sweetness, then enjoy!

Magickal Associations: Joy, relief from depression, sympathy, charity.

History/Lore: Currants get their name from Corinth, Greece, where they were first discovered. In the in the language of flowers they mean, "your frown will kill me." Raspberry branches have been regarded as protective (due to thorns) while the fruit itself is one of happiness.

Alternative: By adding about 6 cups of sugar to this mix after removing the flowers, and bringing to a slow boil until liquid is reduced by half, you can make a tremendous syrup for ice cream, pies, tarts, and even poultry glaze.

BURDOCK BRACER

1/4 oz. Burdock root

1/4 oz. chamomile

2 slices ginger root

1/2 cup sugar

1 qt. water or apple juice

Directions: Place the ingredients together in a large pot and boil for 15 minutes, leaving out the sugar. Pour this through a strainer, then add sugar, stirring until dissolved. Cool and strain again. This is also good served hot or cold.

Magickal Association: Protecting or healing relationships, disperse negativity.

History/Lore: While burdock is an annoying flower when clinging to clothing, it has been much enjoyed as an edible item in Japan where the leaves, roots, and stems are also popular. The aspect of relationships in this recipe has to do with Burdock's ruling planet being Venus. Chamomile adds a sense of peacefulness, and ginger energy towards well-being.

Alternative: Nutmeg can be added to this recipe in place of ginger root to help change a streak of bad luck especially in romance.

CARNATIONS OF CAPABILITY

1 qt. hot water

1/4 cup lavender

2 cups carnation petals

2 to 3 whole cloves

1 cup sugar

1 stick of cinnamon

1 lemon peeled

1/2 cup rose petals

Directions: Steep carnation petals, roses, and lavender in water for 24 hours. Strain, then rewarm this liquid adding sugar, lemon peel, cloves, and cinnamon. Simmer for 20 minutes, strain, and serve warm.

Magickal Association: Skill, expertise, proficiency.

History/Lore: Carnations were the favorite flower of Henry IV of France. Pliny claims that carnations were discovered in Spain during the reign of Augustus Caesar, and recommended they were best picked in July. This may be why one of the folk names for carnation is Gillyflower (July-flower).

Alternative: Substitute lime rind for lemon for competence in matters of love.

A variation on the previous recipe first appeared in 1669 in Kenelm Digby's *The Closet Opened* under "Countess Dorset's Sweetwater."

HEARTENING HAWTHORN

2 cups hawthorn flowers

2 cups water

1 L peach juice

1 tsp. almond extract

1 slice lemon

1 slice orange

sugar or honey to taste

Directions: Place hawthorn flowers in warm water and allow to steep for 30 minutes. Strain and pour this liquid into a larger pan with remaining ingredients. Warm over low flame, adding sugar or honey until desired sweetness is acquired. Serve over ice chips with slivered almonds as garnish.

Magickal Associations: Faithfulness, Productivity, fairy magicks, aspirations.

History/Lore: Known as the flower of hope, hawthorn symbolized fertility and marriage in ancient Greece and Rome. Hawthorn was a favorite flower to adorn May Poles and is part of the sacred fairy tree trinity of Europe, the other two being oak and ash. Additionally, peach enhances this energy being likewise aligned with love and fruitfulness.

Alternatives: To improve devotion and steadfastness in relationships, add some chunks of pineapple to your finished beverage.

DIVINATION DRAUGHT

1/2 qt. marigold petals

1/2 qt. water

1/2 qt. pansy flowers

2 slices ginger root

1 oz. meadowsweet

1/2 qt. cherry juice

1/2 orange, sliced and peeled

honey to taste

Directions: Place your ingredients, except for cherry juice and honey, in a large pan and bring to a low simmering boil. Allow to simmer until flowers are almost transparent, then cool and strain. Rinse out your cooking pot, and return the liquid to it to add cherry juice and sweetening. This is best served cold.

Magickal Associations: Psychic abilities, insight, oracles, prophesy.

History/Lore: John Gerald felt meadowsweet brought joy to the senses. Marigolds, pansies, and meadowsweet have all long been used as components in love divinations. Additionally, marigolds follow the sun, lighting the way for psychic insight. Cherry and orange are also associated with divinatory workings.

Alternatives: For additional oracular power, add a cup of dandelion, and a sliced apple for wisdom.

Alcoholic Recipes

During the Middle Ages, petaled beverages (and foods) found their way to Europe with a flurry. Flower and vegetable wines and liquors established a place on the table alongside the more traditional fruit preparations. They were so admired that they soon became a welcome addition to royal gatherings.

In preparing your own fruit and vegetable wines, two factors rise above all others as crucial for success. The first is freshness. Flowers can be bought dried, but are more effective when freshly harvested. When gathering petals (only petals—no green parts) do so just after the dew evaporates, no later than 10:30 a.m. This helps the petal retain its essential oil. Handle them carefully, storing in a muslin or nylon mesh bag, and use them as soon as possible. Once wilted, their taste is far less enjoyable.

(ROSE GERANIUM ORACLE)

1 qt. apple wine

2 limes

2 oranges

8 rose geranium leaves

1 cup sugar

Directions: Warm the apple wine, sugar, and geranium for five to 10 minutes until sugar is dissolved. To this add sliced limes and oranges and allow to cool. Strain and bottle, aging for one month before consuming.

Magickal Associations: Prophesy, well-being, insight, love, service to others.

History/Lore: This beverage comes to us from Arabia where the prophet Mahomet is given honor as birthing this lovely blossom. Some cunning folk of old would plant specially enchanted geraniums by their door to prepare them for impending guests by foreseeing their arrival.

Alternatives: Geraniums can be replaced with 6 whole bay leaves for similar magickal results.

BROOM BOUNTY

1 gal. broom flowers

2 oranges

1 gal. water

1/2 pkg. yeast

3 lbs. sugar

1 lemon

Directions: Warm the water, sugar, sliced lemon, and oranges together for a half hour. Cool to lukewarm then pour over the broom flowers and stir in yeast suspended in warm water. Let sit covered in warm area for three days. Strain and let sit for 10 more days before bottling. Age six months.

Magickal Associations: Productivity, purification, order, modesty.

History/Lore: Broom was originally used as the floor cleaner of the home, and slowly developed into our modern tool. When used in the home, a properly made broom could sweep good luck in, and bad fortune away. Couples in country ceremonies would often jump over a broom stick to insure their fertility. Broom has an almond-like flavor.

Alternatives: When broom is not available, almonds themselves are appropriate to this recipe. Add them at the same time as the petals, but in 1/2 the proportion.

HONEYSUCKLE SERENDIPITY

4 cups honeysuckle blossoms

1 gal. water

6 cups sugar

2 oranges, sliced and juiced

1/2 pkg. wine yeast

Directions: Place the blossoms in a large crock. Warm 1/2 the water to just below boiling then pour over the petals. Allow to sit until blossoms turn almost translucent. Strain and rewarm slightly to add orange juice pieces, and yeast. Place into a fermentation container with a lock until the liquid becomes clear. Bottle and store in cool dark area for use.

Magickal Associations: Luck, good fortune, and good health.

History/Lore: If you find a honeysuckle plant growing near your home (also known as Woodbine), it is not only a sign of good fortune but a protector of the family's health. The orange in the recipe helps accentuate the healthful benefits of the beverage.

FAIRY FOLK FOLLY

"And I serve the fairy queen, to dew her orbs upon the green, the cowslips tall her pensioners be."

—*Bard of Avon*

2 qts. cowslip heads
1 lemon
2 oranges
1 gal. water
4 lbs. honey
pinch of thyme (optional)
1/2 pkg. yeast

Directions: Cowslips are best brewed in dried form. Place these in a crock. Wash and peel lemon and oranges, putting rinds with flowers and squeezing juice of the remainder into the crock. In a separate pot, mix warm water and honey together until dissolved, pouring this over the flower mixture. Let this cool to lukewarm stirring regularly. Next add yeast dissolved in 1/4 cup warm water. Cover with a towel and let sit for five days, mixing once a day. Strain and move the clear fluid to a glass container with fermentation lock. When all signs of fermentation cease, decant and bottle.

Magickal Associations: Longevity, kinship with fairy realms.

History/Lore: Sometimes known as primroses, the cowslip is one of the most favored flowers of England. It is known by the folk names "fairy cup" or "fairy flower" as it is believed this is where the fey take shelter from storms. It is also thought to hold the power of eternal youth in its petals.

Alternative: Some folks like to add a touch of pineapple sage (about 2 Tbs.) to this mixture for a slightly zesty flavor.

A Persian philosopher, Zarathustra claimed the rose was the mother of all nutritious fruits.

ROMANTIC ROSE WINE

1 to 2 gal. pot filled
1/2 full with rose petals
1 gal. water
3 lbs. sugar
2 Tbs. rose water
1 tsp. orange juice
1/2 pkg. wine or champagne yeast

Directions: Cover the rose petals with water and simmer over a low flame until the petals become see-through. Strain off the liquid, returning it to the original pan to warm with sugar until the sugar is dissolved. Cool to lukewarm, adding champagne yeast (preferably) which has been suspended in 1/4 cup warm water. Cover the pot with a cloth for 24 hours to begin fermentation. The next day, move the liquid to a large container with fitted fermentation lock and add the rose water and orange juice to it. Allow this to age until fermentation has all but ceased. Pour the clear pink liquid into bottles with a sugar cube in each bottle. Cork using champagne corks and store in dark, cool area for one month. Caution is issued upon opening as bottles will have a fair amount of pressure built up.

Magickal Associations: The spirit of love and beauty

History/Lore: Greeks considered the rose to be one of the best symbols of love and loveliness, having been born from the blood of Aphrodite. Romans often covered festival floors with roses in welcome to honored guests. Rose water is called the "dew of paradise" by Arabs.

FORTUNE DRAUGHT

2 qts. dandelion blossoms

2 qts. clover blossoms

1 gal. boiling water

3 lbs. sugar

2 lemons

2 oranges

1/2 pkg. of yeast

1 cup raisins

Directions: Remove any stems and leaves from your blossoms, placing them in a large cooking pot. Pour the boiling water over top of these, adding sugar, sliced lemon, and oranges. Simmer for a half hour, then cool to luke-warm. Add the wine yeast suspended as shown in other recipes herein, stir. This should sit covered with a loosely woven cloth for one week.

Magickal Associations: Luck, opportunity, windfalls.

History/Lore: Dandelions acquire their name from the jagged leaves which resemble lion's teeth (note the French term *dent de lion*). This gives this beverage a bit of a pro-tective bite. More importantly, however, is the associa-tion both clovers and dandelions hold for luck. A four-leaf clover is considered most fortunate, as is dreaming of a dandelion.

LAVENDER AND SPICE

1 cup dried French lavender

1 inch minced ginger root

1 1 inch cinnamon stick

4 whole allspice berries

4 whole cloves

1 tsp. nutmeg
1 qt. water
pinch sage
1 qt. brandy
1 cup raisins
2 cups honey
2 Tbs. rose water

Directions: All dry ingredients except the raisins should be ground finely then put into a large container with honey, raisins, and rose waters. The brandy is then poured over the entire mixture. Cover this container well, and allow it to sit in the sun (or a warm area) for 20 days, shaking regularly. Strain thoroughly, rebottling the clear fluid for use. Store in cool, dark area.

Magickal Associations: Strength, vitality, recuperative powers, the spirit of life.

History/Lore: This recipe is a version of a Medieval Aqua Vitae that Knights often drank before battle. It was also frequently given to those thought dead with the belief that such a potent combination of healthful herbs might restore breath and vitality.

Alternative: Sugar can be substituted for honey here, as can many other culinary herbs for the spices listed. Suggestions include angelica, mint, rosemary, and bay.

MAY WINE

1 qt. warm apple wine
1/2 cup woodruff flowers, freshly picked
2 oz. sugar
1/4 pt. water
slice of orange per glass
stick cinnamon

Directions: Allow the woodruff to set in the warm wine for 30 minutes then remove. To this add sugar and water. This serves about six people and may be prepared warm or cold. Garnish with orange slices and cinnamon. Do not ingest if allergies to certain flowers are known. Brewing may not alleviate the problem, and serious allergies, when taken internally, can prove fatal.

Magickal Associations: Victory, protection, banish negativity.

History/Lore: Woodruff is called the Master of the woods in Germany, with a rich smell similar to that of cinnamon. Its white flowers are sacred to the Goddess and it has often been used in magick to protect against impishness.

Alternative: To make the wine even more special, consider making the apple wine base from scratch approximately 4 months before your May Day celebration. The number four is associated with success.

Celebrations: Any May observance, Royal Oak Day, Memorial Day, Patriots Day, Old Dance.

Chapter 8

Joyful Juicing

> *"Tis a little thing to give a cup of water*
> *yet its draught of cool refreshment*
> *drained by fevered lips*
> *may give a shock of pleasure to the frame*
> *more exquisite than when nectarine juice*
> *penetrates the life of joy in happiest*
> *hours."*
> —Sir Thomas N. Talfourd

> *"Fill me with the old, familiar juice."*
> —Omar Khayyam

Most of us live in a state of perpetual busyness. Any number of daily duties can leave little time for three square meals a day. This makes easy, healthful beverages very important. That is probably why juicing is a popular "fad" of the 1990s.

Most fruits and vegetables contain considerable levels of fiber, iron, calcium, potassium, vitamin B and C, beta carotene, and sodium, all of which can be beneficial to most diets. Some of these beverages help stave-off cravings for candy by supplying our bodies with natural sugars. Thus, juicing can be an integral part of sound weight loss efforts, with no artificial colors or flavors to hinder revitalization.

You do not have to buy a special juicer for this product. A good blender or food processor and straining equipment will do. The major advantage to juicers is that they are specifically constructed to make your job a lot easier. If you decide to purchase one, look for good quality, safety, and a clearly stated warranty.

Because the process of juicing is basically the same for most fruits and vegetables, I am going to give generalized directions here to avoid repetition throughout the chapter. Any special instructions pertaining to a specific recipe are provided below. Additionally, each recipe includes nutritional information to help those using these preparations to improve physical well-being.

General Instructions

First, make sure to clean your ingredients under warm water. If possible, buy organically grown fruits and vegetables to eliminate the ingestion of pesticides. Remove all leaves, seeds, rinds, and bruised parts before putting the components in your blender/juicer. With the exception of potatoes, fruits and vegetables are predominantly juiced raw to obtain the highest content of nutrients. Then all that remains is pulping the ingredients thoroughly with your equipment.

If you do not want chunky drinks, use a good sieve and strain off the juice. To recycle the left over pulp, put it in an equal portion of hot water and bring to a low rolling boil for one hour and strain again. This juice will not be as high in vitamins as the first extraction, but it uses your components economically. Be sure to refrigerate any unused portions. The remaining pith can be composted.

CIDER IMPOSTER

1 1/2 lbs. of pulped apples, boiled

5 gal. cold water

3 1/2 lbs. brown sugar

1 Tbs. cream of tartar

1/2 orange, sliced

Directions: Peel and rinse your apples, then put them through a blender or food processor to achieve pulp. Boil this in 2 gallons of the cold water to express the juice. Let sit until cold then strain thoroughly through cheese cloth. Add remaining ingredients into a large pot over low flame to properly incorporate sugar. Feel free to add sweetening slowly to get a personally pleasant taste. Remove and let cool again before bottling in air tight containers for use.

Magickal Association: Long lasting love or revitalizing a romance gone stale.

History/Lore: As mentioned earlier in this book, apple beverages, and specifically cider, have participated in a wide variety of rites which honor the gods and nature. It is an appropriate fruit for the altar in any festival for Diana or Venus and has been accepted by many cultures as the symbol of immortality.

Nutritional Value: Pectin which helps decrease cholesterol, vitamin C, and potassium.

Alternative: For a lovely and refreshing twist, decrease apples by one pound and add 1/2 pound of cherries and 1/2 pound pineapple juice made from fresh fruit. This can be achieved by macerating fruit and pouring 1/2 gallon of hot water over it to stand for 48 hours, then strain. Add this juice into the remaining ingredients as per the previous directions. This mixture is for a little extra luck with relationships.

CRAN-TALOUPE ENCHANTMENT

1/2 lb. cranberries

1 pt. strawberries

1/2 cantaloupe

1/2 orange

honey to taste

Directions: Follow general directions given previously.

Magickal Associations: Well balanced relationships with others or the self. Proper motivations for long-term commitments.

History/Lore: Both melons and strawberries are strongly associated with love, being round juicy fruits. This energy is balanced in this recipe by the Mars energy in cranberries for protection, and orange for purity.

Nutritional Value: Rich in vitamin C, beta carotene, potassium, and fiber. An excellent choice to help clean out urinary tract.

Alternatives: Black or red raspberries can be substituted for strawberries in this recipe to improve happiness.

GLORIOUS GRAPE JUICE

Preparing home made grape juice is slightly different than other juicing processes described herein. In this instance, you can make as little or as much as you personally desire, keeping in mind that each 1 1/2 pounds of grapes yields about 1 cup of juice.

Directions: Begin by washing your grapes (preferably seedless) in warm water. Please note the grapes should be well ripened but still firm. These should be placed in a pan where you can use the flat of a wooden spoon to crush and press them by hand. This pan is then transferred to a low flame until the entire amount is steamy but not boiling. Let this mixture cool in a glass container for twenty four hours then strain off the sediment. Place the juice in open bottles, which have been cleaned with boiling water, on the top portion of a double boiler. Warm the juice again until steaming, cool to lukewarm, and then seal up immediately. It is a good idea to use paraffin in this final step to alleviate the possibility of mold. When sealed properly, this juice will last almost indefinitely. Upon serving, you may find it is too thick or sweet for your tastes. At this point, dilute the juice according to personal preference using spring water or for more zest, a bit of soda.

Magickal Associations: Successful end to a project, a welcome windfall, conception, productivity.

History/Lore: Sacred to both Bacchus and Dionysus for obvious reasons, the grape was a favored symbol of fertility in ancient Rome. Because of their use in wine making, grapes are also associated with celebrations and momentous occasions.

Nutritional Value: beta carotene, iron, potassium and low levels of vitamin C.

Alternatives: For a cleansing quality, to a glass of shaved ice add the juice of 1/2 lemon, 1/2 orange, 2 tsp. pineapple nectar, 1 1/2 ounces of grape syrup, and soda water decorated with a fresh lemon slice.

LEMON-LIME ZINGER

6 lemons, peeled

6 limes, peeled

1 lb. sugar (or honey)

2 qts. water

Directions: Save the peels of three lemons and limes, from which the white pith has been removed. Place the peels in a large pot, covered with 1 quart boiling water and allow to sit and infuse like a tea. Meanwhile, express the juice of all six lemons and limes, adding the remainder of the water, sugar and the juice from the peels. Taste to see if additional sweetening is required, then serve over ice.

Magickal Associations: Purification, cleansing and protection.

History/Lore: Anyone who has used lemon or lime juice and water for cleaning knows firsthand what a terrific cleanser they make. Lemon juice is often used to help purge magickal tools of unwanted energies, while lime is considered an effective protection against negative magicks.

Nutritional Value: Lots of vitamin C, potassium, low levels of beta carotene. Consumed hot with honey, this makes an excellent cold tonic.

Alternatives: For a really fruity flair, add the juice of six raspberries and 6 strawberries to each glass, or simply float the fruit on top. Another refreshing alternative is to add two whole mint leaves to the rind tea to infuse. The first blend is good for improving joy in a relationship, while the latter can help rejuvenate sexual interest.

ELIXIR OF HEALTH

1 cup pineapple juice
Watercress (opt)
1/2 cup cucumber peeled and seeded
crushed ice
1 sprig parsley

Directions: Use general directions given in the introduction.

Magickal Associations: General well being, physical fitness and protection of ones vitality.

History/Lore: Because of its spiny exterior and cutting flavor, pineapple is regarded as a shielding fruit. Cucumber peels have long been recommended by folk healers to relieve headaches and the decorative sprig of parsley on our plates dates back to Roman superstition about it keeping the food safe from contamination.

Nutritional Value: Rich in vitamin C. Good levels of calcium, iron, potassium, and beta carotene. An excellent choice for those watching cholesterol counts.

Alternative: A whole, peeled apple may be added to this mixture. The metaphysical effect here is for positive efforts and energy towards magickal wholeness.

CARROT KEEN

3 large carrots
3 stalks of celery
6 radishes
2 cups diced cabbage
1 tsp. thyme

Directions: Follow general directions given in introduction. Please take extra care in scrubbing your carrots. Fresh thyme, if available, is preferred and best added into the cup after straining.

Magickal Associations: Psychic awareness and insight.

History/Lore: Most of us know the old saying that eating carrots will improve eyesight, so why not take advantage of this on a spiritual level by internalizing the beneficial qualities!

Nutritional Value: High quantities of beta carotene. Fair amounts of sodium, potassium, vitamin C, and calcium.

Alternative: Substitute caraway for thyme and parsley for radishes. This potion can help improve sexual desire, fertility, and possibly aid impotence.

In the Pink

2 pink grapefruit

1 orange

1 banana

1 cup strawberries

1 cup raspberries

honey or sugar to taste

1 cup soda water

Directions: Juice and strain fruits before adding honey or soda water. Mix thoroughly.

Magickal Associations: Overall well-being, friendship, the first buds of romance.

History/Lore: I have used the combination of color (pink) here with the natural love energies of the berries in this drink to produce a beverage which encourages good thoughts about self and others. Pink is considered a color of kinship, and it is also can be symbolic of the beginning of a romance (toned down red).

For those who are curious, the grapefruit did not become part of popular diets until about 1700, probably being a mutant strain of the pomelo from Jamaica or Barbados.

Nutritional Value: Excellent source of vitamin C, potassium, and fiber.

PROPHETIC PUNCH

1 cup dandelion flowers

2 cups spinach

1 clove garlic

1 cup romaine lettuce

1 medium onion

1 tsp. rosewater or 1/2 cup diced rose petals

Directions: Keep rosewater or petals out of juicing process. Instead, add them at the end, either by stirring in or floating on top for a garnish.

Magickal Associations: Foresight, divination, oracles, psychic awareness.

History/Lore: The scent of roses is thought to encourage prophetic dreams. In the language of flowers, the dandelion means "oracle." Garlic is to purify the visions and the green vegetables are for growing awareness.

Nutritional Value: Large quantities of vitamin C, iron, and calcium. Some potassium, vitamin B, and beta carotene. Garlic contains a natural antibiotic and even the rose petals in this recipe are beneficial!

Alternative: Use red cabbage instead of lettuce and a tomato for the onion. Magickally this is to improve one's fortune in matters of the heart.

FIRE FESTIVAL

2 large tomatoes

2 cloves garlic

2 red peppers

1 cup chopped red cabbage

1 tsp. lime juice

1 tsp. hot sauce

rosemary (garnish)

Directions: Follow the directions given in introduction. Please note however, that hot sauce may be increased or decreased according to your tolerance. A fresh sprig of rosemary is placed in each glass.

Magickal Association: Fire Magick, drastic change, the energy of the Phoenix, purification.

History/Lore: The traditional herbs, plants, and colors of fire combine in this drink to quite literally spark your creative source from inside out! An appropriate beverage for Beltane and many summer observances.

Nutritional Value: A good purgative and blood tonic, high in vitamin C, it also has some potassium and calcium.

Alternatives: Fire related ingredients not listed in this recipe, but which work well for juicing are carrot, celery, basil, bay leaf, dill, leeks, and a dash of curry blended together.

GREEN PROSPERITY

1 cup diced broccoli

2 stalks celery

4 brussel sprouts

3 scallions

1 sprig parsley

1 cup asparagus

1 cup tomato juice (or 2 whole tomatoes)

salt and pepper to taste

Directions: Follow general directions at the beginning of the chapter.

Magickal Associations: Abundance, good fortune, success.

History/Lore: Asparagus was thought to be one of Julius Caesar's favorite foods, contributing to his strength, and celery was used in Rome to try and prevent hangovers! In this case, the color of this beverage is a rich green to help encourage growth or improved finances. Visualize your needs while you drink!

Nutritional Value: High amounts of fiber, vitamin B and C. Additionally a good mix of minerals, most notably iron.

Alternatives: For prosperity which more specifically pertains to money matters, add a cup of alfalfa sprouts to your mixture.

Hot Apple Toddy

1 cup pineapple juice
3 large apples
1/2 lemon
1 orange
dash cinnamon
dash ginger
1 Tbs. brewers yeast

Directions: Follow basic recipe, adding ginger and cinnamon with brewers yeast after juicing. Serve warm.

Magickal Associations: Centering, balance.

History/Lore: Apples are associated with spiritual wisdom, which can only come through personal insight. The warmth of this drink draws your attention directly to your center of gravity helping you to focus energy and bring improved inner harmony through meditation.

Nutritional Value: Excellent source of vitamin C and pectin.

Alternative: Add mint in lieu of cinnamon to encourage spiritual purging during this process.

BAKED POTATO PIE

2 baked potatoes, peeled

1 large onion

2 scallions with tops

2 cloves garlic

1 cup skim milk

salt and pepper to taste

Directions: Once your potatoes are baked and peeled you can follow the basic recipe. This is best enjoyed without straining, and has the consistency of mashed potatoes or cream of potato soup.

Magickal Associations: Health and healing, Earth magick.

History/Lore: Potatoes, being a root plant, help us connect more directly with Gaia energies. Carry one with you into circle when working Earth Magick and hold it in your palms as a focus. Potatoes have also played an intricate role in folk medicine especially for wart removal. Thus, potato halves or pieces are good components in spells for well-being.

Nutritional Value: Surprisingly, baked potatoes are rich in vitamin C, fiber, vitamin B complexes, and potassium. Onions improve this content.

Alternative: Try sweet potatoes in a recipe where the health and welfare of a relationship is the issue.

MELLON-CHOLY BABY

1/2 cantaloupe

2 cups watermelon, seeded

1/2 musk melon

1/2 honeydew

1 cup skim milk

Directions: Follow basic recipe.

Magickal Associations: All Lunar and Goddess Magicks, especially those for completion of any creative project.

History/Lore: These round, watery fruits are under the ruling of the moon and as such are perfect ingredients for beverages pertaining to artistic or imaginative endeavors.

Nutritional Value: Vitamin C, beta carotene, potassium, calcium, and electrolytes, making this an excellent hot summer drink to revitalize bodily fluids.

Alternative: For conception magick, add a banana for fertility, a mango for love, and a touch of ginger for success.

FRUIT SALAD

2 peaches
1/2 cup apricots
2 kiwi fruit
1/2 cup strawberries
1/2 cup raspberries
1 banana
1 cup skim milk or seltzer water
1 cup vanilla yogurt
1 whole cherry (garnish)

Directions: Juice together the first six ingredients of this recipe, then add the liquid to the milk and yogurt, garnishing with a cherry.

Magickal Associations: Abundance of energy, joy, productivity, and love. A good celebratory beverage.

History/Lore: Apricots had their origins in Asia where they were known as "sun eggs" because of their rich golden color. This magickally allows them to become an active energy source for your beverage on which the symbolism

of the other fruits is conveyed like bright beams of sunlight through your body.

Nutritional Value: A bevy of good vitamins and minerals are exhibited here. A terrific pick-me-up!

Alternatives: Almost any fruit you enjoy can be added
to this blend. Try grapes to enhance the festival spirit or
passion fruit for harmony.

VEGETABLE TOSS

2 cups diced romaine lettuce

1 cucumber

3 scallions with tops

4 to 5 radishes

2 tomatoes

2 stalks celery

1/4 tsp. thyme

1/4 tsp. basil

salt and pepper

Directions: Follow general directions.

Magickal Associations: Peace, resolve, trust in the future.

History/Lore: While mostly associated with a tranquility about one's personal resources, this peace can really
extend to anything. Lettuce leaves have been used in folk
medicinal teas to help calm the nerves. Additionally, celery juice is thought to help cure tension headaches.

Nutritional Value: for those who tend not to get enough
greens in their diet, this is one very tasty alternative rich
in fiber, vitamins, and minerals. Helps improve energy tremendously.

Alternatives: Just like the fruit salad, this beverage lends
itself to creativity. Add broccoli for stronger lunar influences or mushrooms for increased awareness.

Chapter 9

Sorcery Soda Pop Magickal Malteds, and Fun Frappes

> *"Let us have wine and women,*
> *mirth and laughter,*
> *sermons and soda-water*
> *the day after."*
> —Lord Byron

> *"With headed bubbles winking at the rim."*
> —John Keats

Malted milk shakes and soda pop were dispensed carefully by the glassful, often by the local pharmacist, the latter sometimes being prescribed for health, as far back as 100 years ago. Also known as sweet water and fizz water, soda pop is one of the largest beverage industries in the United States.

To get an idea about the beginnings of fountain beverages, let's look at one company. Its originator, Charles Hires, had a dream to establish mail-order sales of homemade beverage kits. Mr. Hires carefully selected 18 ingredients including roots and herbs, and packaged them with directions for the frugal housewife. This package sold for

25¢ and made five gallons of root beer. Slowly, the Hires Root Beer Company formed, and with them a number of other popular favorites followed.

People continue to enjoy soda pop, malteds, and other "fountain" drinks. As of 1982, each person in the United States consumed approximately 38 gallons of pop per year. In other words, we annually drink as many soft drinks (and related beverages) as we do water.

Soda Pop

Older formulas for soda pop call for forced carbonation or the addition of yeast. Yeast leaves an average alcohol content of about 1 percent, which is not acceptable if one is allergic to alcohol! Thankfully, home brewed soda pop today can be much simpler. The basic formula is carbonated water, sweetener, and added flavoring(s). Sweeteners may be adjusted to suit your dietary needs, including substituting honey or Nutrasweet for sugar.

Make a syrup of your sweetening agent so it mixes well with room temperature soda water. The proportions are the same for honey and sugar; 2 cups sweetener to 1 cup water, brought to a low rolling boil then refrigerated. Then, you can make soda pop by the glass using 1 1/2 cups carbonated water, and 1 to 2 tsp. syrup plus your fruit, vegetable or flower essences and extracts. Choose flavorings made by juicing (see Chapter 8), or those readily available in the supermarket's cooking isle.

If you don't like the taste of plain soda water, try ginger ale instead. This makes a zestier drink. Additionally, please take care to add your sweetener slowly. Sugars activate the carbonation even further to the point where your glass may froth over. Here are five examples soda pop to try at home:

COLA COLADA

1/8 tsp. lemon extract
1/8 tsp. vanilla extract
1/8 tsp. coconut extract
slice of lime, juiced
slice of sweet orange, juiced
dash of nutmeg
1 1/2 cups carbonated water
sweetener to taste

Directions: Follow the general directions, taking care to taste-test for personal enjoyment.

Magickal Associations: Fidelity, devotion, and integrity specially in relationships.

History/Lore: Because coconut is associated both with protection and chastity, when combined with common love flavorings, it is a perfect beverage to become art of engagement or hand fasting rites.

Alternative: For friendship, float a bit of sweet pea or passion flower on top of the glass.

SUGARED GINGER

1 cup room temperature carbonated soda
2 pieces candied ginger root
1 lemon balm leaf
dash of cinnamon (optional)

Directions: Follow general directions, except place this mixture in an air tight container for about an hour before serving over ice for best flavor. If time is short, use some sweetener and ginger extract instead.

Magickal Associations: Sweet success, victory, positive culmination of efforts.

History/Lore: Ginger is considered an herb which accentuates energy towards specific goals. The additional benefit of this beverage is that it also tends to settle the stomach allowing you to really focus on your magickal rites.

Alternative: For success specifically in areas of personal aspirations, add some expressed pomegranate juice to this mixture. About 2 Tbs. is good.

BLOOMING SYMMETRY

1 small bundle of lilac petals

1 white rose (no leafs or green parts)

2 tsp. lavender

1 tsp. chopped violet petals

2 tsp. pennyroyal

1 1/2 cups carbonated water

sweetener to taste.

Directions: For this recipe, it will be necessary to infuse your floral essence before adding it to the carbonated water. For this simply add the flower petals, once cleaned, to a cup of warm (not boiling) water and allow to simmer until their coloration is all but gone. Cool this mixture and add enough so that your soda has the lovely bouquet of fresh blossoms.

Magickal Associations: Harmony, accord and peace especially among families or groups.

History/Lore: All the flowers chosen for this recipe are strongly associated with the energy of agreement and compatibility. This might be a good ritual beverage to mark the acceptance of a new member into a study group or coven.

Alternative: Actually, any member of the mint family is fine for this recipe. Mint tends to have a calming effect on the human nervous system. An alternative to the flowers in this recipe is to simply use a cup of warmed apple juice with a fresh sprig of mint.

FREEDOM FOUNTAIN

1/2 cup peach juice

1 1/2 cups carbonated water

1/2 tsp. apple extract

dash anise

sweetener to taste

1 bay leaf (garnish)

Directions: Follow the basic recipe, placing a large bay leaf on the side of the glass. This is best accomplished by splitting it up the middle and sliding it over the rim.

Magickal Associations: Breaking bondage, changing bad habits, personal transformation.

History/Lore: According to cunning folk, peaches help to rid negativity and improve wisdom while the apple encourages healing, anise increases awareness, and the bay leaf is an icon of strength.

Alternatives: If you feel your problems are directly related to mal-intended magick, add a leaf of fresh wintergreen to this beverage and nibble on it after partaking. This is thought to dispel the wizardry.

SPARKILING MENTAL MIGHT

1 tsp. grape extract

1/3 tsp. mint extract

1 cup carbonated water

sweetener to taste

mint leaf (garnish)

Directions: Follow general directions.

Magickal Associations: The conscious mind, matters of study, education, logic.

History/Lore: Eating grapes is believed to improve concentration and mental faculties. Perhaps that is why the leaders in Rome and Greece were fed them so frequently by servants. Additionally, the aroma of mint is also supposed to aid these types of efforts.

Alternative: If available, spearmint is the most highly recommended member of the mint family for this recipe.

Malteds

Gone are the days when you can readily find ice cream shops that offer chocolate malteds on their menu—and that is a pity. The rich, bubbly taste is something truly remarkable on a hot summer day. But the first question that comes to most readers' minds is, "Exactly what is a malted made with?" Malt extract, of course. This is not as difficult as you think to obtain, just check with a local brewers supply store where you can usually find this substance at reasonable prices.

As you read these recipes please keep a bit of ingenuity handy. A scoop of ice cream can be added to any one of these for a thicker, richer beverage. For health, add some plain yogurt.

CHOCOLATE COVERED CHERRIES

1 8 oz. glass of cherry soda
1 Tbs. chocolate syrup
1 tsp. cherry extract
1 Tbs. malt extract
dash cinnamon
cherries (garnish)

Directions: Place ingredients together in a blender and whip until frothy. Pour into glass, sprinkling cinnamon on top and decorating with fresh cherries.

Magickal Associations: Sweet, romantic love. Please use two straws!

History/Lore: In lands to the east, the beautiful cherry tree has long been associated with amorous pursuits, and chocolate is a food which inspires passion in most people I know (if only for the chocolate itself!).

Alternatives: For orange and mint lovers, either of these extracts can be substituted for cherry in this recipe for similar magickal effects. Mint, however, is a little less romantic and a bit more "lusty."

ORIENTAL ROSE

one orange sliced and seeded (no pith)

1 Tbs. malt extract

1 tsp. sugar or honey

2 capfuls rose water

4 oz. skim milk

4 oz. orange soda

Directions: Place your ingredients together in a blender, first on low speed to dice the orange finely. Then turn to high until a orange-white foam is forming on top. Serve over crushed ice.

Magickal Associations: Steady happiness, constancy of good feelings, and physical health.

History/Lore: Oranges played an integral role in offerings to the gods of the East, being a very valued commodity thought to provide joy and abundance to all who receive them. Rose water helps promote health, thus allowing your pleasures to be balanced with judgment.

Alternative: This beverage may be warmed over a low flame and served with a cinnamon stick to help settle the stomach and calm nerves. If rose water is not available, use fresh flower petals as a garnish instead.

VERY BERRY

3 whole strawberries

6 blueberries

6 raspberries

10 black berries

1 tsp. sugar

1 Tbs. malt extract

6 oz. skim milk

2 oz. soda water

Directions: Rinse your fruit thoroughly, then blend all ingredients together until frothy. Serve as is or over ice. Please note that sundae sauces can be used in lieu of fresh fruit, about 1/2 tsp. being all that's necessary.

History/Lore: When properly prepared, this malted comes out a lovely violet hue, the color most commonly associated with spiritual pursuits and metaphysical learning.

Alternative: Consider floating a fresh violet on top of this drink to further accent the magickal energies. These flowers are often grown in the home to promote sacred pursuits.

Alternative: Try adding a scoop of raspberry sherbet!

MALTED MILK

1 tsp. vanilla syrup (or 1/4 tsp. extract and sugar)

2 Tbs. heavy cream

1 Tbs. malt extract

8 oz. milk

apple slice (garnish)

Directions: This may either be stirred or blended, but I prefer a frothy malted. It is also excellent with vanilla ice cream added in. Place the apple over the rim of the glass sliced so the internal pentagram design can be seen.

Magickal Associations: Goddess, energy, maternity.

History/Lore: Milk, being the first source of food for all humankind, has always been sacred to the Goddess. In her Mother aspects, She teaches us about nurturing ourselves and others, healing, and self-awareness.

Alternatives: The options on this recipe are almost as endless as personal taste. Consider substituting chocolate and mint flavorings for vanilla, for example. Magickally, this is to refresh romance.

TOFFEE COFFEE

8 oz. milk

2 Tbs. heavy cream

1/4 tsp. vanilla extract

1 Tbs. sugar

1 tsp. instant coffee dissolved in 1 tsp. water

1/4 tsp. butterscotch flavoring

Directions: Beat the heavy cream to peaking and put in a large glass. Separately, blend your other ingredients until bubbly, then pour over cream. This may also be prepared warm.

Magickal Associations: Energy, vigor, initiative, stamina.

History/Lore: Coffee beans originally were made into wine by African nations, not the hot beverage we know today. It was not until nearly 1,000 years after Christ that Arabs considered this alternative. The stimulating effect quickly became popular and also gives us its natural magickal associations.

Alternatives: Try this substituting a herb-spice apple tea bag infused in 1/4 cup water in lieu of vanilla.

> The slang term *Java* for coffee stems from the fact that Java itself produces a fair quantity of coffee beans, most of which are spicy with full bodied flavor.

Frappes

Frappes are semi-frozen drinks served in iced cups. Usually frappes are made from fruit juices or flavored waters and sweetener, which are blended, then half frozen to take on a snow-like consistency. To quote modern commercials, in this beverage, "the thrill is the chill!"

In all recipes below, except where noted, the following basic directions should be used. As was the case with soda pop, it is best to use a sweetener in syrup form to mix evenly with the juice(s). Next, combine the syrup with hot juice and flavor with any additional ingredients desired. Please add these components slowly, testing for personal taste preferences at this point. Cool and pour into a shallow pan for freezing. Stir this occasionally so the liquid freezes evenly.

When the entire batch has equal amounts of ice throughout, remove it from the pan and crush it with the back of a wooden spoon. Once a uniform consistency is reached, fluff with a fork in the same manner you would beat an egg. The beverage can be placed in a tall, chilled glass at this point and garnished with fruit, flavored whipped cream, some sundae syrup or whatever seems fitting.

ORANGE COFFEE CRUNCH

1 pot extra strong coffee
whipped cream
1 whole orange, seeded
whole almonds
1 cup orange juice
3/4 to 1 cup sugar syrup
1 cup slivered almonds

Directions: Blend together your hot coffee, orange, and juice with sugar until frothy. Freeze as per directions above. When flaking with the fork, mix in slivered almonds. Garnish with almond or orange flavored whipped cream and two whole nuts.

Magickal Associations: Energy for healing relationships of any nature.

History/Lore: Almonds have been used readily in early medicine for insomnia and headaches. Oranges are a love fruit, their blossoms often being carried by brides at ancient weddings. Coffee adds active energy to this beverage-spell.

Alternative: Try changing the flavor and meaning of this recipe by using any one of your favorite gourmet coffees for a base.

MELLOW YELLOW

4 lemons, juiced

1 egg

1 tsp. vanilla

2 bananas, mashed

2 scoops of lemon sherbet

1 star fruit, sliced

1 cup heavy cream

3/4 cup sugar syrup

Directions: Place lemon juice, vanilla, and sherbet in a pan to warm. Meanwhile, beat cream until fluffy. Slowly mix this with the warm liquid adding your sugar, and a beaten egg. Freeze at this point, moving the frozen crushed beverage to the blender with the bananas. Pour from the blender into glasses decorated with star fruit. Serves two.

Magickal Associations: Divination, prophesy, creativity, and any Air-related magick.

History/Lore: Yellow is associated with the energy of inventiveness and the Air Element allowing our dreams to take flight. Additionally, bananas are for fertility of efforts and lemon for clarity in goals. The star fruit is a wonderful addition here, already bearing the shape of the magickal pentagram.

Alternatives: Specifically for Air Magick, you may wish to substitute a paper fan or umbrella for the garnish.

HONEY LICOR-ICE

2 Tbs. licorice extract

3 cups hot water

2 Tbs. honey (or to taste)

2 licorice twists (garnish)

Directions: Warm extract, water, and honey together until honey is dissolved. Add more honey or extract to be personally pleasing in taste. Follow general for freezing and serving, placing one licorice twist in each glass before filling. Serves two people.

Magickal Association: Providence, especially with regard to essentials.

History/Lore: Bees were always considered messengers of the Gods. When their byproduct, honey, is combined with licorice, believed to help relieve hunger, the message sent to the universe was for immediate aid during times of severity.

Alternative: Try a little mint with this recipe to help refresh your outlook.

FALL FROLIC

6 cups hot apple juice

dash nutmeg

2 Tbs. maple syrup

dash ginger

2 tsp. honey

2 to 3 whole cloves

2 bay leaves

2 to 3 whole allspice

1/2 stick cinnamon

juice of one orange

Directions: Mix the syrup and honey with the apple juice until dissolved. Add your spices and allow to infuse like a tea until cool. Strain off whole spices, adding orange juice before freezing. Finish by following the general directions. Possible garnishes include rum sauce, a slice of apple or orange or a little sweet cream.

Magickal Associations: Any fall-related festival, the harvest of labors, outcomes, and results.

History/Lore: This is a wonderful autumn beverage, which is also good warm, by the way. It tastes like all of the favorite traditional flavors of fall and is especially nice for Thanksgiving gatherings.

Alternative: Peach juice, sacred to many Chinese deities, may be substitute for apple in this recipe for magickal energy towards helping bring wishes into reality.

PINEAPPLE PASSION FOR TWO

1 1/2 cups pineapple juice

1 1/2 cups passion fruit juice

1/2 cup crushed pineapple

2 tsp. sweetener syrup

1 tsp. vanilla extract

dash cinnamon

Directions: Follow the general directions given in the introduction to this section.

Magickal Associations: Desire, affection, romantic passion toward one person.

History/Lore: Just by its name, passion fruit elicits certain expectations. Pineapple is the balancing point to this recipe, allowing our desires to be centered on one special individual. This is a nice love potion for serving at weddings, an anniversary party, and so on.

Alternative: For even more sensual vigor, try using blackberry or mango juice instead of the pineapple.

Chapter 10

Mystical Meade, Metheglin, and Horilka

> "I rise to sing at midday feasts
> from tables filled with mead
> of knights who ride on fabled beasts
> perfecting noble deeds"
> —Marian Singer

> "The Druids and Old British bards were
> wont to carouse thereof (mead) before they
> entered into speculations."
> —Dr. Howells, Oxford, 1640

For the purpose of this chapter, I will discuss only wines that use honey as their main source of sweetening. The section on wine later in this book is restricted to sugar-based beverages. The substitution of sweetening agents for variations in flavor between both these chapters is very feasible, in equal commodities.

Achieving the greatest success with these beverages comes through a little experimentation with flavor components, and contentious skimming of honey sediment as it rises to the top of your pot during boiling. Also, when possible, try to purchase a good quality, raw honey. This improves the overall body and taste of the finished mead.

Mead

"From the mead horn —the pure and shining liquor, which the bees provide but do not enjoy, Mead distilled I praise."
    —*Book of Taliesin, Mabinogion*

BASIC MEAD

This recipe will serve as a good foundation for all your efforts in mead related drinks. Simply change fruits, fruit juices and spices for different and uniquely flavored results. All proportions given are for one gallon yields.

1 gal. water

5 lbs. dark honey

2 oranges

1 lemon

1/2 package sparkling yeast

Directions: Place the honey with water in a 2-gallon pot over a medium flame. To this, slice in the oranges and lemon in large enough pieces to easily remove by slotted spoon later. Bring the mead to a rolling boil, skimming off any scum which rises to the top over the next hour. Cool to lukewarm, strain our fruit pieces and add the yeast dissolved in 1/4 cup warm water. Allow this mixture to sit with a woven cover (such as a dish towel) for seven days until the first fermentation has slowed considerably. Strain again, trying to pour off only the clearer top fluids into a bottle to age. These bottles should be lightly corked for about two months, then tightly sealed for six months before using.

Magickal Associations: Vary with ingredients. Basic associations are good health, artistic inspiration, romance, and religious observance.

History/Lore: Because it was honey, not sugar, which was the main source of sweetening for many centuries, simple mead recipes like this show up in almost every nation with only minor variations appropriate to that culture.

HOPS MEAD

The hops in this recipe is not added as a flavor, but a clarifier which allows the finished mead to be unclouded with a distinctively less dense taste.

1 gal. water
2 oranges
1 oz. cascade hops
1 lemon
4 lbs. light honey
1/2 lb. white raisins
1/2 pkg. yeast

Directions: Place water, hops, honey, and sliced fruit into your pot boiling as in the basic recipe, but only for thirty minutes. Reduce heat and add chopped raisins, stirring for another five minutes before removing from flame. Cool, strain, and add yeast as previously instructed. Place five raisins in each bottle before closing. Aging time after secure corking is one year.

Magickal Associations: Sweet dreams, smooth versatility, and adaptation.

History/Lore: Hops is a very multifaceted herb, being used not only to brew beer, but also to make paper and linen. A tea made from hops is sometimes used to improve sleep and encourage a healthy appetite.

QUICK WINE MEAD

1 gal. red wine (medium dryness)
2 lbs. honey
2 sliced oranges
1/4 fresh lemon
spices as desired

Directions: Warm the wine over a very low flame, adding honey slowly to dissolve thoroughly. Place this back into two equally divided gallon containers with equal portions of fruit and spices in each. Cork and shake daily for three days before serving warm. Please note that the honey in this recipe can be decreased to suit personal tastes.

Magickal Associations: Expediency, swift action

History/Lore: As the name might imply, this mead is a charlatan in that it is not made from scratch, but prepared when immediacy is called for. The traditional name for such mixtures in medieval Europe was *Pyment.*

Alternative: This is incredibly tasty when prepared with an apple wine instead of the traditional red, then served with a cinnamon stick on a cold winter's night.

PINEAPPLE MELOMEL

1/2 gal. water
3 16 oz. jars pineapple chunks (in juice)
1 orange
4 lbs. honey (orange blossom)
1/2 gal. pineapple juice
1/2 pkg. of yeast

Directions: Place pineapple chunks and juice from the can in a large pan with the water, sliced orange, and honey. Bring to a low rolling boil for 30 to 40 minutes, skimming any residue off the top, then add pineapple juice reducing heat to a simmer for 10 more minutes. Cool, then follow directions for yeast and bottling given in basic recipe. Aging time after final corking is about 6 to 8 months for a sweet wine; one year for dry.

Magickal Associations: Hospitality, joyful meetings or discoveries.

History/Lore: As a fruit native to tropical Americas, the pineapple was unknown until the New World was discovered, going by the native name *na-na* which translates to mean "fragrance." Slowly images of the pineapple worked themselves into all manner of American furniture, architecture, and so on as an emblem of welcome.

Alternative: I really like to add 1 to 2 inches of freshly bruised ginger root to this beverage for zealous energy and a matching rich flavor. Another interesting twist is to substitute two pounds of brown sugar for half the honey in this recipe.

Apricot-Banana Melomel

1 gal. water

1 1/2 lbs. dried apricots

6 ripe bananas

1 orange, juiced

2 cups apricot nectar

3 lbs. honey

Directions: Place the apricots in cold water until they soften and swell a bit. Place this pot on the stove and begin to warm it over medium flame as you slice in the bananas (peeled). Add the orange rind and juice along with your honey, boiling slowly for 45 minutes again skimming off any scum. Cool and add yeast as in the basic recipe, then move entire mixture to a temporary container where it can clear for three weeks (corked only loosely). Strain off the clarified wine and bottle with secure lids for at least three months before serving.

Magickal Associations: The mysteries, insight, oracular vision.

History/Lore: There are some scholars who argue the Tree of Knowledge in the Garden of Eden was actually an apricot because of their abundance in Israel. The Persians regard apricots as the "seed of the sun," and in China, apricots are considered a tremendous aid to prophets.

Interestingly enough, the Hondurans and Indians believe that the banana is actually the fruit of paradise. So, herein the two sweet fruits of biblical debate are blended together for a marvelous mead!

(NUTTY MEAD)

1 qt. hickory nut leaves

1 qt. black walnut leaves

1 lb. almonds, crushed

1 gal. water

4 lbs. honey

1 lemon

1 orange

1 Tbs. almond extract

1/2 pkg. of yeast

Directions: Be sure your leaves are fresh, with no signs of wilting or infestations. Crush them by hand and place them in a large pan with almonds. In a separate container, warm water with honey and fruit to a low rolling boil for 20 minutes, skimming. Add extract and follow as with the basic recipe, aging wine for one year.

Magickal Associations: Divine intervention, safety especially from severe weather. The God aspect.

History/Lore: In Lithuania, the God Pekun was said to be eating walnuts during the time of the great flood. When any of the shells reached a needful human, it grew to the size of a boat and brought them to safety.

Alternatives: Try adding or mixing personally favored nuts to this recipe for different taste sensations. Another tree leaf which can be added is that of the great Oak, sacred to Ceres, Zeus, and the Druids of old. This produces a mead with a sherry-like undercurrent and engenders energy for fertility and luck.

> In South America there is a deity dedicated to honey known as the Honey Mother, who receives offerings, prayer, and worship.

Metheglin

"Trefoil, vervain, John's wort, dill, hinder Witches at their will."

—Old English nursery rhyme

CLOVE METHEGLIN

1 gal. water

3 lbs. dark honey

2 oranges

1/2 pkg. yeast

1 lemon

1 to 1 1/2 oz. clove (adjust to personal taste)

Directions: Place all your ingredients except the yeast together in a large pot and boil for one hour, skimming as you go. Fruit should be sliced with rind on. Cool to lukewarm, removing the cloves and fruit which should be squeezed to extract the juice into the pan. Next add your yeast leaving covered in a warm area for two weeks. Siphon off the clear fluid into bottles and age seven months for sweet wine, one year for dry.

Magickal Associations: Protecting marriages, close friendship and the spirit of kinship.

History/Lore: Persians used cloves to rekindle the fires of a relationship gone cold, often mixed with rose water and a bit of prayer from the Koran. The potent flavor and scent of the clove has also given it associations with energy for protection, perhaps best directed towards relationships.

Alternatives: Instead of water, try a base of apple juice or half water, half orange juice instead.

GINGER-CINNAMON WARM UP

1 gal. water
3 lbs. clover honey
3 oz. fresh ginger root, bruised
2 lemons
1 orange
1 cup raisins
2 large cinnamon sticks (broken up)
1/2 pkg. yeast

Directions: Dissolve the honey in warm water, adding the ginger root (cut up), cinnamon, and raisins. Bring this to a boil for one hour then strain liquid into a separate container. Peel the lemons and orange, squeezing their juice into the container with the gingered water and add the rinds. Dissolve the yeast in warm water then add, stirring well. Follow as per basic recipe, allowing mead to age eight months to a year before use.

Magickal Associations: Sympathy, cordial feelings, affection, health.

History/Lore: This is similar to the Irish beverage Usquebaugh, which adds nutmeg and spirits to the recipe, and is used to warm chilled bones. Recipes such as this were common during the Middle Ages to ward off the plague and extend life.

Alternatives: A few cloves added to this recipe will provide even more gusto!

BALM-MINT MEDLEY

1 qt. packed balm leaves
1 qt. packed mint leaves
1 gal. water
1 inch piece vanilla bean
2 lbs. dark honey
1/2 pkg. yeast

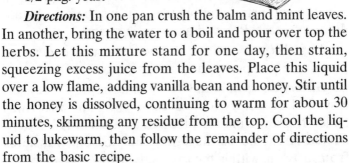

Directions: In one pan crush the balm and mint leaves. In another, bring the water to a boil and pour over top the herbs. Let this mixture stand for one day, then strain, squeezing excess juice from the leaves. Place this liquid over a low flame, adding vanilla bean and honey. Stir until the honey is dissolved, continuing to warm for about 30 minutes, skimming any residue from the top. Cool the liquid to lukewarm, then follow the remainder of directions from the basic recipe.

Magickal Associations: Happiness, rejuvenation, amicable feelings.

History/Lore: Mint is the herb of wisdom, being considered helpful in improving spirits and curing stomach discomforts. The Israelites were known to cover the floors of their temples and homes with mint leaves to refresh

their guests. Balm is very compatible to this energy, helping to make people more agreeable and joyous.

PARSLEY-SAGE SUCCESS

1 qt. pineapple sage leaves

1/2 lb. parsley

1 gal. water

1 lemon

1 orange

3 lbs. orange blossom honey

1/2 pkg. yeast

Directions: Place the herbs in a large crock. Bring the
water to a full boil, then pour it over top the sage and
parsley, allowing it to sit for a full 24 hours before straining. Squeeze to express any liquid from the herbs, then
rewarm the herb water with the sliced fruit and honey
until mixed well. Continue warming for 20 minutes, then
allow to cool, straining off the fruit just before the addition of yeast. Proceed as in basic recipe.

Magickal Associations: Protection in new endeavors,
preserving prosperity, and achievements.

History/Lore: In both Greece and Rome, parsley was
a symbol of victory and success. The plant itself was
fabled to grow from the blood of an ancient fallen hero
named Archemorus. Sage, by comparison, translates
from a term which means "salvation" because the
Virgin Mary was thought to have used these plants to
protect herself from Herod's men, and blessed the leaves
for their protection.

FALL METHEGLIN

1 cup dried apple
7 bay leaves
2 large cinnamon sticks
1 inch bruised ginger root
1 Tbs. dried lemon peel (or fresh from 1 whole fruit)
1 Tbs. dried orange peel (or fresh from 1 whole fruit)
12 whole cloves
7 whole allspice berries
1 Tsp. nutmeg
1 gal. water
3 lbs. dark honey
1/2 pkg. sparkling yeast

Directions: Try to begin this yeast in November of one year so that it will be ready for the next Fall's celebrations. Place all your ingredients except the honey in a two gallon pan with water. Simmer for one hour so that the water takes on a tea-like quality. Now, add the honey, bringing the entire mixture to a boil to skim off scum. Boil for 15 minutes, then follow the basic recipe. This mead has a marvelously crisp Fall flavor and is good both hot and cold.

Magickal Associations: The harvest, thankfulness, prudence.

History/Lore: This is basically a mulled beverage which is traditionally made for enjoyment during Lamas, Fall Equinox, and Thanksgiving into the Yule season. It has all the scents and flavors of the holidays to inspire your magick for the season.

In the Middle Ages, a favored recipe to ease wrinkles included newly laid eggs, roses, honey, and quince seeds applied to the skin.

Horilka

"If earth loved not the wine, the Wine
Spring would not on the earth be."

—Li Po

GRAPEFRUIT RUM HORILKA

(from Yukihanna)

12 ripe grapefruits

1 L dark rum

1 gal. water

4 lbs. dark honey

1/2 pkg. sparkling yeast

Directions: Peel your grapefruits, carefully removing the white pith from the peels and the fruit itself. Cut up peels from four of the fruits and place in a large pot with the sectioned fruit itself. Bring to a low rolling boil for 20 minutes, then cool. Strain the fruit, juicing carefully, then return the liquid to the pan to add honey. Boil again for 15 minutes to clear residue, then follow as with basic recipe for mead. After three months of aging, strain the base liquid again, testing for sweetness, and add rum along with any additional honey you feel is necessary for flavor. Age for a minimum of six months.

Magickal Associations: Purification, knowledge, health.

History/Lore: In some rural areas of England, the grapefruit is still called "forbidden fruit" as it is one of many thought to be the actual fruit of Eden. Additionally, the tart yellow juice has a cleansing, protective nature.

Hint: Continue to monitor your horilka even after the alcohol is added as I have had batches that continue to ferment, meaning certain precautions must be taken with your bottling techniques. If using screw tops, check at weekly intervals to be certain no pressure is building up. If after three weeks there are no signs of fermentation, you can seal securely for aging.

Alternatives: For richer flavor, try adding one can of frozen grapefruit or pineapple juice at the same time as the honey.

RASPBERRY-BLACKBERRY HORILKA

1 lb. fresh Raspberries
1 lb. fresh Blackberries
1 16 oz. can frozen raspberry-cranberry juice
1 gal. water
2 lbs. light honey1/2 package yeast
1/2 L raspberry brandy
1/2 L blackberry brandy

Directions: This recipe is prepared the same as the grapefruit except that you do not strain out the raspberries until just before you add the brandy. The left over fruit makes excellent conserves when mixed with coconut and apple plus 6 cups sugar.

Magickal Associations: Divine help and messages.

History/Lore: It is told to us that the blackberry has the unique distinction of being the Burning Bush of biblical fame. In the Americas, certain Native American tribes used blackberries mixed with honey as ceremonial food. The raspberry was similarly honored among the Native Americans with a special ceremony upon their first harvest where they would ask the spirit of the fruit for help with all endeavors of peace and war.

Alternative: If the price of brandy is prohibitive, try a fruit flavored vodka in this recipe instead.

APPLE-ALMOND AFFECTION

1 gal. apple juice or cider
2 oz. sliced almonds
1 Tbs. almond extract
2 lbs. honey
1/2 pkg. yeast
1 cup almond liqueur
1 L vodka or white rum

Directions: Warm your apple juice with the almonds over a low flame for 20 minutes. Add honey, turning up the heat to boil for 15 minutes, skimming all the while. Cool and add almond extract. Add yeast and allow to sit in the open air for 24 hours before straining into fermentation vessel. This will need a balloon or lock to clarify for two months before siphoning off and adding spirits. Age another year.

Magickal Associations: Pleasant relationships, robust life, fondness.

History/Lore: In Genesis, Israel sent almonds as a gift to show friendship and love. Ancient Phrygians considered this tree to be the Father of all life, making this nut sacred to Attis and Cybele. In many lands, especially among ancient Greeks, the apple is regarded as a fruit which insures both fertility and love, alongside its other healthful qualities.

TROPICAL FANTASY

1 cup diced, peeled papaya
4 kiwi peeled and sliced
1 cup drained, cubed pineapple
1 cup coconut (dried or fresh)

1 cup diced, peeled mango

3 ripe sliced bananas

1 orange, peeled and sliced

1 16-oz. can frozen tropical juice (any)

1 gal. water

2 lbs. honey

1 L rum

Directions: Follow the directions given for grapefruit horilka, straining twice if necessary because the bananas make a very thick stock. Aging time is one year.

Magickal Associations: Respite, luxury, adventures, and travel.

History/Lore: There is something about the smell and taste of tropical fruits which engenders day dreams of beautiful beaches and long, relaxing winter holidays beneath the sun. Bring a little vacation time into any day with a sip of this beverage!

Alternatives: Many of the tropical fruits are regarded as love enhancers, and as such this drink could make a good aphrodisiac!

STRAWBERRY SURPRISE

1 lb. frozen strawberries

1 16 oz. can strawberry daiquiri juice

1 gal. water

1 gal. light honey

1/2 pkg. sparkling yeast

1 L scotch or whiskey

Directions: This recipe is closer to the raspberry horilka in the making, as the fruit is left in the beverage for the initial fermentation process, then strained following the same procedures. The left over strawberries are very tasty for tarts and jams if you don't want to throw them out.

Magickal Associations: Kindness, charity, benevolence.

History/Lore: This fruit, sacred to Freya, was often the center of a unique country custom as late as 100 years ago. Strawberries which dropped on the ground were left there for the poor, and when people who had been picking passed a church, three berries were left conscientiously on the doorway as an offering.

Alternatives: If you can not find the juice mentioned in this recipe at your supermarket, use at least twice the amount of frozen strawberries to insure fullness of flavor.

> In East Africa, certain tribes require those who make honey wine to be specially prepared by being chaste from two days before preparation until the work is completed and the wine is ready to drink.

Final Note on Horilka

In the instance when you do not have time for a long fermentation process, it is possible to make a horilka that is ready in 24 hours. This method is probably more traditional than the one herein, which I have found provides better flavor and body.

In this instance you take your fruits, spices, fruit juice, and water together adding only enough honey to be pleasing to you. This should be cooked over medium flame for one hour then cooled. You then immediately add your chosen spirits, taste test for sweetness, and bottle. This mixture will not ferment without the addition of yeast and can be consumed after one day. However, aging takes a lot of the "bite" off.

Chapter 11

Seasonal Brews

*"There is no season such delight can bring
as summer, autumn,
winter and the spring."*
—William Browne

"The poetry of Earth is never dead."
—John Keats

No matter where you live, all year round something, somewhere on the Earth blossoms while another falls to seed. This simple cycle is a majestic teacher if we take the time to watch. How graceful Gaia is, how generous with her bounty and how accepting of the ever-turning wheel.

It is this subtle movement, and the symbolism for each season, that this chapter presents. Please bear in mind that seasonal significance can vary tremendously depending on your climate. However, the traditional magickal succession has four definitive parts, thus I am writing this in terms of four seasons.

In considering winter and summer beverages, I encountered one small problem which bears explaining. Depending on your view point, summer drinks should be hot to honor the sun, or cold to bring down your body temperature. Conversely, winter beverages might be frosty to honor the cold hush falling across the earth, or warm, giving strength to the sun that sleeps. To be honest, I couldn't find a good answer to this quandary. So, in the tradition of a true peace maker, both hot and cold beverages are included for all seasons!

Additionally, because each season has a central theme, the beverages in that section pertain, in some manner, to that focus. The magickal application is the "title" of the beverage in this instance, instead of a separate listing.

Nonalcoholic

Spring (ReBirth—the Child)

Spring is the dawn of creation. A pale blue light sneaks across the horizon to announce a creamy yellow sun. The aroma of fresh rain reaches the window, and a sense of reawakening touches our hearts. This is the time for beverages pertaining to refreshment, fertility, intuitive explorations, and creative work. Commonly associated with the element of Air, the energy for growth and vision is abundant, and ready to be poured into each drop of liquid.

Ideas to Consider for Spring Components:

- Daisy, pansy, woodruff, dandelion, lilac, and other early blooming flowers.
- Air spices such as almond, anise, hazel, marjoram, pecan, and sage.

- ⚬ Other flavorings such as maple, citron, lavender, and hops.
- ⚬ Any beverages which are yellow, pale green, or clear like rain.
- ⚬ Preparing beverages at dawn, the time of beginnings.

> Victorian Maidens believed if they heard the first dove of spring coo they would marry that year.

CLOVER DAISY TEA

1 tsp. dried clover flowers
1 tsp. daisy petals
1 cup hot water
honey to taste
1 daisy bud with leaf (garnish)

Directions: Place the petals in a gauze wrap or tea ball and steep for 15 minutes. Remove and flavor with honey. The daisy bud should be snipped so that it barely appears over the edge of your cup, like a young spring sprout.

Magickal Associations: Beginnings, inceptions.

History/Lore: The daisy is a flower which represents youthful innocence and wishes. Clover enhances this with a bit of luck and the power of protection to keep our goals plausible.

Alternatives: A stick of cinnamon can replace the daisy garnish in this recipe for successful energies.

PANSY, BORAGE BOUNTY

1 handful each pansy and borage flowers
4 cups water, warm
juice of one lemon
sugar to taste

Directions: Leave the pansy and borage flowers in warm water for 12 hours to infuse. Strain, adding lemon juice and sweetener. Garnish with a slice of lemon or fresh, cheerful petals.

Magickal Associations: Refreshment

History/Lore: Borage has often been thought to sooth the melancholy that often accompanies long, arduous winters. Pansy is known by the alternative folk name "hearts ease" and is likewise felt beneficial to restore one's wits. The additional benefit is that this beverage is full of healthful minerals including calcium.

Alternatives: To specifically promote physical strength and health, delete flowers and add two tea bags each of apple and orange to this recipe.

FERTILITY

1 banana
1 peach
1 cup milk
2 Tbs. heavy cream
1 tsp. almond extract
1 tsp. vanilla extract

Directions: Dice the banana and place it in a blender with milk, flavorings, and a skinned peach cut finely. Mix this until frothy. Meanwhile, using a hand mixer or wire whisk, beat the heavy cream until thick. Pour the juice into a tall glass, 1 inch at a time, adding a layer of cream until topped off.

History/Lore: In this recipe, I have used the banana to represent the masculine energy, the peach for feminine, the milk for maternity, almond for love, and a little vanilla to aid desire.

Alternatives: At present, this drink may be consumed by either sex. You can, however, change the beverage slightly by eliminating the banana for a woman and adding avocado instead. For a man delete the peach and add a mint leaf.

IN THE PINK

2 cups pomegranate seeds, juiced

1 cup ginger ale or soda

dash ginger

dash cinnamon

1 lemon balm leaf (garnish)

Directions: Juice the pomegranate seeds by placing them in a bowl and pressing with the back of a spoon. Strain this off, adding it to your ginger ale with the spices sprinkled on top and the leaf hinged on the edge of your serving glass.

Magickal Association: Creativity and inventiveness

History/Lore: Pomegranate encourages fertile ideas while both ginger and cinnamon add energy for achievement. The carbonated soda is for effervescence!

Alternative: For spontaneity in love, try passion fruit juice or raspberry juice instead of pomegranate.

GLORIOUS GREENERY

1 lime, juiced

8 seedless green grapes

3/4 cup white grape juice

1 to 2 drops green food coloring

sugar to taste

1 whole peppermint leaf (garnish)

Directions: Use a tall slender glass which will show off the grapes. Mix grape juice, lime juice, and food color together. Chill and serve with mint leaf. This is a singular serving.

Magickal Associations: Growth.

History/Lore: The pale green color of this beverage looks much like the healthy first bits of grass to reach the sun. It is a color that, along with the mint, promotes consistent, but paced, maturation.

Alternatives: In summer use red fruits and coloring such as cherries or strawberries. For spiritual growth, move to purple grape juice and grapes—the color of metaphysical pursuits.

Summer (Life—the Maiden and Son)

Earth is vitally awake now; Her senses, keen. Every leaf and bud reaches towards a glowing sky as if to praise the Sun's return. Summer is the season of Fire; a time when the energy of life itself is plentiful. It is a good time to consider cultivating new virtues and enacting fire related magicks (such as scrying). It is also the season for purification and drastic change. The hot solar disk offers the opportunity to burn away the old, so, like the phoenix, we can return better than before.

Ideas to Consider for Summer Components:

- ❧ Rose, marigolds, geranium, hyacinth, nasturtium, violets, and other summer blossoms. (Please check a book on edible flowers before using flowers to brew!)

- ❧ Fire herbs such as allspice, basil, bay, clove, dill, fennel, ginger, nutmeg, and peppermint.

- ❧ Other flavorings such as cashew nut, lime, orange, pomegranate, pineapple, and walnut.

- ❧ Any beverages which are bright red or golden yellow in color.

- ❧ Preparing beverages at noon, when the sun is most powerful.

> To be certain the weather will be fair for your summer outings, check to see if any new spider webs are evident. Spiders usually spin before fair skies.

PAPAYA POWER

1 cup papaya juice
1 cup milk
1 tsp. sugar
1 egg white, beaten
4 crushed strawberries
2 Tbs. honey

Directions: Blend together the papaya juice with milk and sugar. Meanwhile, beat the egg white until frothy. Scoop one heaping tablespoonful on top of the glass. Mash together the strawberries and honey and drizzle in the middle of the egg. Serve chilled.

Magickal Associations: Energy.

History/Lore: The visual effect of this drink is not unlike a sun in splendor with yellow rays beneath, and bright red in the center. In the West Indies, papaya is known as the Medicine Tree and is rich in vitamin A.

Alternative: Add a dash of cinnamon to this beverage to increase its potency.

SUMMER SUNSET

8 whole strawberries

2 cups orange juice

1 cup raspberries

1 cup crushed ice

Directions: Place all ingredients together in a blender, adding more ice if you desire a thicker beverage. Sweetening is not usually needed.

Magickal Associations: New virtues.

History/Lore: While berries are generally considered a "love" food, we have to love ourselves before we can really incorporate new qualities into our lives. The orange is for a "healthy" outlook!

Alternative: It is nice to garnish this drink with carnation which symbolizes pride in your progress.

PATRIOT PUNCH

1 dozen white nasturtiums

1/2 lb. sugar

6 rose geranium leaves

1 qt. apple juice

2 limes

1/2 qt. ginger ale

red rose geranium petals

1/2 cup blueberries

Directions: Make a paste from the nasturtium petals and sugar. To this, add the juice of one lime. Meanwhile warm the geranium leaves with the apple juice, cool, and strain. Slowly blend this juice with the nasturtium and ginger ale. Garnish with a thinly sliced lime, rose geranium petals, and blueberries for a red, white, and blue day!

History/Lore: In the language of flowers, nasturtium means patriotism, so all that remains is a bit of creative coloring to encourage energy which supports your native land.

Alternative: For those who live abroad, food coloring and different shades of flowers can be substitute to mimic the hues of your national flag. To eliminate flowers, find alternative fruits, sodas, or colorings to substitute in equal measures.

PURIFICATION POTTAGE

Directions: To a tea kettle of hot water add 1 tsp. each of the following: anise, bay leaf, chamomile, fennel, lavender, lemon juice, peppermint, rosemary, and thyme. Steep for 15 minutes then serve piping hot before meditation.

History/Lore: The herbs for this tea were chosen for their cleansing effect on both the body and psyche.

Alternative: To increase the effect of this tea specifically for divination efforts, add a slice of orange and a bit of onion to the stew. This tastes a little like a weak soup.

Fall (Maturity—the Mother and Father)

Fall is the harvest of our youthful days. The earth turns on its voyage once more and grows cooler. Rains fall across the land like a cleansing wave, and slowly trees begin marking the transition from vitality to sleep.

This season is one of fruitfulness; we gather the earth's bounty even as we gathered the gifts planted in our hearts months ago. It is an excellent time to focus on social activities with family and friends, and to share your abundance with those in need. Through these months, work on water magick, matters of the heart, protection of health, and generate some magickal "projects," such as updating your book of shadows.

Ideas to Consider for Fall Components:

ᕳ Any late-blooming flowers including squash blossom.

ᕳ Water herbs such as cardamom, chamomile, poppy, mint, and thyme.

ᕳ Other flavorings such as berries, apple, avocado, birch, banana, coconut, grape, lemon, peach, pear, and vanilla.

ᕳ Any beverages which are dark russet, burnt orange, muted yellow, or pale brown in color.

ᕳ Preparing beverages at dusk, when the sky fills with the hues of the season.

> *If you can catch an oak leaf before it falls to the ground in fall, you will have a winter free from colds and flu.*

SWEET HEALTH

1 cup orange juice

1 Tbs. rosemary

1 tsp. vanilla

2 Tbs. whipped cream

1 slice of orange (garnish)

Directions: Make a warm tea of the orange juice, rosemary, and vanilla, then strain. Serve slightly warm with 1

Tbs. whipped cream blended in, and one on top for garnish with a slice of fresh orange.

History/Lore: While many people think of rosemary only in terms of remembrance, in the Middle Ages it was lauded as having many restorative qualities for health. The high content of vitamin C in oranges aids this feature.

Alternative: This is also good cold, served over chipped ice with a mint leaf for extra energy.

MATTERS OF THE HEART

1 cup dried jonquil petals

1/2 cup dried French lavender

2 cups warm water

sugar to taste

Directions: Infuse the petals with warm water for 12 hours, preferably during a waxing to full moon. Strain and sweeten. Serve over ice with a fresh flower to bring hope.

History/Lore: In the language of flowers, jonquil means the return of affection, while lavender speaks of appreciation and response.

Alternative: If you are sharing this on a special occasion and want it to be remembered, add a fresh sprig of rosemary to adorn the cup. Any love fruit may be added in this recipe in place of the flowers including strawberry, cherry, or oranges. This creates a hot fruit juice tincture high in vitamins.

FALL HARVEST

1 cup currants, juiced

1 cup cherries, juiced

1 cup blackberries, juiced

1 Tbs. honey
1 orange, juiced
1 bundle of grapes
2 cups apple juice

Directions: Place all ingredients after juice extraction into a blender and mix at high speed until bubbly. Serve in a glass with the grapes hinged on the side.

Magickal Associations: Abundance.

History/Lore: Most of the fruits chosen for this drink are connected with financial prosperity, however the energy can be put towards other areas of your life where some opulence is needed such as creativity.

Alternative: Citron or pomegranate juice may be added to this drink specifically to aid in energy towards the arts.

CHARITY COOLER

1 large glass pineapple juice
minute dash tarragon
1 tsp. walnut extract
sprig of basil (garnish)

Directions: Pour pineapple juice mixed with tarragon and extract over ice. Finish off with basil.

History/Lore: Pineapple is the universal symbol of welcome and warmth. The basil is added for compassion and to ease a distressed heart. Tarragon is for calm nurturing and walnut is to improve our mental keenness to recognize needs as they occur.

Alternative: For empathy specifically in matters of love, add a few fresh berries to this beverage.

Winter (Death—the Crone and Grandfather)

Winter marks a kind of death, but it is not one lost in hopelessness. In fact, winter is the time of expectation. Just beneath the surface of the land, seeds and plants rest quietly, knowing the sun will find its way back to them.

Winter is filled with themes of sleep, contemplation, nurturing, economy, and conservation of personal resources including spiritual ones. It is an excellent season for in-depth meditation and study about one's Path. Also, don't forget your animal friends. Leave the birds your left over crumbs, and work magick for the Earth and her creatures to sustain them through until spring.

Ideas to Consider for Winter Components:

- Any indoor flowers, or frozen petals such as roses which keep well.

- Earth herbs such as mugwort, magnolia, primrose, and tulip

- Other flavorings such as barley, beet, oats, quince, and rhubarb.

- Any beverages which are white, bluish-white, brown, or black in color.

- Preparing beverages at midnight, when silence and rest fall across the land.

> Greater fur growth in animals and thicker skins on vegetables in the fall are fairly certain signs of a long, cold winter.

SNOW SONG

2 cups pear juice

1 slice of lemon

1 egg white, beaten

Directions: Pour pear juice into a large glass. Squeeze lemon slice into the juice with one heaping teaspoon of beaten egg white and stir. Place remaining egg white on top to look like peaks of snow.

Magickal Associations: Clarity in thought.

History/Lore: Not only does this beverage have a pale white glimmer of snow, but the lemon adds precision to our contemplative processes. Additionally, this beverage can improve your focus in an emotional situation.

Alternatives: To improve wisdom with regard to spiritual insights, add fresh or juiced peaches to this recipe.

WINTER HOPE

1 cup white grape juice

1 cup pineapple juice

1 cup persimmon juice

2 cups warm ginger ale

Directions: Warm the juices together over a low flame. Add this to the ginger ale, which should be at room temperature. Garnish with a fresh flower to remind yourself spring is not that far away.

History/Lore: Persimmon is the fruit of hope while the other components of this beverage give it a bright yellow color to remind us of warmer days.

Alternatives: For improved outlooks specifically for finances, add cinnamon and ginger to your juices. Please note, too, that while this beverage is served warm to bring comfort within, it may also be chilled if you prefer.

THE TODDY

1 cup apple juice

1 tsp. lemon juice

1 tsp. honey

cinnamon stick

1 cherry

1 beaten egg white

Directions: Warm the apple juice just to the point of almost boiling, then add lemon and honey which are stirred with the cinnamon stick. Place egg white over the top of the drink with a cherry in the middle (sundae style)!

Magickal Associations: Contemplation and rest.

History/Lore: The apple juice brings wisdom balanced against lemon's cleansing clarity. The entire hot beverage is immersed in snow, with the cherry on the top to help improve personal focus and balance. Visualize this in the middle of your gravity center.

Alternatives: Eliminate the egg and add a dash of ginger, 1/4 tsp. of rosemary, and a shot of whiskey (optional) for a terrific winter cough remedy.

COCONUT OF NUTURING

1 cup fresh coconut

1 cup milk

1 cup water

Directions: Open a hole in your coconut and pour the juice in a pan (not aluminum). To this add 1 cup of fresh coconut meat shredded, milk, and water. Simmer over very low flame for one hour, strain and enjoy.

History/Lore: For this recipe I have chosen ingredients and alternatives which are often associated with the Mother aspect of the Goddess to encourage energy for personal development or the growth of parental instincts.

Alternatives: A vanilla bean sliced and blanched almonds can be added to the beverage during the cooking process for richer flavor and similar magickal results.

Alcoholic

Spring

FLOWING TRANSFORMATION

1 ltr. vodka

1 cup maple syrup

2 cups pecans, ground

2 cups almonds, ground

Directions: Warm the vodka slightly with maple syrup so that the syrup mixes completely with it. Meanwhile, place the nuts in a wide mouth container (with lid). Pour the warm vodka mixture over top and seal tightly. Leave in a dark, breezy place and shake daily for eight weeks, then strain and enjoy.

Magickal Associations: Personal changes, reversing cycles, modifying habits.

History/Lore: The number eight (months) is the number of change. Additionally the ingredients here are all aligned with the Air Element to encourage the winds to bring a refreshing metamorphosis in your situation.

Alternatives: Replace vodka with one liter of water and increase syrup to three cups, adding wine yeast as directed in the wine chapter. This produces a lovely golden beverage with lower alcohol content.

DATE-FIG FERTILITY

2 lbs. pitted dates

1 orange

2 lbs. figs

1 lemon

1 gal. white wine

2 cups sugar (to taste)

Directions: Cut up the dates and figs into 1/2-inch chunks and place them in a large container with the wine. To this add the orange and lemon sliced. Warm the sugar in just a little water to make a syrup, then mix this with the wine-fruit blend. Close tightly and shake daily for six weeks before straining and serving.

Magickal Associations: Productivity, child-bearing, resourceful energies.

History/Lore: The date palm is a unique tree with two distinct sexes. The Greeks regarded it as the perfect emblem of fertility, and the Israelites often named female children after it, as a symbol of beauty.

MAY PUNCH

1 qt. warm apple wine or hard cider
1/2 cup woodruff flowers, freshly picked
2 oz. sugar or honey
1/4 pt. water
stick cinnamon
1 orange, sliced
1 lemon, sliced

Directions: Allow the woodruff to set in room temperature wine or cider for a half hour then remove. To this add sugar and water. Pour into punch bowl, garnishing with sliced fruit and cinnamon stick. May be served hot, if desired.

Magickal Associations: Success, safety, relieving a heavy heart.

History/Lore: Woodruff is a traditional May decoration. Germans call this lovely white blossom the master of the woods. Its white petals are considered sacred to the Goddess. Magickally woodruff is used to protect against negative energies.

Alternatives: Other early blooming, edible flowers such as the daisy might be added to the bowl to further encourage vibrant Spring energies. For more ideas regarding edible petals, look to the flower beverage sections of this book.

CREATIVITY COOLER

1 ltr. peach brandy or liqueur
1 cup milk
6 ice cubes, chopped
2 Tbs. heavy cream
1 banana, sliced

Directions: Place the brandy, milk and ice together in a blender. Whip until frothy. Pour into glasses topped with a thin layer of heavy cream and sliced bananas for garnish.

Magickal Associations: Fruitfulness, productivity, sexual symmetry, Yin-Yang balance.

History/Lore: The banana and peaches in this recipe combine to create a harmonious balance of male/female energies perfect to bring fertile energy into any creative effort.

Summer

FIRE FESTIVAL

1 tsp. allspice
1 tsp. nutmeg
1/4 tsp. basil
1/2 tsp. peppermint
2 bay leaves
1 tsp. black tea
1/2 tsp. cinnamon
1 whole orange, sliced
6 whole cloves
1 small lime, sliced
1/4 tsp. fennel
2 Tbs. pomegranate juice
1/2 tsp. ginger
1 cup honey
1 L whiskey

Directions: Place all your ingredients together in a large container which can be securely sealed. Leave in a sunny window, shaking daily for one month. Do not open during this time. Strain and enjoy hot or cold (hot is probably more magickally appropriate).

Magickal Associations: Vibrant energy, increasing power, the God aspect, mental awareness.

History/Lore: Each of the ingredients for this beverage, including the Whiskey as "fire water" are strongly associated with the Element of Fire itself. Magickally, Fire is related to the Southern portion of the Circle and the attributes of vigor, strength, and leadership.

Alternatives: Try making other elemental drinks simply by reviewing some lists of correspondences and putting together complimentary herbs and fruits. Or for cyclical balance, have one beverage that accentuates all four elements!

LAMMAS TIDES

1 qt. apple mead

1 tsp. nutmeg

1 tsp. rosewater

5 sprigs fresh thyme

Directions: Mix the first three ingredients together and chill. Serve in five glasses with one sprig of thyme each on August 1st.

Magickal Associations: Kinship with the fairy kinds or Devic realms, psychic vision, and insight.

History/Lore: Rose, honey, and thyme are all thought to be excellent temptations to the Wee Folk to come for a visit. And because they are active during Lammas, the first harvest festival, the goal is accentuated by apple mead and a little nutmeg for perception.

Alternatives: To further improve your sense of inner vision, decorate the glasses with an additional peppermint leaf, or use one as a breath refresher.

GOD ASPECT

1/2 cup crushed almonds

1 tsp. nutmeg

1/2 cup crushed cashews

1 whole walnut, per person

1/2 cup crushed hazelnuts

1 pt. vodka

1 pt. almond liqueur

Directions: Place the first six ingredients together in a large glass container with lid for two months in the sunlight, shaking daily. Strain. Add almond liqueur and test for sweetness. Add honey if desired. Note that, although this beverage is quite tasty without the almond liqueur, this last ingredient serves to accent the magickal aspects and improve flavor.

Magickal Associations: The Huntsman, male virility, Pan, the Horned One, and other fertile god images.

History/Lore: Nuts in general have often been associated as an emblem of male sexuality. An old Phrygian tale tells about how one of their great Gods, Attis, was born from an almond nut placed in the heart of the Goddess.

PURIFICATION POTION

2 Tbs. anise

1 qt. warm water

2 Tbs. fennel

1 cup sugar

2-inch strip of lemon peel

1 tsp. yeast

Directions: Place the anise, fennel, and finely sliced bits of the lemon peel in the water and allow to soak for one hour. Strain and return the water to a low flame, adding sugar and stirring until dissolved.

While this cools to lukewarm, suspense the yeast in 1/4 cup warm water. Mix into the tea-like water then bottle with a loose cork for about 10 days. Slowly tighten cork, then age until liquid in bottle looks clear (about three months).

Magickal Associations: Cleansing, turning negativity, safety from malevolent magick.

History/Lore: Anise has been used since the time of Virgil to protect against the evil eye. Fennel mirrors this in Medieval Europe where it was rubbed on the body to keep mischievous witchcraft away.

> Both anise and fennel are sometimes included as ingredients in dream pillows with the belief that they will protect against nightmares.

Fall

HARMONIC DRAUGHT

2 cups boiling water
any white flower (garnish)
1/2 cup sugar
1 jigger gin
9 mint leaves
slice of lemon

Directions: Stir sugar into the boiling water until it is totally dissolved. Steep the mint leaves and lemon for about 10 minutes, then remove adding gin. May also be chilled and served. Garnish.

Magickal Associations: Peace, serenity, reconciliation.

History/Lore: Nine is the number of universal law and symmetry. Mint has been honored with such folk names as "heart mint" and "lamb mint" as an indication of its peaceful nature. Greeks and Romans often used mint in baths to help calm tensions. The white flower is added as an emblem of amicable intentions.

Alternatives: Change the type of flower according to your needs. As an illustration, use a rose to accentuate peace in relationships.

HARVEST HORN

2 cups white grape juice
1 cup berries (any)
2 cups apple juice
2 cups ginger ale
1 bottle mixed fruit wine
grape bunches
1 orange sliced

Directions: Mix the juices with the wine, adding sliced orange and berries. Allow this to sit at room temperature for 30 minutes then chill. Add ginger ale when pouring into a punch bowl. Garnish sides of the bowl with grape bunches.

Magickal Associations: Abundance, providence, gathering natural bounty, gratefulness.

History/Lore: The Horn of Plenty appears in various forms in a diversity of folklore as an object which pours unceasingly of divine goodness—usually in the form of foods or blessings.

Serving Idea: If you have some readily available, the magick of this beverage is accentuated by serving it in a drinking horn instead of a glass.

TEMPERANCE TONIC

1 cup coconut juice

1 black tea bag

1 tsp. ginger

1 pt. peach brandy

2 cups pineapple juice

Directions: Warm the coconut juice with the tea bag and ginger allowing to simmer for 10 minutes. Strain and chill. Add this to the pineapple juice and peach brandy, whipping with a wire whisk until frothy. Serve in chilled glasses with a slice of fresh pineapple as garnish.

Magickal Associations: Moderation, self control, restraint, forbearance.

History/Lore: In order of appearance, the ingredients in this recipe have been chosen for their magickal associations with restraint, strength, energy, protection, and wisdom.

SNIFFLE STOPPER

1/2 cup whiskey

dash ginger

1/2 cup warm water

1 to 2 Tbs. honey

2 to 3 eucalyptus leaves

1 Tbs. fresh lemon juice

1 Tbs. fresh orange juice

Directions: Heat the water until almost boiling with the eucalyptus leaves in it. Remove the leaves, then add all remaining ingredients, drinking before bed time. The remedial value of this beverage can be accentuated magickally by working during a waning moon, so the sickness will likewise shrink.

Magickal Associations: Return to health and well being (more on the physical level than emotional or spiritual).

History/Lore: This recipe comes from my own "backyard," so to speak where I have tried to combine the best herbal decongestant with other healthful fruits for best results. I have found this drink helps improve sleep and breathing during cold and flu season.

> It is said that if you catch the first Autumn leaf to fall from the trees before it reaches the ground you will be free of colds all winter.

Winter

PEACEFUL PLEASURE

3 cups boiling water

1 L brandy

12 quinces, peeled and diced

2 chamomile tea bags

Directions: Place the quince and chamomile in the boiling water in a large bowl. Allow to sit until cool. To this, add the liter of brandy and store together in an air-tight container for three months. Strain. May be served warm with a cinnamon stick, or chilled over ice.

Magickal Associations: Accord, restfulness, relaxed visits with friends, serenity.

History/Lore: To the ancient Greeks, the quince was a fruit which insured joy and harmony especially in relationships. They sometimes called it the golden apple, much as they did the orange. Chamomile likewise encourages this tranquility.

Alternatives: The flavor of the quince is similar to the pear, and can be enhanced by any number of other fruits such as nectarines, which magickally produces a blend of sagacity, peace, and health.

VISIONARY VIBRANCY

2 cups carrot wine

2 cups onion wine

1 cup boiling water

5 pinches angelica (approx. 1 tsp.)

5 whole nutmeg beads

Directions: Place the angelica and nutmeg in a tea ball to steep in hot water for 15 minutes. Mix this, the onion and carrot wine (which should be chilled and well blended). Serve to five people on the fifth day of the week for best results.

Magickal Associations: Psychic awareness, oracles, divination efforts, spiritual insight.

History/Lore: Five is the number for psychic endeavors, combined powerfully with herbs for spiritual awareness, nutmeg, and angelica. Onions are thought to produce prophetic dreams, and carrots are said to improve vision.

LEFTOVER CORDIAL

1 lb. left over fruit (any, even fruit cocktail)
1 12 oz. can frozen fruit juice (your choice)
2 cups sugar or honey
1 ltr. Vodka

Directions: Place your left over fruit and fruit juice (undiluted) in a medium sized pan to warm. Add sugar or honey and bring to a low boil. Allow this mixture to cool completely, then pour it into a wide mouth jar with vodka. Cover securely and age for three months before straining and serving.

Magickal Associations: Frugality, economy, conservation of resources.

History/Lore: In a variety of older brewing recipes, I found reference to uses for fruit strainings as part of other wines, meads, and even food items. In this way, our ancestors were wont to waste nothing. For the modern magician, this approach represents a chance to live in greater reciprocity with nature.

Alternatives: For those who find this drink a little strong for their liking, mix the cordial with equal portions soda water or ginger ale.

YULE GLOGG

2 cups red wine
1/3 cup white raisins
2 cups brandy
1 tsp. almond extract
12 whole cloves

1 cup apple juice
2 medium sized cinnamon sticks
2 cups sugar

Directions: Combine all your ingredients except the sugar in a large pan and warm slowly. Once the liquid is all but boiling, light the surface carefully with a match. While it burns, slowly sprinkle in the sugar until expended. Place a cover over the pot to extinguish the flame. Pour your ingredients into a large container to age for 12 weeks before serving, straining first and serving hot.

Magickal Associations: Happy celebrations, kinship, joyous parties of old friends and family.

History/Lore: A favorite Swedish drink for the holidays, this beverage is thought not only to warm the body but the spirit of any gathering as well!

Chapter 12

Social Cauldron: Pagan Party Punches

"At the punch bowl's brink let the thirsty come and drink."

—Edward R. Sill

"Nature never did betray the heart that loved her."

—William Wordsworth

There are many occasions when Pagans, Wiccans or friends and family gather for meetings—be it a ritual, reunion, or festival. In this setting, magickal punches would make a wonderful accent. Match the theme of the beverage to the season, the occasion, or a specific need in the group. Since these mixtures get served from one cauldron, like a communal cup, they link everyone in unity of purpose.

Party punches also afford the perfect opportunity for extra creativity. There are hundreds of flavored sodas, additives, and natural juices on the market that can replace any of the components in these recipes. One of my personal favorite twists is to substitute raspberry ginger ale for regular, magickally bringing joy and abundance. The flavor is subtle, but exhilarating and fun. So, by all means, experiment!

Nonalcoholic

CELEBRATION JUBILATION

1 qt. ginger ale

2 cups sugar

1 qt. soda water

1 cup lemon juice

1 qt. white grape juice

1 cup raspberries

2 cups apricot juice

borage flowers

Directions: Mix together your sodas and juices, slowly adding sugar until the taste is pleasing. Float whole raspberries on top of the punch and chill. Place borage around the edge of the punch bowl before serving.

Magickal Associations: Jubilee, merry-making, glad tidings

History/Lore: Sparkling waters have long been used in various forms of celebration and were even considered lucky. Raspberry is added for pleasure, and borage flowers for joy.

Alternatives: Add a whole strawberry and pineapple bite on a toothpick as a garnish to celebrate love.

PEACHY KEEN

1 qt. peach juice

1 tsp. rum extract

1 cup sugar

1 lemon juiced

1 lemon thinly sliced

Directions: Mix the first four ingredients in a blender before pouring into the punch bowl. For a frothy top, add one egg white. Float lemon slices on top as garnish.

Magickal Associations: Sagacity, good judgment, prudence.

History/Lore: The peach is a fruit of wisdom and its pit (the core of growth) is a good addition to medicine bags.

Alternatives: If you have a group who has a particularly difficult time with funding, add pineapple juice or chunks to this punch to encourage wisdom in spending.

(WEE PEOPLE NECTAR)

1 qt. apple juice

1 Tbs. rose water

2 oranges, juiced

1 tsp. thyme

2 cups honey

1 qt. soda

sliced pineapple

sliced lemon

whole grapes

whole cherries

clover flowers (garnish)

Directions: Place the apple juice, orange juice, honey, rose water, and thyme in a blender and mix well. Pour this into a bowl, slowly adding the soda water. Stir in some ice (about 12 cubes) and float the whole fruits and flowers on top. The amount of whole fruit is according to your personal taste.

Magickal Associations: Understanding and vision of the "unseen" world; fairy friendship and welcoming.

History/Lore: Perhaps best served at Lammas, May Day, and Midsummer when the fey are thought most active, clover is to help your astral vision, while rose, thyme, and honey are to attract and appease the Wee folk. Lots of color is added here, knowing that faeries like gaiety.

Alternative: If you can serve this punch near a thorn, oak or ash tree your results might be more favorable; where these three grow together fairy homes are more abundant. Also, be sure to leave some miniature cups filled with the beverage for your visitors to enjoy.

(MAY DAY BOWL)

1/2 qt. white grape juice

1/2 qt. apple juice

handful woodruff flowers

sugar to taste

Directions: Chill the May bowl, pouring the juices in to mix. Steep only the flowers of woodruff in the juice for about 15 minutes, then move them to the edge of the dish. Add sweetener if desired.

Magickal Associations: Safety during celebration, joy in abundance, flourishing energy.

History/Lore: The blossoming of woodruff marks the suns victorious return to the sky and the joyous energy of spring. Woodruff, however, is a masculine herb and since May Day is a festival of fruitfulness, a bit of apple juice is added to honor the Goddess.

Alternative: Orange slices may be added to encourage the return to health for all participants who may have been plagued by winter colds. If woodruff is not available in your area, skip the step for steeping it and simply float one or two fresh spring daisies on top of your bowl instead.

LOVE GROG

4 cups apple cider
4 whole cloves
2 cinnamon sticks
1 cup raisins
1/2 cup blanched almonds
sugar or honey

Directions: Warm the cider over low flame with other ingredients incorporated. Once sugar or honey is dissolved this is ready to serve. If desired, the beverage may be chilled or even enjoyed as a frappe. You can leave spices in or strain, depending on what is most personally pleasing.

Magickal Associations: Warm feelings, kinship, the love of friends.

History/Lore: A favorite Swedish drink during winter celebrations, this grog may be enjoyed hot or cold. For a special treat, roll the almonds after cooking in a bit of honey and offer them to someone special to spark some romance.

Alternative: Add some diced figs during the heating process to improve fertility.

In Asgard, the Gods were believed to draw their strength and youthful vigor from magick apples.

BOWL OF PLENTY

1/2 gal. apple cider
1 cup whole strawberries
1 12-oz. can raspberry juice
1/2 peeled grapefruit

cinnamon to taste

1 orange, sliced

ginger to taste

1 cup whole cherries

1 cup blueberries

1 thinly sliced lemon

ginger ale (optional)

Directions: Mix cider with undiluted raspberry juice and spices. If you prefer, use whole cinnamon and ginger-root so spices can be removed. Stir in fruit slices and chill. Add ginger ale just before serving, if desired.

Magickal Associations: Abundance, providence, prosperity.

History/Lore: Being representative of the bounty of earth, this makes an excellent beverage for rituals of thankfulness or during holiday gatherings to bless all in attendance with good fortune.

Alternative: Try using this same idea with thematic colors. Add only yellow fruit or juice for rich creativity or only red fruit and juices for growing passions.

Cool as a Cucumber

1 thinly sliced cucumber

1 qt. tomato juice

1 cinnamon stick

6 whole cloves

salt and pepper to taste

Directions: Mix the spices with juice and cucumber and allow this to set at room temperature for one hour. Remove the spices and chill. Serve with a stalk of celery.

Magickal Associations: Calmness, peace, tranquility.

History/Lore: The power of the aphorism in this recipe is undeniable. Actually, cool cucumbers have been used to relieve pain, especially for headaches, in folk medicine, which could have led to the idea that they ease stress.

Alternatives: Feel free to add any spices that you enjoy with a vegetable juice such as basil (for peace in relationships) or rosemary to bring quiet to a restless mind.

COFFEE EXCITEMENT

2 qts. dark coffee

1 cup milk

1 cup cream

1 tsp. vanilla

1/2 cup sugar

1 pt. ice cream (your choice)

Directions: Brew your coffee and let it cool adding milk, cream, vanilla, and sugar to taste to a punch bowl. Once chilled, float small scoops of ice cream on top.

Magickal Associations: Abundant energy!

History/Lore: This beverage is an especially nice pick-me-up after a long evening of magick. The cream makes for a smooth transition in energy and the ice cream is just for fun!

Alternatives: You can make some luscious punches by matching gourmet coffee with distinctive ice cream. Make sure to whisk your components to whip up the energy!

MULLED ALE

5 cups non alcoholic ale

1 lemon

5 whole cloves

1 cinnamon stick

1 Tbs. brandy flavoring

2/3 cup brown sugar

1 tsp. ginger

1 tsp. nutmeg

Directions: A very easy punch to prepare, simply stew all your ingredients over a low flame for about 30 minutes. Cool until palatable, then pour in the punch bowl. Please be careful with this last step. Some glassware does not take to drastic temperature changes well, so rinse your bowl in warm water first.

Magickal Associations: Honoring the gods, or deeds of those close to us.

History/Lore: We have spoken often about how beer was the common man's offering to the Divine. In this case, pour a bit of your warm brew to the ground first, then lift your cup to toast whatever is appropriate. An excellent choice for cold winter rituals!

Alternative: This is also very tasty when prepared with nonalcoholic red wine.

DIVINATION DRAUGHT

2 cups cheery juice

1 cup orange juice

1 cup pomegranate juice

1 tsp. hazel extract

1/2 L ginger ale or soda water

dandelion or broom flowers (garnish)

Directions: Pour your first four ingredients together and chill well before placing in the punch bowl. Add ginger ale and float the flowers, after washing them well, atop the dish.

Magickal Associations: Psychic energy, improved insight, foresight, prophesy.

History/Lore: Each ingredient in this beverage has at one time been linked with the ability to divine information with the exception of ginger ale. The soda adds bubbly energy to your efforts.

Alternatives: Try changing your garnish to reflect the goals of the question being asked. For love, use rose petals, or in matters of weather, float heather.

APPLE BEER

6 apples baked till soft

1/2 cup brown sugar

1 tsp. nutmeg

1 tsp. ginger

5 cups hot nonalcoholic beer or apple wine.

Directions: Peel the apples, pulping the fruit with brown sugar and spices (more sweetening may be added, if desired). Mix this with ale or wine and enjoy as a liquid dessert!

Magickal Associations: Earth Magick, wisdom, ecology.

History/Lore: In certain parts of Europe a version of this drink was often served on August 1st (Lammas Tide) to honor the spiritual protector who presides over fruit, seeds and earths bounty. Not surprisingly, Lammas was sometimes referred to as "the day of the apple fruit."

Alternatives: Nice when served with sweet cakes, you can try substituting apple cider or pear juice for the ale. Pear, however, is more appropriate to help extend or give life to a living thing or project that is ailing or stagnant.

WASSAIL

6 cups apple juice or cider

1 tsp. cinnamon

1 tsp. ginger

1 tsp. nutmeg
1 qt. non alcoholic beer
1 sliced lemon
1 cup sliced apples baked in sugar

Directions: Warm all ingredients except the apples and lemon over a low flame until well spiced. Serve out into cups immediately, adding a thin slice of lemon and one to two slices of sweet apple to the top. If you like, a little sweet cream is nice on this too. The apple topping is easily made by peeling the fruit and placing the slices in a pan. For each apple add about 1/8 cup of water and brown sugar. Cook until slices are tender.

Magickal Associations: Good health, good fortune, happiness, and a prosperous year.

History/Lore: A traditional beverage for the period between Yule and New Years, the word *wassail* is literally a wish for well-being to all who partake of the bowl.

Alternatives; In place of the beer, try adding various flavors of juices or soft wines which match your magickal goals. For example, with health matters use soft apple wine instead of beer.

EOSTRE EGG BOWL

12 eggs
2 cups sugar
2 tsp. vanilla extract
1 to 2 tsp. brandy extract
1 tsp. lemon juice
1 tsp. orange juice
grated lemon peel
grated orange peel
nutmeg (garnish)

Directions: In a double boiler, place your eggs and sugar beating constantly until fluffy over low flame. Next, add extracts and juices, continuing to beat until warm. To garnish, place a dab of whipped cream on each cup and a sprinkle of lemon, orange, and nutmeg on top.

Magickal Associations: Fecundity, fertility, productivity.

History/Lore: The egg is a traditional symbol of spring in that farmers mark the season by when their hens begin laying. Many ancient myths use eggs as part of the creation story.

Alternative: This can also be very refreshing if chilled before serving. In this case, only garnish after the beverage is completely chilled.

(KANDEEL)

3 cups nonalcoholic white wine

4 whole cloves

1 cinnamon stick

1 Tbs. lemon peel

1 tsp. nutmeg

1/3 cup milk

2/3 cup sugar

12 egg yolks

Directions: Place the spices in wine over a low flame to create a tea, then strain. Mix sugar with egg yolks beating until frothy, then slowly incorporate tea. The final texture should be rich and creamy. Serve with a tablespoon of heavy cream or swirl of chocolate syrup on top.

Magickal Associations: Baby blessing, children's birthdays, Wiccaning.

History/Lore: This treat comes from the Netherlands, where it is traditionally given to guests when visiting a mother and newborn. It is thought to bless both the guest and the family.

Alternatives: There is no reason why this might not also make a good beverage to be employed in fertility and conception rites. In this setting the milk and eggs would help encourage maternal energies.

BERRY-MINT MEDLEY

1 L raspberry ginger ale

3 to 4 whole mint leaves

1 12 oz. can red raspberry juice

1 cup blueberries

1 cup blackberries

1 cup strawberries

Directions: Open the bottle of ginger ale and stuff the mint leaves inside. Close securely and leave at room temperature for at least two hours. Pour the undiluted raspberry juice over ice, slowly adding ginger ale and topping with berries. Float a few more mint leaves on top if they don't come out of the soda bottle.

Magickal Associations: Joyful gatherings, good feelings, friendship, and community.

History/Lore: Berries have always been regarded as a special gift from the earth, appearing in the most surprising places to bring a smile to our face.

Alternative: Other theme punches are really fun to try. Orange juice with orange soda and all orange fruits (tangerines, cantaloupe, and so on) are one example for magick pertaining to warmth, empathy, or consequences.

TEA TIME

1 tsp. mint tea

2 cinnamon sticks

1 tsp. apple tea

1/4 cup honey

1 tsp. berry tea

orange peel (fresh)

1 tsp. black tea

lemon peel (fresh)

4 cups boiling water

2 tsp. lemon juice

Directions: Steep the four types of tea in hot water using a tea ball or bag, then remove tea. To this, while hot, add your cinnamon, honey, fruit rinds (one whole fruit each), and lemon juice. This is wonderful hot, or maybe chilled and served over chipped ice.

Magickal Associations: Relaxation, healthy leisure, introspection that provides refreshed insights.

History/Lore: Tea was one of the plants sacred to Buddha, and considering all its uses in religion and medicine it is certainly no wonder. Tea has played a major role in folk remedials for hundreds of years, and during the Victorian era was often associated with the pleasurable moments of quiet sharing with friends.

Alternatives: Use any type of herbal teas that you personally like. Also, some people like to add a cup or two of apple juice to this mixture.

PINEAPPLE-GINGER SURPRISE

2 bottles sparkling white grape juice

1 12-oz. can pineapple with syrup

1 inch bruised ginger root

Directions: Drain the syrup from the pineapple and place in a small pan with 1 Tbs. of water. Add ginger root and warm for 15 minutes. Strain off root. Pour this liqueur into the grape juice and garnish with fresh green grapes or pineapple chunks.

Magickal Associations: Protection.

History/Lore: Both ginger and pineapple are considered as protective, the first because of its biting flavor and the second because of its prickly exterior. These are especially protective of health.

Alternative: To further accentuate energies for physical well-being add a little orange rind to the syrup while cooking.

Alcoholic

TEA TOT'A-LING

1/2 qt. boiling water

4 lemon verbena tea bags

1 cup honey

1/4 cup lemon juice

4 cups lemon-lime soda

4 cups vodka

Directions: Prepare tea as you usually would, steeping the bags until water is very dark and adding honey to dissolve. Chill. Next add lemon juice, soda, and vodka over a bed of ice. Serve with garnishes of fresh lemon slices.

Magickal Associations: Paced recuperation, calm adjustment

History/Lore: Lemons still play an important role in the Jewish Feast of the Tabernacles where they are brought to the Temple to enjoy their refreshing fragrance. Tea is a quieter balance to the energy of lemon, offering repose.

Alternatives: This beverage offers a bounty of options just based on the number of flavored teas available. Match your chosen goal with the flavor of the tea, juice, and soda for an amazing variety of taste and magick!

WINE AND SONG

1/2 qt. strawberries hulled

1 cup sugar

3 sliced peaches

1/2 gal. sangria

2 cups fresh diced pineapple

1 bottle champagne

Directions: Put both the fruit and sugar in a large bowl, stirring to cover the fruit well. Crush half of the fruit while you blend, then let this sit for one hour to produce juice. Next add the sangria and champagne (both chilled), adding ice just before serving. Makes just under one gallon.

Magickal Associations: Joyful celebrations, cessation of cares and worries, exchange between new companions.

History/Lore: In the late 1600s, when sailing voyage was popular, some sailors who landed in India got quite a surprise. They were greeted with a fruity liquid, mixed with spirits that was very refreshing. The potency however was deceptive and the crew quickly found themselves intoxicated and quite giddy to the point of spontaneous song.

ICE CREAM PASSION

1 qt. passion fruit juice

2 cups pineapple puree

1 qt. rainbow sherbet

1 ltr. ginger ale

1/2 ltr. Vodka

2 cups whole cherries

Directions: Mix passion fruit with pineapple puree until well incorporated. Next, using a hand mixer, beat together the sherbet slightly softened, ginger ale and vodka. Slowly mix this blend with the juice and pour into your punch bowl. Float cherries on top. Makes about 3 1/2 quarts.

Magickal Associations: Young love, exchange of good feelings, romance, adoration.

History/Lore: The combination of tropical fruit and ice cream here make a powerful vehicle for the imagination and flights of fancy especially with regard to relationships. All the fruits included here have, at some time, been magickally associated with love.

Alternatives: Any "love" fruit can be substituted for the puree, flavor of ice cream or floating fruit as your personal tastes or creativity dictate. Possibilities include apples, apricots, lemon, peach, pear, plum, and raspberries.

HOT ORANGEADE

2 pts. water

4 oz. sugar

6 oranges juiced

2 pts. rum

1 tsp. whole cloves

2 whole cinnamon sticks

1 tsp. whole allspice berries

Directions: Mix the juice of oranges with the two pints water in a quart sized pan. Warm over low flame with spices and sugar until a tea-like consistency is reached. Add rum and serve with pieces of cinnamon stick. Makes one quart.

Magickal Associations: Balance, fruitfulness, symmetry, abundance

History/Lore: The orange tree is unique in that it bears its leaves, flowers, and fruits all at the same time, making it an excellent symbol of bounty and the triune nature of both Gods and humankind.

Alternatives: For more of a purifying beverage, substitute the juice of four lemons for the oranges.

PLANTERS PUNCH

1 L dark rum
1 orange, sliced
1 1/2 cups brown sugar
1/2 lime sliced
3 tsp. grenadine
1 cup pineapple cubes
1 cup soda water
3 to 4 mint leaves
1 maraschino cherry per person

Directions: Dissolve brown sugar with grenadine and water in a small punch bowl, then slowly stir in rum adding an ice cube tray full of ice (crushed). Float your fruit slices and mint on top. Makes just over one liter.

Magickal Associations: Completion of projects, fulfillment, following through on aspirations.

History/Lore: While the Puritans often balked at beverages such as this as being too potent, variations were a favorite among farmers who enjoyed it as a refreshment during planting and harvesting season.

Alternatives: This is a very strong drink, so you may wish to dilute it some using a fruity ginger ale, plain soda water, or perhaps pineapple juice.

JUMPIN' GINGER!

6 to 12 oz. bottles ginger beer
1/2 cup honey
3 cups ginger ale
1 pt. ginger liqueur
2 oranges sliced thinly

Directions: Use one bottle of ginger beer to warm the honey in until it is dissolved. Add ginger ale to this mixture and stir until well incorporated. Chill remaining ginger beer and liqueur, pouring this with the honey blend into a medium sized punch bowl. Float oranges on top. May be served hot if desired.

Magickal Associations: Improved energy, return to health, Fire Magick, mental keenness, power.

History/Lore: Ginger was one of the nine great herbs of the Middle Ages purported to cure plague, and it was heralded by Pythagoras as an antidote for poison.

Alternatives: If you would like to focus the enhanced power of this beverage on a specific goal, simply change the garnishing fruit to reflect those intentions, such as raspberries for love or strawberries for luck. Please note that if you do not like honey, brown sugar in equal commodity may be substituted (add slowly and test for sweetness).

MILK PUNCH

2 beaten eggs
3 qts. milk
1 lemon peeled
1 cup sugar
4 cups brandy

Directions: Place beaten eggs and milk in a sauce pan and stir. Carefully remove as much white pith from the lemon peel as possible then shred and place with milk mixture. Slowly warm, adding sugar, until the liquid almost boils, then remove from heat, immediately removing the lemon. Slowly add brandy, using a wire whisk to beat until frothy. May be served in a punch bowl with whipped cream, if desired.

Magickal Associations: Maternal nature, Goddess energy, nurturing, feminine fertility, and power.

History/Lore: The Gaelic word for milk translates to "mean heart," and truly milk has been the heart of the Mother in all civilizations. As the first food we experience, it is a powerful emblem of the nourishment and care of both human and Divine mothers.

English Ale Bowl

4 to 12-oz. bottles dark ale

1 orange peeled

1/2 cup cognac

nutmeg (garnish)

4 tsp. honey

Directions: Slowly heat all your ingredients until the honey is well blended then pour into a warm punch bowl. Sprinkle the top with nutmeg and a bit of cinnamon, if desired. Makes enough for eight people.

Magickal Associations: Flowing discourse, free parlay, ease of communications.

History/Lore: In the Elizabethan era, punches similar to this were considered quite able to encourage free speech among the celebrants to the point of rumor mongering!

OLD FASHIONED EGGNOG

1 dozen eggs, separated
nutmeg (garnish)
1 1/2 cups sugar
1 qt. brandy
1 qt. light cream
dash orange water (optional)
2 pts. heavy cream, beaten

Directions: Beat the whites of your eggs until stiff, then set aside. Next, beat your egg yokes, slowly adding sugar. Pour this mixture into a large saucepan and heat until very warm, but not boiling. Stir in the brandy, light cream, and orange water pouring all into the punch bowl. Fold in egg whites then top with whipped cream and a sprinkling of nutmeg.

Magickal Associations: Generation, inception, creative energy, fertility.

History/Lore: Eggs, being one of the oldest symbols of beginnings and reproduction (some even being credited with the birth of gods) make this the perfect beverage for Eostre and many spring festivals.

Alternatives: Instead of rum, some people like to substitute whiskey, brandy or a combination of all three into this punch.

BUBBLING RASPBERRY BREWPOT

5 cups fresh raspberries
1 orange sliced thinly
1 L gin
mint leaves (garnish)
1 orange, juiced

5 tsp. sugar

1/2 L raspberry ginger ale

Directions: Crush 3 cups of the raspberries and place them in the punch bowl. Add gin, the juice of the one orange and sugar, beating with a wire whisk. Next add ginger ale, floating sliced orange, and mint on top. Serve with ice for eight people.

Magickal Associations: Protection, especially from wandering spirits. Boldness in the face of adversity.

History/Lore: In the Philippines, raspberry vines are considered very protective. They are often draped near a doorway shortly after a loved one's death to keep an unsettled ghost from entering. One wonders if this early connotation of safety eventually lead to the idea of "giving a raspberry" as a sign of defiance—in this case even of the afterlife!

Alternatives: To enhance the raspberry flavor, use some raspberry-cranberry juice in place of the orange (about 1/2 cup). An especially fun beverage to serve with a little dry ice at Samhain.

Eggnog II

5 egg yolks

1 qt. milk

8 Tbs. sugar

1 1/2 cups cognac

1 1/2 tsp. vanilla extract

nutmeg

2 drops yellow food color

Directions: Beat egg yokes with sugar until well incorporated. Add the vanilla next with the milk which has been heated to very hot. Stir in cognac, food color, and a dash of nutmeg, pouring into the punch bowl. If possible, serve in yellow cups.

Magickal Associations: Creativity, imagination, sun magick.

History/Lore: This version of eggnog was popular in the 17th century throughout France. It is a wonderful golden color, bringing a little solar warmth to any winter celebration.

WELLNESS BOWL

9 cored apples (small)

dash nutmeg

1 cup packed brown sugar

12 whole cloves

1 1/2 qts. dark ale

3 eggs separated

1/2 inch ginger root sliced

Directions: Roll the apples in 1/2 the brown sugar, using all of it. Place these in an oven set at 375 degrees oven for 40 minutes. Meanwhile, warm the ale with ginger and other spices. Beat egg whites and egg yolks separately until thickened, then fold them together, slowly pouring this mixture into the ale, beating with a wire whisk quickly as you go. Makes enough for six to eight people.

Magickal Associations: Health, well-being, good wishes, and fruitfulness.

History/Lore: A version of the Anglo Saxon treat, Wassail, which literally translates to "be well," this beverage found itself consumed throughout the Yule season. Sometimes such parties were followed by carols to the fruit trees in order that there would be an abundance again next year.

HIPPOCRAS

2 oranges studded with cloves

1 cup sugar

2 sticks cinnamon

1 lemon, juiced

6 allspice berries

3 bottles sweet red wine

Directions: Use a toothpick to poke holes in your oranges before trying to adhere cloves. Feel free to pattern the cloves decoratively, with magickal symbols appropriate to your goals. Bake these in a 375-degree oven for about 35 minutes. When finished cooking, cut each in four pieces, placing them in a sauce pan with sugar, cinnamon, allspice and the lemon juice. Add wine and simmer making sure the sugar dissolves. Pour into a warmed punch bowl and serve immediately.

Magickal Associations: The deep crimson color of this drink gives it marvelous applications for blood mysteries, Fire Magick, and spells to improve energy and strength.

History/Lore: Also known by the less romantic sounding title of spiced wine, this version of Hippocras was enjoyed regularly by Dutch sailors who shared their favored beverage with the English.

Alternatives: For the wine, champagne is sometimes substituted. However, I would suggest using only a small amount of this beverage to warm with the spices, then chill, adding the rest of the champagne afterwards.

HIPPOCRAS II

1 qt. red wine
1 inch ginger sliced
1 1/2 cups sugar
2 mackintosh apples
1 tsp. chili pepper
1 Tbs. almond extract
1 large cinnamon stick
1 Tbs. rose water (opt)
6 whole cloves

Directions: Warm your wine to a medium temperature, then pour it into a large bowl with all remaining ingredients, (note: apples should be peeled and quartered) and save the extract and rose water. Allow this to sit, making a tea-like base, for one hour. Strain, adding extract and rose water and serving over ice. Garnish with fresh rose petals, if desired.

Magickal Associations: All the ingredients in this recipe make it an excellent choice for improving friendships and romantic feelings between people.

History/Lore: This recipe was popular in the 17th century, when various perfumes were often added (like musk) to improve its aroma. For this purpose, the rose water is included as an option in this recipe.

TIERED TREASURE

1 pt. grenadine
1 Tbs. orange juice
1 pt. triple sec
2 Tbs. sugar

1 pt. crème de menthe

2 pts. heavy cream

Directions: Pour the grenadine into a small punch bowl. If you'd like, add some fruit in this layer (such as cherries). Next, very slowly pour the triple sec on top of the grenadine by touching the bottle to the rim, and letting it seep down the side of the bowl. Follow this procedure again with the crème de menthe, succeeded by one pint of the heavy cream. Next, beat the remaining pint of cream until thick and frothy adding juice and sugar. Float this *carefully* on top of the whole drink. The end result looks much like a layered mountain with snow at the peak!

Magickal Associations: Removing divisions, reunion into a whole.

History/Lore: It has been an adventurous pastime of many bartenders to learn techniques of layering liqueurs. This particular punch bowl only looks pretty until you serve out of it, then the layers get blended by people dipping in their cups.

Serving Hint: These three liqueurs together may be a little strong for some guests. Have plain soda water or ginger ale available as a mixer.

MYSTIC APPLE BOWL

1/2 gal. apple juice

3 broken peppermint sticks

1 cup sugar

2 cups soda water

2 cups whiskey

3 broken cinnamon sticks

Directions: Using two cups of apple juice over a low flame, dissolve the sugar. Mix this with the rest of the juice and pour into punch bowl with whiskey and spices. Allow this to sit covered for a half hour before chilling, then add soda water just before serving.

Magickal Associations: Occult insight and ability; psychic talents being manifest.

History/Lore: It is not commonly known that the apple was not regarded popularly as the fruit of Eden until after Milton's epic poem was written. During the time of the Greek Gods, to own an apple tree was to possess supernatural powers. Cinnamon and peppermint enhance this energy.

Chapter 13

Mellow Meads, Soft Beers, and Wine

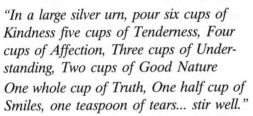

"In a large silver urn, pour six cups of Kindness five cups of Tenderness, Four cups of Affection, Three cups of Under-standing, Two cups of Good Nature One whole cup of Truth, One half cup of Smiles, one teaspoon of tears... stir well."
—Count De Mauduit

"Observe when mother earth is dry, she drinks the droppings of the sky."
—Tom Moore

Soft wines and beers now appear frequently on our supermarket shelves. Yet, despite easy-access, the question remains, what of the home-brewer? With little professional equipment, how can we recreate these substances adding our own magickal vision?

To be honest it's not always easy. The fermentation process is such that it leaves a distinctive flavor with your beverage along with its alcohol. So, what I'm presenting herein is the closest substitute I could devise through research at home, without the advantage of fancy equipment. While the results are pleasant, don't expect them to taste exactly like modern mead, beer, and wine or you will be disappointed.

Mead

I made an interesting discovery when I first tried to find recipes for nonalcoholic mead. Right through the 1920s, mead was not considered a spirituous beverage! This is probably due to the fact that mead was made very thick, with more than the necessary amount of honey, fermented only a short time, then drawn off and mixed with juice or carbonated water (circa 1919). The ratio given in a turn of the century cookbook for the second option was two ounces mead to 12 ounces additive. The original preparation was anywhere from 1/5 to 1/2 honey by proportion to the water base. This would yield a beverage with a root-beer-like head and only the very slightest percentage of alcohol.

In the interest of pleasing the purist, I have provided recipes for straight, fruited, or spiced meads without using yeast. This eliminates the need to wait for the beverage to age, however a little aging (about three weeks) to clarify and rack does improve the flavor. This combined with careful taste-testing during preparation is the key to success. Because there is no yeast to eat up your honey, if you make it too sweet that's the way it will stay unless diluted or infused with juice.

Additionally, because there is no alcohol to act as a preservative, I do not suggest making any more mead than you will consume in a three to four week period. Honey, fruits, and flowers have the capacity to carry wild-yeast that can slowly activate and begin fermenting. Alternatively the mead may turn (yuck). Keep your finished meads in a cool storage space and in air tight containers for best results.

BASIC RECIPE

This recipe will act as a foundation for the others given in this section. The process is the same, with the exception of the addition of fruits and spices, or other minor variations as noted in each.

1 gal. water

1/2 to 1 lb. of honey

1 lemon, juiced

1 orange, juiced

Directions: Bring your water to a low, rolling boil in a nonaluminum pan. Stainless steel or stoneware is recommended. Slowly add the honey, allowing it to fully mingle with the water. Taste periodically until a personally pleasant level of sweetness and honey flavor is achieved. Add juices of the fruit at this point and bring the entire mixture to a full boil. Scum from the honey will start to rise. It is very important that you skim this off until it all but disappears from the top of the pot. Doing this will help your mead to be clearer and less heavy in body. Finally, cool the mixture completely and place in sterilized bottles with secure tops for storage.

Please note: that your mead can be served hot with a cinnamon stick, or cold over crushed ice with a slice of lemon or orange to refresh the flavor.

Magickal Associations: The God-self within, Divine inspiration, sacred visions.

History/Lore: There are few nations in the world that at one time or another have not considered honey a heavenly substance because of its vast applications including cooking, brewing, and medicine. By partaking of it, we can internalize a bit of that Divine energy and allow it to be revitalized within us.

Alternatives: As mentioned earlier in this book, mead took on a wide variety of forms, some of which added fruit and/or spices. This leaves the options for this beverage wide open to your imagination. Some samples follow in this section.

GINGER-ROSE

3 oz. ginger root, bruised

1 qt. pot full of rose petals

1 gal. basic recipe

Directions: Ginger root and rose petals should be added to the basic recipe after honey has been dissolved. Turn off the heat underneath the pan so the rose scent is not damaged by too high a temperature. Allow both ginger and roses to infuse until flower petals turn translucent.

Magickal Associations: Success in relationships, especially those which are intimate or spiritual.

History/Lore: The combination of ginger and roses was not unknown to Middle Eastern recipes, especially those of Egypt and Asia. These items found their ways to altars as part of offerings and incense to help commune with the gods. Both are considered "love" foods.

Alternative: For peace and success in the work place, use white roses as the color of truce and add a few drops of pecan extract, a nut associated with employment. For a non flower option, replace rose petals with 1 lb. of fresh strawberries without losing loving connotations.

GRAPPLE MEAD

1 gal. apple cider

1 1/2 lbs. grapes

basic recipe with the following alterations

Directions: The recipe here is fairly simple, except that your cider replaces the one gallon of water in the basic recipe. Additionally, I suggest using seedless grapes which have been mashed to extract the greatest amount of juice.

Magickal Associations: Offerings for peace among people. In a group setting this should be shared from a communal cup.

History/Lore: Here we have combined a cyder-like apple beverage popular in Europe and this recipe, which is reminiscent of an ancient wine from Egypt known as Pymeat for a truly international drink to encourage a one-world perspective.

Alternatives: Choose your grapes according to your goals. White can be for harmony and purity, or purple for spiritual insight.

TANGERINE-BERRY

1 lb. strawberries

1 lb. tangerine fruit, seeded

1 gal. basic recipe

Directions: Bring the berries and tangerine fruit to boil with the rest of the basic recipe. After cooling, strain once before bottling.

Magickal Associations: Safeguarding the sanctity of close relationships. Reaffirming love.

History/Lore: Because of their zesty flavor and bright, sunny color tangerines have been associated with protection in Asian lands, and often adorn Buddhist shrines.

Alternative: To protect the accord or serenity of any situation, consider substituting passion fruit juice for the strawberries in this recipe. You will need one, 12-ounce can of frozen concentrate.

HERBAL HARMONY

1/4 cup French lavender dried
3 leaves fresh mint
3 to 4 allspice beads
1/4 tsp. thyme
1/4 tsp. angelica root
1/2 lemon rind
1/4 tsp. sage
1 gal. basic recipe

Directions: Follow the basic recipe, adding herbs after the boiling process to create a tea. Lemon rind may require the use of additional sweetener.

Magickal Associations: Accord, agreement, unity.

History/Lore: Lavender and mint are employed here to promote happiness and harmony. The next two components are for healing. Angelica will aid in dispersing negativity, lemon to building friendships, and sage is for wisdom.

Alternative: Where a tremendous amount of discernment is required, add a cup of freshly diced peaches to the mixture. If this is going to be consumed in a group setting, I suggest adding one allspice bead or mint leaf to represent each person to the pot. This way, their desire to become unified is literally cooked right into the brew! In this case, lavender can be regarded as an optional ingredient.

WEATHER LIBATIONS

1/2 cup broom blossoms
1 cup heather blossoms
1 cup rice
1 gal. basic recipe

Directions: Rice should be added even before the honey in the basic recipe to allow it to fully cook. The broom and heather are added after boiling. Note that while some people enjoy heather mead, it has an unusual flavor, making this beverage better for sacrifices than drinking in most cases.

Also, when you drain off the rice, don't just throw it away. Dry it and place it in sachets as a protective amulet for each member of your group.

Magickal Associations: Weather magick.

History/Lore: Rice, dried heather flowers. and broom tossed to the winds, are all believed to affect the weather, specifically wind and rain. Thus, this beverage is a good choice to participate in rituals or spells as a offering for needed weather changes.

Alternative: For sunshine, try chrysanthemums, marigolds and the juice of one orange in this recipe. As an alternative to flowers, try fruits which are naturally aligned to solar or lunar (fire and water) spheres, maintaining the same proportions.

Beer

In actuality, these are "small" beers in that a minute amount of alcohol content is created in the production. If you feel you need to totally eliminate this, once the beverage is ready to drink, boil it, effectively evaporating any alcohol, then chill and serve. The only problem with boiling is that it deters the "head" of the beer. To compensate, prepare your batches slightly stronger than desired, boil them, and then serve with a little seltzer water to achieve "fizz."

These beverages should not be stored for more than four to six weeks if you want to keep the alcohol content at a minimum. To alleviate this problem, after the first brief fermentation period, keep the bottles in a refrigerator. This will inhibit the yeast, while extending the shelf life to about six months.

SPRUCE BEER

5 gal. water

1/8 lb. hops

1/2 cup bruised ginger root

1 lb. outer spruce fir twigs (rinsed)

3 qts. molasses

1/2 pkg. active yeast

Directions: Place the first four ingredients in a large pot for boiling. Allow this to cook on a low rolling boil for about 45 minutes, then strain. Slowly stir the molasses into the filtered liquid while still fairly hot so it is well incorporated. Cool to lukewarm, then add yeast suspended in warm water. This needs to sit for 48 hours before a second straining and securing with caps or corks in glass bottles. Age for five days then enjoy.

Magickal Associations: Getting things in shape, finishing touches, embellishment.

History/Lore: For this recipe, I have fallen back on the colloquialism, "spruce things up." This originated because the branches of a spruce tree were so dense with foliage that they became useful in cleaning, especially sweeping. The only difference here is that we are using the metaphor for improvements or clean up in metaphysical terms.

Alternatives: To further accentuate the spiritual aspects of this potion, add 3 sticks of cinnamon to the recipe, one each to represent your body, mind, and soul.

SPICED LEMON

1 gal. boiling water
1 inch bruised ginger
1 stick cinnamon
4 to 5 whole cloves
4 to 5 allspice beads
1/2 tsp. cream of tartar
1 lb. sugar
2 lemon peels grated
1/2 cup hop flowers
juice of two lemons
1/4 pkg. active yeast

Directions: Place the first nine ingredients together in your brewing pan and boil vigorously for 15 minutes. Strain and cool adding the juice from the two lemons previously peeled and yeast, suspended in warm water. This needs to sit for 24 hours uncovered (or put some cheese cloth on top the pan to keep dust out). Strain and bottle. Ready to drink in five to seven days.

Magickal Associations: Wisdom, caution, clarity, prudence.

History/Lore: In the language of flowers, the lemon is a sign of discretion, tolerance, and forbearance. Its tangy flavor helps to bring lucidity and precision to mental functions.

Alternative: To further accent the cognitive energy of this beverage, add 2 tsp. of rosemary with the other herbs. The additional benefit to this beverage is that it makes a super marinade for chicken.

DANDELION-MINT BEER

1 gal. water
4 cups fresh dandelion flowers
6 to 10 whole fresh mint leaves
1/2 lemon, diced
1/2 cup hop flowers
1 mint tea bag
1 lb. sugar
1/4 pkg. active yeast

Directions: Boil together the first six ingredients for 25 minutes and strain. Add sugar immediately thereafter, stirring in suspended yeast when liquid cools. Follow as per other recipes this section for bottling.

Magickal Associations: Growing awareness, improved clarity of psychic gifts, vision, foresight.

History/Lore: Oliver Wendell Homes said that dandelions leapt from the kindling sun's fire, and they did so with a bounty as any spring lawn will show. In the language of flowers they are symbolic of ancient oracles. For health, they are high in vitamins B and C.

Alternatives: A whole orange or 1 cup pomegranate juice can be added to this recipe to increase its effectiveness for divinatory work. To eliminate the dandelions, add two peeled, sliced citron in their place for similar magickal applications.

MAPLE BEER

4 gal. water
1 qt. maple syrup
2 cups hop
1 pkg. of yeast

Directions: A nice, simple recipe, your water, syrup, and hops are brought to a low rolling boil for about 20 minutes. Strain and allow to cool before adding suspended yeast. This needs to sit for another 24 hours, be strained again, and then bottled. Ready in one week.

Magickal Associations: Tapping inner-wells, centering, peaceful transitions.

History/Lore: The maple leaf, having three distinct sections, is representative of the three-fold nature of both God and humankind. Each aspect of these is bound together in a smooth stream (the syrup) that gives attention to the whole person to encourage balance.

Alternatives: Any berries added to this beverage will help encourage self-love to bring well-being.

Birch Beer

1/4 lb. black birch bark

2 pts. boiling water

1/2 oz. hops

1/8 lb. ginger root, bruised

3 qts. boiling water

3 pts. sugar syrup

1 oz. active yeast

Directions: Boil the bark separately in two pints of water until liquid reduces by half, then strain and boil the remaining liquid rapidly until it is very thick. Meanwhile, simmer the hops and ginger in three quarts of water. As it boils, add sugar syrup. Then add this mixture to the bark extract. Add another five gallons of water to the entire mix, testing for coolness. You need to add yeast, previously suspended for 15 minutes in warm water, when the liquid is lukewarm. Let this sit covered with a clean, dry cloth for three days. Strain into bottles and cork, storing in cool area for another three to five days before drinking.

Magickal Associations: Rituals for Thor, protection from unseemly weather, earth and tree magick.

History/Lore: The birch is regarded as the queen of the woods, under whose bows protection from evil or ill luck could be found. Frequently, birch branches have become the base for a Witch's broom.

Alternative: Another item under Thor's domain is the hazelnut. Adding a few drops of extract to this beverage will increase its potency.

Wine

Wines, like beer, can not be properly prepared without some amount of fermentation. Because wine, by definition, is fermented fruit juice, somehow the effect in taste just wouldn't be the same. Because of this, I have employed a similar method in preparing soft wines as those previously used for homemade soda pop. As with the beers, you can eliminate any alcohol content by boiling, then rejuvenating the bubbles with carbonated water. Additionally,

one part soda to one part soft wine makes an effective non alcoholic wine cooler where the bubbles help carry your magick to the surface!

BASIC RECIPE

(for 6, 12 oz. bottles)

1 Tbs. extract or flavoring
3/4 cups sugar
72 oz. juice
1/16 tsp. yeast

Basic Directions: Heat your juice(s) in a large kettle until it is lukewarm. Dissolve the sugar, feeling free to add more if you want a sweeter wine. Likewise dissolve the yeast and add any flavorings desired at this point. It is a good idea to test the beverage at this point for full-bodied flavor, adding more extract, if needed.

Next, move the wine into clean glass bottles which can be either capped (like pop), corked, or a screw top which is secure. Keep the bottles in a warm (not hot) area for about four days. Open one carefully to see if it is bubbly enough for your tastes. If not, allow to sit about two days more. Store these in the refrigerator to inhibit further fermentation (and possible explosion of the bottles due to pressure). Here is one sample recipe for you to try:

GRAPE APE

36 oz. white grape juice
36 oz. purple grape juice
2 Tbs. banana extract.

Directions: Follow basic recipe using the preceding ingredients.

Magickal Associations: Commitment, adoration, freely given love.

History/Lore: Grapes are a celebratory fruit. This combined with the fact that bananas often adorned Hindu temples during marriages makes this a good choice for the communal cup at hand fastings or vow renewals.

Alternative: For a more passionate approach, eliminate purple grape juice, adding instead an equal amount of strawberry-kiwi juice, which can be obtained at most health cooperatives.

Chapter 14

Tea Talismans
and Coffee Charms

"And Venus, Goddess of the eternal smile,
Knowing that stormy brews but ill become
Fair patterns of her beauty, hath ordained
celestial tea; a fountain that can cure
the ills of passion and can free from
frowns, and sobs and signs the dissipated
fair. To her, ye fair, in adoration bow!"
—Robert Fergusson

"...Arrayed in the most gorgeous Oriental
costumes, they served the choicest Mocha
coffee in tiny cups of egg-shell porcelain,
hot, strong and fragrant, poured out on
saucers of gold and silver..."
—Issac D'Israeli

On a metaphysical level, coffee increases power, energy, or conscious alertness. Conversely, tea is a tranquil
plant, full of rest, serenity, renewal of health, and introspection. This intrinsic quality to both beverages gives us
some unique variables to consider. I would not suggest, by way

of example, using coffee as part of a ritual for peace. Instead, it might be better added to improve mental acuity, which could help in obtaining viable resolutions. This way your ingredients are magickally compatible to the ends desired.

Nonalcoholic

Coffee

There is a marvelous Arabic story about a goat keeper who was very responsible and sober by nature. One night his goats failed to return home. When he went searching for them, much to his dismay, he discovered the goats dancing with a red berried shrub. The caretaker quickly surmised that the berries must have been the cause of jubilation, and he soon found himself waltzing too.

Amidst all the merriment, a studious monk came by, observing with far more caution than the caretaker. After some experimentation, he placed the berries in hot water and happily found that he could stay awake during prayers. From this sole monk and simple servant, the fame of coffee quickly spread through Arabia, where it is still regarded with sanctity.

Thus, it is not surprising to discover that the Arabian traders or possibly the Persians are responsible for advertising the coffee beans' qualities. Back in the desert, where people learned to boil water around 1000 A.D., hot coffee was used in medicines and for the religious observances of the Whirling Dervishes. This also marked the very first beginnings for Coffee Houses.

In the Arabic home, people extol coffee more than anywhere else on Earth. During the Middle Ages (and probably long before) except in the most impoverished areas, one could find a special furnace for preparing coffee in every house. Around this feature the host and guests sit in a circle, the most honored seated closest to the sacred flames. The coffee is hand ground, roasted, and brewed while everyone chats.

Next, the host adds a bit of cardamom and continues cooking the coffee until it boils three times. Then it is strained into a serving vessel. Following, cups are prepared for each guest by pouring one full of coffee to warm it, then reusing this coffee in each cup. When finished, they pour the remainder to the honoring Sheikhesh Shadhilly, the patron saint of coffee lovers.

Finally, the coffee is served in the same circular fashion, the host and guests each honoring the name of God. The circle is repeated at least once as the cups are small, and this affords more enjoyment. Some Arab families still follow this tradition today.

During the reign of Louis XIV, coffee was raised to a distinction unlike any other time in history. A new grandeur was born around a growing ritual and social standard for coffee consumption. Every middle class table exhibited elegance with fine imported porcelain ware for this beverage. Voltaire, a contemporary of the King, was addicted to the substance, enjoying as many as 50 cups a day. It was during this period that our contemporary habits of having breakfast coffee and after dinner coffee as a tonic took shape.

No matter where we live, however, we have not completely escaped some of the ceremonial feelings transported with coffee along with the Pilgrims to Mecca. We still find ourselves considering the personality of those who drink coffee sweetened instead of pure. At most formal tables the sugar and creamer dish hold a place of honor. And, in many homes there is a personally favored coffee cup that is not used by other household members unless they want to receive indignant stares.

COFFEE FROST

4 ice cubes crushed

1 to 2 Tbs. sugar

4 cups strong coffee (your choice)

1 tsp. amaretto flavoring

amaretto whipped cream

Directions: Place the crushed ice with sugar, coffee, and flavoring in a blender on medium speed for two to three minutes. Pour into a tall glass or cup and top off with whipped cream. Most supermarkets now stock the amaretto flavored aerosol cream, or you can make it fresh and simply add 1 tsp. of extract during the beating process.

Magickal Associations: Calming energies, cooling tempers.

History/Lore: The icy nature of this beverage tends to put a distinctive chill on emotions or energy which have gotten out of control.

Alternatives: Orange flavoring is an excellent choice if you wish to sooth undesired feelings of romance or passion, especially those which are ill-timed.

SOUTH OF THE BORDER

2 cups strong cinnamon coffee

5 tsp. chocolate syrup

1/2 stick cinnamon

1/4 tsp. nutmeg

1 Tbs. sugar

1/2 cup heavy cream

Directions: Begin by whipping the cream with nutmeg and sugar and setting this aside. Meanwhile pour 1 tsp. of the syrup into each small cup, adding the hot coffee and stirring with a cinnamon stick that can be left for garnish. Top with a teaspoon of cream.

Magickal Associations: Perseverance, dedication.

History/Lore: Cinnamon in oil form was an important part of many ancient religious rites including the anointing oils of the Hebrews and the Egyptian mummification process. This combined with the steadfast nature of nutmeg makes for an excellent beverage to help keep you consistent in your spiritual studies and goals.

Alternatives: Instead of chocolate syrup, try this with butterscotch. This will improve your creativity in magick.

> Retain your old coffee grounds for gardening. They help deter ants and enrich the soil.

VIENNA HOLIDAY

2 cups Viennese coffee

4 to 5 cloves

4 allspice berries

2 tsp. sugar

1 cinnamon stick (broken in half)

1 bay leaf (broken in half)

Directions: Brew your coffee according to directions given on the bag or can. Add the allspice to the hot liquid and let stand 15 minutes to steep. Strain and top with cream and a sprinkle of nutmeg. Place the cinnamon and by leaf into each cup as a garnish.

Magickal Associations: Victory over lust or love.

History/Lore: The bay leaf is the ancient Greek symbol of success. The cinnamon stick is linked with passion through Venus, an associated Deity. Here, both items are carefully broken in two to help peacefully separate individuals who have an unhealthy relationship.

Alternatives: For fuller bodied flavor, leave the bay leaf and cinnamon stick in each cup.

Cafe L'Orange

6 cups strong orange coffee

6 slices fresh orange without rind

6 cups hot chocolate

1 cup heavy cream

1 tsp. vanilla extract

orange peel

cinnamon

Directions: In each cup place one orange slice, pouring over equal quantities of hot cocoa and freshly brewed coffee. Top with cream, grated orange peel, and cinnamon.

Magickal Associations: Prosperity, abundance, accomplishment.

History/Lore: In the Middle Ages, oranges were a very rare and costly commodity to most European homes and, as such, were used frugally or to show off one's wealth. Magickally speaking, this precious association slowly attached itself with the fruit even after it was readily available.

Alternative: This beverage is often enjoyed in Belgium, but sometimes cinnamon takes place of hot cocoa with a dash of orange extract.

Summer Relief

3 cups mocha coffee

6 Tbs. strawberry syrup

1 pt. strawberry ice cream

Directions: Prepare mocha java as per directions on the label of your grounds. Chill this in the refrigerator until refreshingly cold. Pour 3 cups of the coffee in a blender with syrup and ice cream for a marvelous shake that cools the body and sweetens disposition.

Magickal Associations: Relief of anxiety, especially in relationships. Energy for accord and love.

History/Lore: There is nothing which elicits fond, happy memories like going strawberry picking in a wild field. This vision is one of repose and a break from turmoil. Additionally, the strawberry is a love food, making this beverage especially helpful with overactive imaginations or tempers.

Alternative: Try matching up other syrups and ice creams for unique results. Chocolate would be for passion, or pineapple for hospitality and protection.

CHRISTMAS IN DENMARK

6 eggs

grated lemon peel

1/2 cup sugar

3 cups strong fruity coffee

1/2 cup apple juice

1 Tbs. brandy flavoring

Directions: Beat eggs until frothy, then slowly add grated peel from one lemon and sugar until thick. Set aside while you mix together the remaining ingredients. Fold this into the egg mixture very slowly. Serve in chilled glasses.

Magickal Associations: Joyful gatherings, sojourns to see friends and family.

History/Lore: A version of this recipe is often served at Yule festivities in Denmark.

Alternatives: For abundantly happy energy, choose a raspberry coffee base, and use strawberry syrup in place of sugar to taste.

EASTERN PASSION

2 Tbs. sugar

1/5 cups water

2 Tbs. dark coffee beans

Directions: Begin by grinding the coffee beans to a flour-like powder. In a separate saucepan, stir sugar and water together over low flame until dissolved. Blend in coffee powder and boil. Remove this from the stove heat and let settle. Repeat the boiling process two more times and serve in small cups. Add a twist of lemon rind, nutmeg, cloves, cardamom, or nutmeg for extra flavor

Magickal Associations: Energy for building friendships and good lines of communication.

History/Lore: This drink is enjoyed popularly in Turkey and Russia with similar reverence to the Arabic coffee house, where friends and associates can gather for light conversation and simple companionship.

Alternatives: Any number of flavor additives besides those already mentioned can be mingled for various magickal goals. For improved awareness in relationships, try rosemary or to heal rifts, sample mint.

COFFEE SHAKE

2 scoops cappuccino ice cream

1 cup chocolate ice cream

1/2 cup dark roast coffee, cold

1/4 cup cream

grated dark chocolate

Directions: A marvelously easy beverage to make, all of your ingredients, except 1 tsp. of the cream, are placed in a blender and mixed until smooth. Serve by pouring into a glass with the teaspoon of cream on top and chocolate shavings for garnish.

Magickal Associations: Rewarding good actions, delight.

History/Lore: To be honest, this recipe is not so much magickal as it is personally pleasing and down-right decadent. The rich flavor brings a smile to the face of any coffee or chocolate lover I know.

Alternatives: Change the flavors of your ice cream for a wide variety of taste combinations, any of which can reflect your magickal goals. Cookies and cream might be appropriate for youthful vision while vanilla is for improved mental energy.

> When brewing, try making your coffee blends 20-percent chicory. This yields a heavier, darker beverage.

Vanilla Soda

2 cups vanilla coffee, chilled

1 cup soda water

3 scoops vanilla ice cream

1 tsp. vanilla extract

whipped cream

Directions: Another cold coffee drink, this is mixed most easily in a blender, leaving the whipped cream for a garnish on top. Serve in soda glasses.

Magickal Associations: Love, rituals honoring Venus or Aphrodite.

History/Lore: Vanilla is actually a member of the orchid family, grown in Mexico and Central America.

Once discovered, it managed to topple rosewater as the favored flavoring of Medieval Europe, and has been used widely as a magickal attractant for romance.

Alternative: Try adding some almond extract in place of vanilla. Magickally this still accentuates your goals while adding a lovely, light nutty flavor.

Hazelnut Nog

4 eggs

3/4 cup sugar

2 cups milk

1 cup hazelnut coffee

1 Tbs. hazelnut extract

1 cup cream

Directions: Beat eggs and sugar together until thick and frothy. Add milk and coffee which have been warmed together with extract slowly to the sugar mixture. Separately beat heavy cream and gradually mix 1 Tbs. of this into each cup as its poured. Serve warm.

Magickal Associations: Fertility, wisdom, and luck.

History/Lore: A favorite wood for dowsers, hazel trees offer their fruit for a number of other magickal applications including increasing funds and as gifts to a young bride for joy in her new life.

Alternatives: Replace the milk in this recipe with 100-percent cream for smooth transitions especially with regards to attitudes and personal ambition.

Tea

There is a wonderful Chinese tale about how tea came to this country. Daruma, who was the founder of the Zen sect, retired to meditate in a secluded area. There, for nine years, he prayed until he unintentionally fell asleep.

As he dozed, he began to dream of a beautiful woman. When he awoke from the vision, his longing for her left him deeply ashamed. For such sin, he cut his eyelids off and threw them to the ground. Much to his amazement, the eyelids formed themselves into a tea bush, the leaves of which keep a person awake, even during prayer. Many years later when Daruma left this world for another existence, his followers honored him by enjoying the leaves of this plant steeped in water (plain tea) drunk from bowls before his image.

By definition, the word "tea" specifically pertains to the leafy shrub of China and India. In that context, rose hip tea and beef tea are not really teas at all. Instead they are beverages with tea-like quality. Here is just a brief sampling of the herbs employed for tea impostors and their magickal or religious significance:

- **Anise**—A popular spice during the time of Virgil, anise wards against the "evil eye" and tastes very similar to licorice.
- **Basil**—Buried with those of Hindu faiths to insure passage in to paradise. Rich, spicy flavor.
- **Chamomile**—Lauded as the physician's plant, it was sacred to the Egyptians and has a slightly bitter flavor.

- ☙ **Cinnamon**—In the mythology of China, this tree grows in paradise offering immortality to all who eat it. Cinnamon tea is sweet and fragrant.

- ☙ **Marjoram**—The touch of Venus gave this herb its aroma, and thus it often crowned the heads of newlyweds in ancient Greece and Rome. Sweet taste similar to thyme.

- ☙ **Mint**—Used by the Hebrews as a strewing herb for sacred temple floors, mint has a refreshing vibrant flavor.

- ☙ **Rosemary**—Thought to improve memory by Greek students, it was sometimes worn as a crown. Rosemary has a cool flavor.

- ☙ **Vervain**—Known to the ancient druids to improve spell potency, in Persia an aid to wish magick and an ingredient in many Medieval love potions. Vervain has a fairly neutral taste which can be improved by combining it with other herbs.

It would be inappropriate not to take one moment extolling the ancient, dainty art of tea leaf reading. To use tea for divination, choose a hearty leaf tea and leave it loose in your cup. Drain off as much liquid as possible, then tip your cup upside down with a light tap of the finger on the bottom.

Reverse the cup to see what patterns emerge in the remaining sediment. You can interpret these images symbolically, knowing they often pertain to the questions strongly on your mind at the moment. Designs near the rim of the cup are things closest to occurring, while those in the bottom are in the future. For extra effectiveness, choose the type of tea according to your question. For example, use marjoram in matters of love.

Besides divination, there are certain social graces that linger around tea. There are formal teas, social teas, and sick-room teas. There is also the Japanese tea ceremony, Cha No Yu, spoken of earlier. Here, green tea is whipped in special bowls to form a frothy beverage. This gets passed in silence to all in attendance. In the quiet moments, this ritual becomes a group meditation about matters of eternity, the spirit, and universal truths. This makes our ordinary, "generic" tea bag, steeped via microwave, look rather bland by comparison.

These diverse cultural approaches give us pause to consider unique serving arrangements for our own magickal teas. If you want to have a Victorian tea, or a thematic oriental-style tea for a special occasion, these examples serve as a starting point. However, you do not have to get that fancy. Plain or elaborate, tea is a rich addition to the magickal pantry.

TEA PUNCH

5 cups hot apple juice

10 apple tea bags

3/4 cup sugar

juice of one lemon

1/2 cup orange juice

6 cloves

2 cinnamon sticks

Directions: Warm the apple juice in a large saucepan over a medium flame. Add the apple tea bags to steep for at least 15 minutes before removing. Next add sugar, juice, and spices, allowing to simmer for another 10 minutes. This can then be poured into a punch bowl and served hot, with cinnamon sticks for cup garnishes.

Magickal Associations: Healthy inter-relationships and wisdom in communications.

History/Lore: Tea is a social beverage, especially in the form of a punch. The apple juice and tea in this recipe encourages well-being among the drinkers so that dialogues are pleasant and tempered with sagacity.

Alternative: Chill the entire mixture for two hours before serving, adding 1 qt. of ginger ale to the punch bowl. Magickally this will lift uneasy feelings in a group.

LEMONADE TEA

2 qts. water

10 lemon verbena tea bags (or zinger)

1 cup sugar

3/4 cup lemon juice

sliced lemons (garnish)

Directions: Heat the water to boiling, then steep the tea bags for 20 minutes. Remove. Keep the mixture over a low flame while you add sugar and lemon juice. Especially refreshing when chilled or served over chipped ice.

Magickal Associations: Cleansing and purification.

History/Lore: The purgative abilities of lemon are well known. Without any sweetener, this tea can be used to aspurge a magickal circle, consecrate magickal tools, or as the base for a ritual bath before special occasions.

Alternative: Substitute honey for the sugar in this recipe and drink hot for effective cold relief.

DRIED FRUIT TEA

6 dried apricots

1/2 cup dried apple

1/4 cup dried pear

4 cups hot water

2 fruit tea bags (your choice)

Directions: While this tea must be prepared hot for proper flavoring to occur, it is delightful served warm or cold. Boil the water to rolling, add the fruit and tea bags. Simmer for 15 minutes then remove from the heat and strain. Sweeten as desired.

Magickal Associations: Preservation, sustenance.

History/Lore: Drying of food, perhaps best evidenced by dried meats, has been a traditional means of conserving it for difficult times to many lands and time periods. In the magickal setting, this association can be applied to any situation in which you need to conserve energy, preserve your sanctity or a relationship, and so on.

Alternative: Adding a few favorite nuts during the boiling process would bring greater fertility to your magickal effort.

SUN TEA

6 cups water

6 tea bags

sugar to taste

slice of lemon and orange

Directions: For this recipe, you will need a large glass container that can be easily and securely sealed. Place all the ingredients inside the container together, leaving it directly in the sunlight until the color is rich and full. Chill and serve over ice.

Magickal Associations: Solar magick and associated attributes.

History/Lore: There is a wealth of superstition and lore pertaining to the sun, most of which regards it as a protective and powerful ally. When the sun shone on special occasions, it was a beneficent sign accepted almost universally as a blessing from the gods. Magickally speaking, solar energies are best employed for matters of learning, the conscious mind, leadership, and communion with the God aspect of the Divine.

Alternatives: To further accentuate your energies here, try using herbal teas which are solar in nature. Good choices include angelica, chamomile, cinnamon, ginseng, and orange.

PINEAPPLE-MINT MERRIMENT

1/2 qt. hot water

7 mint tea bags

2 to 3 fresh mint leaves

1/4 cup lemon juice

1/2 cup sugar or honey

1/2 cup pineapple juice

pineapple bites

Directions: Another beverage which is tasty either hot or cold, begin by warming the mint tea bags and leaves in hot water for 15 minutes, then strain. Keep the remaining liquid warm so that the sugar or honey is dissolved properly and the pineapple juice can be well incorporated. Pour into cups, adding pineapple bites and a mint leaf for garnish.

Magickal Associations: Joyful hospitality.

History/Lore: There is an old Greek tale which tells us that Zeus and Hermes, when disguised as travelers, were entertained at the cottage of Philemon and Baucis. They welcomed the strangers to their home by rubbing the table with mint leaves.

Alternative: If you use specifically peppermint in this mixture, it can also be magickally associated with increasing power or virility as it was to both the ancient Arabs and Romans.

RICE TEA

1 Tbs. tea leaves (your choice), crushed

2 cups water

1 Tbs. butter

1 1/2 Tbs. flower

1/2 cup milk

1/2 cup cooked, long grain rice

salt to taste

Directions: Boil tea leaves in a sauce pan over low heat for 15 minutes. Meanwhile, in a separate pan melt the butter, slowly adding the flour to make a thick paste. Blend in the milk which will yield a gummy but cream-like consistency. Add rice and pour into tea seasoning as desired.

Magickal Associations: Providence and fertility.

History/Lore: Western weddings are not the only place where rice is thrown. It is also evident in Oriental cultures as well where rice was the heart of the land. In Japan especially it is considered terrible to burn or waste rice, as it was once so valuable it was used for currency. In both the Eastern and Western settings, rice is an emblem of prosperity and productivity.

Alternative: When served with dry toast, this makes an excellent tea for upset stomachs.

GINGER NUT

2 cups blanched walnuts, crushed

4 thin slices fresh ginger, bruised

1 tsp. black tea

2 cups boiling water

sugar or honey to taste

Directions: Bring the water to a full rolling boil then remove from the heat adding all ingredients except sugar. Let this mixture sit for 25 minutes. Drain and rewarm, adding sweetening as desired.

Magickal Associations: Resourcefulness, innovation

History/Lore: Nuts are foods for fertility, including improving one's imagination. Meanwhile, ginger adds stimulation and overall energy to your endeavor.

Alternative: In Korea, dates and pine nuts are sometimes used to flavor a similar tea. Magickally, Romans associated both dates and pine nuts with physical strength and endurance.

TEA TONIC

1/4 cup Paraguay tea (Mate)

1 tsp. chamomile

1/8 cup rose-hips

1 qt. boiling water

1 slice lemon

honey or sugar to taste

Directions: Prepare as you would any tea, using a tea ball or cloth bag for the loose chamomile and rose hips. Lemon and sugar are added in the cup per personal tastes.

Magickal Associations: Return to normalcy, adjusting erratic energies, centering and balance.

History/Lore: This beverage, besides having magickal restorative features, is rich in caffeine, vitamins, and physically rejuvenate qualities.

Alternatives: The base materials can be reused with other personally enjoyed additives to make less potent, but magickally creative batches. For example, to help return to well being, add nutmeg to the base. A high vitamin option in place of rose hips is to use the juice of one orange instead.

VIOLET-ANISE ICE

2 cups boiling water
1 tsp. dried violets
1 Tbs. aniseed
1 cup cream
1 tsp. strong, loose black tea
sugar to taste
crushed ice

Directions: Bundle the aniseed, black tea, and dried violets together in a tea ball or gauze bag to steep in the hot water for about 20 minutes until the water smells heady. Stir in sugar to dissolve then chill. When cold, add one cup of cream and serve over crushed ice.

Magickal Aspects: Safety, protection from negative magick or malignant spirits, peaceful sleep.

History/Lore: In the time of Virgil, anise was considered a potent protection against the "evil eye," as well as an effective deterrent to nightmares. Violets were similarly used by the Ancient Greeks to bring peaceful sleep and safety from spirits.

Alternatives: Add 1 tsp. of chamomile or valerian root if you are making this specifically for sleep. Both herbs have a relaxing effect on nerves. Please note: this beverage can be served hot simply by adding the cream while the tea is still warm and eliminating the ice. If dried violets are not available, try a stick of cinnamon or 1 tsp. of fennel for similar magickal results.

Alcoholic

Coffee

LUCK OF THE IRISH

1 tsp. sugar or honey

2 Tbs. whipped cream

1/2 cup Irish Whiskey

2 drops green coloring

1/2 cup black coffee

2 Tbs. heavy cream

Directions: Mix honey, whiskey, and black coffee together in a large cup. Float the heavy cream on top, then add a mound of whipped cream which has been tinted green—the color of shamrocks!

Magickal Associations: Serendipity, good fortune, godsends.

History/Lore: The Irish claim to be the most fortuitous people on the Earth, with the shamrock and blarney stone to aid them. This coffee is a favorite beverage there and has become quite popular abroad.

Alternatives: For a more Scottish tone, leave the whipped cream white and use drambuis in place of the whiskey. Magickally speaking this is for hospitality.

PROSPERITY PUNCH

2 cups dark rum

2 medium cinnamon sticks

1 cup Kahlua

4 whole cloves

2 tsp. sugar

3/4 tsp. nutmeg

1 sliced orange

1 whole almond per person

1 1/2 qts. orange coffee

Directions: Place rum, Kahlua, and sugar together in a large heat-proof serving bowl. Ignite the liquid, using the coffee to extinguish it slowly. This allows the entire mixture to reach your guests warm. Add spices and allow to sit to comfortable sipping temperature with oranges floating on top. Serve in cups with one almond each.

Magickal Associations: Wealth, abundance, resources.

History/Lore: All the spices, nuts, and fruits in this recipe have been chosen for their money-attracting attributes. Oranges were a symbol of prosperity in the Middle Ages due to their high import cost.

Alternatives: Have a little fun with your choice of gourmet coffee in this recipe. For example, if you hope to have an abundance of love, try raspberry.

COFFEE ACCORD

4 Tbs. butter, unsalted

1/4 tsp. lemon juice

1 cup brown sugar

2 cups dark rum

1/2 tsp. nutmeg

6 cups hot coffee

1/4 tsp. mint extract

1 tsp. catnip

Directions: Allow the butter to soften, then mix it thoroughly with sugar, nutmeg, mint, and lemon. Set this aside. Brew your coffee leaving a tea ball with the catnip in your brewpot, then add the rum. Now place 1 Tbs. of butter mix in each coffee mug, pouring coffee over top and stirring until melted. May be garnished with a cinnamon stick.

Magickal Associations: Clearing misunderstandings, truce between people, agreement.

History/Lore: This version of buttered rum is accentuated by mint for reconciliation, catnip to encourage the return of happiness, and lemon for friendship. Coffee functions as the activating energy to promote healing.

COFFEE SHAKE FOR TWO

1 1/2 cups milk

1 1/2 cups dark roast coffee

1 cup strawberry liqueur

1 cup strawberry ice cream

whipped cream

slivered almonds and chocolate

Directions: Place milk, coffee, liqueur, and ice cream in the blender on medium speed and whip until frothy. Garnish with heaping mounds of whipped cream topped with shaved almonds and chocolate. Drink by candle light!

Magickal Associations: The spirit of true romance.

History/Lore: In the tradition of Mohammed, almonds are considered the symbol of Divine hope which can be applied to your relationship, aided along by strawberries and chocolate, two wonderful love foods.

Alternatives: For similar magickal results, substitute almond ice cream and liqueur for the strawberry.

In the 1700s coffee houses were very popular for their open democratic forum for conversation and news. By this time, there were 2,000 established in London alone, which anyone could enter for a penny.

WISHES ARE BREWING

1/2 cup heavy cream
4 cups water
1 tsp. vanilla extract
2 Tbs. dark roast coffee
1 egg white
1 tsp. ground dandelion root
1 Tbs. sugar
1/2 tsp. ginseng

Directions: Mix your coffee with finely ground dandelion root and ginseng, then place in a pot to brew with water. While this drips, beat your heavy cream and egg white on high until peaks begin to form. Add extract and sugar at this time, placing a hefty portion into each serving cup. Pour the coffee into the cup by slowly letting it slip down the sides. This allows some cream to mix in and the rest to remain on top like mountain peeks.

Magickal Associations: Goals and aspirations, hope and fancy.

History/Lore: Ginseng roots, besides being regarded as a tonic, were sometimes carved or tossed into running water to help bring wishes into reality. Dandelion is similarly regarded, its ground roots often acting as a coffee substitute.

Alternatives: To encourage wisdom in your wishful jaunts, add 1/4 of a peach (peeled and diced finely) into your whipping cream once it begins to peak. Continue as directed.

Earth's Winter Wonder

2 cups coffee, chilled
1 jigger dark rum
3 jiggers coffee liqueur
whipped cream
3 jiggers Irish cream liqueur
grated coconut

Directions: Shake your coffee, liqueurs and rum together in a large container until well blended. Pour this mixture over shaved ice and garnish with whipped cream and coconut. Serves two.

Magickal Associations: Earth healing, Earth Magick, rest, an accent to any winter festival.

History/Lore: The Earth in this recipe is the rich, dark color like fertile soil. This is neatly hidden by a tuft of snow on top (cream and coconut) the later of which protects the sleeping land.

Fires of Cleansing

1/2 pt. brandy
1/4 cup Curacao
2 cinnamon sticks
4 cups hot coffee
7 whole cloves
2 Tbs. sugar
1 orange rind, slivered

Directions: Heat brandy with cinnamon, clove, sugar, orange and Curacao until it almost boils. Turn off flame and move to a heat proof serving dish. Carefully light the top of this mixture with a match allowing to burn for about three minutes before pouring in hot coffee to extinguish. Serve immediately.

Magickal Associations: Purging, total transformation, sun and Fire rituals.

History/Lore: Versions of this beverage are very popular in New Orleans, especially in darkened rooms where they can be exhibited with true flamboyance. Magickally speaking, Fire is the Element of drastic change, purification, and refinement.

Serving Idea: Traditionally, this beverage is served in a demitasse cup (literally, "small cup"). If you can find some of a yellow, gold, or red coloration to accent the magick, all the better.

SOUTH OF THE BORDER

1/2 cup warmed tequila
1 cup dark roast coffee
brown sugar to taste
cinnamon stick (for stirring)

Directions: Mix your tequila, coffee, and sugar together in a personally pleasing balance. Stir with a cinnamon stick, envisioning the Element of Fire filling your inner wells, and sparking creativity.

Magickal Associations: Vision, illumination, divination by fire.

History/Lore: A truly Mexican beverage, this drink is dedicated to the Southern quarter of our magick Circle which not only represents the sun, but the devic energy of salamanders—creatures that live and dance in the fires. Thus, this recipe is an excellent libation for fire scrying and the power light has to fill any darkness in your life.

Alternatives: Consider adding other solar flavors to this beverage by way of a slice of orange, bay leaf, or sliver of lime.

CAFE EXHILARATION

3 cups banana flavored coffee

1/2 tsp. cinnamon

1 tsp. vanilla

1 cup heavy cream

1/2 ripe banana

sugar to taste

5 ice cubes

Directions: This is a marvelously easy beverage to prepare. Place all your ingredients in the blender except for the ice and whip until thick and frothy. Then add ice to chop finely so that the consistency is like a frappe. Garnish, if desired, with a cherry!

Magickal Associations: Conception, fertility, sexual pleasure and prowess.

History/Lore: Banana is used in this beverage to encourage sexual potency, while vanilla and cinnamon are to improve desire.

Tea

WINE TEA

2 pts. strong tea

4 whole cloves

4 Tbs. orange juice

1 slice lemon rind

4 Tbs. sugar

1 pt. sangria

1 stick cinnamon

1 sliced orange

Directions: Heat all of your ingredients together except the orange slices. Once warmed to a tea-like consistency, pour into a punch bowl and garnish with oranges. Or you may chill first, and then serve cold.

Magickal Associations: Kinship, leisurely pursuits, friendly conversation.

History/Lore: Both wine and tea have a cordial, comfortable appeal, making this a very relaxing beverage perfect for quiet afternoons with friends. This drink has the additional benefit of clearing the throat during allergy season.

Alternative: Try dark rum in place of the sangria.

SPICY ORANGE FITNESS

1 qt. mulled mead

2 qts. orange picot tea

1 cup orange juice

1 sliced lemon

1 sliced orange

1/2 cup honey (to taste)

6 pieces cinnamon stick

6 whole cloves

Directions: Make your tea and pour it hot into a large container with the cinnamon stick pieces (one inch each is good), cloves, and honey. Likewise warm the mead and orange juice together and add this to the tea blend mixing thoroughly. Serve hot with a slice of orange and lemon in each cup.

Magickal Associations: Health and well being, vitality, a return of physical balance.

History/Lore: The Portuguese believe that the original orange tree transplanted from China to Europe, and which birthed all other orange bearing trees still lives quite heartily today in Lisbon.

Alternatives: Try an apple-spice tea with apple juice in this recipe in place of the orange for similar and very tasty magickal results.

HARD CIDER TEA

1 qt. water

1 qt. apple wine

12 apple spice tea bags

1/2 tsp. lemon juice

1 qt. hard cider

1/2 cup sugar

Directions: Boil the one quart water, turning off the heat and allowing tea bags to steep. Strain, and add to the remaining ingredients which may be served hot or cold. In hot form, cinnamon sticks make great stirrers. When cold, serve over chilled ice with a slice of fresh apple on the side.

Magickal Associations: Perspective, keeping a cool head, calming temper.

History/Lore: There is an old brewer's custom which added honey to cyder (a kind of fruit wine) which basically created a fortified mead of sorts. According to the ancient alchemists, this created a "cold" beverage that can cool and temper the body, especially fevers.

Alternatives: For a beverage with purgative, cleansing qualities, try substituting lemon tea bags, and increase lemon juice to 1/4 cup.

RUM MATE

1 qt. boiling water

2 cups dark rum

1/4 cup mate leaves

4 Tbs. honey (optional)

Directions: To make mate traditionally, the leaves are placed in a pot, and the boiling water is poured over them and allowed to sit for about 15 minutes. Then honey and rum can be added, and poured out. If you'd like, the mate is of a goodly size and may be used for tea leaf reading when you get to the bottom of your cup. Otherwise, strain the tea leaves before adding rum and honey.

Magickal Associations: Return to normal attitudes and manners, improved personal energy.

History/Lore: Mate is usually prepared with Paraguay tea which is considered a stimulant and tonic.

Alternative: Mate is also sometimes flavored with a slice of lemon and kirsch.

CHAMOMILE COMFORT

1 cup boiling water

1 cup hopped beer

1 chamomile tea bag

honey to taste

1/2 tsp. lavender

1/2 tsp. lemon verbena

Directions: Place the lavender and lemon verbena in a gauze cloth. Steep these with the chamomile in the boiling water for 10 minutes. Meanwhile warm the beer to a palatable temperature, and stir in honey. Blend these in equal proportions with the tea and enjoy two cups. This is especially useful just before bed.

Magickal Associations: Peacefulness, tranquility, gentility, consolation.

History/Lore: Chamomile is known for its sedative quality. The scent of lavender helps calm the nerves, lemon verbena helps encourage rest, and hops improves sleep.

LEMON ICED TEA

4 lemon tea bags

1/2 cup orange liqueur

1 qt. boiling water

1/2 cup raspberry liqueur

1 cup sugar

2 cups soda water

Directions: Steep the tea bags in boiling water and dissolve the sugar allowing to sit for 10 minutes before removing. The amount of sugar may be decreased for personal taste. Chill the tea, adding it cold to the liqueurs and soda (both likewise chilled). Pour this over ice, garnished with a lemon wedge. This beverage has a flavor similar to rainbow sherbet.

Magickal Associations: Positive experiences in relationships, especially new romance. Moon Magick.

History/Lore: Lemons appearing in dreams, especially for women, portend good luck in romance and possibly love soon to follow.

Alternatives: Try dry champagne in place of soda water on celebratory occasions.

PINEAPPLE PRIZE

1 qt. boiling water

2 cups pineapple juice

12 fruit n' spice tea bags

12 pineapple spears

1 lemon juiced

whole cloves (optional)

1 lemon sliced

fresh mint (garnish)

1 pt. rum

Directions: Steep the tea bags for 15 minutes in the boiling water, then add lemon juice. Chill. Pour into a two-quart serving bowl with ice, then stir in pineapple juice and rum. Stud pineapple spears with two to four cloves each and float them on top. Garnish the side of the bowl with a fresh sprig of mint, or more pineapple pieces.

Magickal Associations: Pleasant surprises, unexpected windfalls, suddenly improved prosperity.

History/Lore: The pineapple was regarded by travelers to the new world as a unique, tasty treasure. One clergyman of the 1700s even went so far as to claim it should only be picked by the hands of Venus!

Alternatives: To add a bubbly body to this beverage check small local stores for pineapple soda pop. I have seen this most frequently at Hispanic markets and 1/2 quart tastes great in this recipe!

APRICOT ORACLE

1/2 cup apricot brandy

1 apricot or orange tea bag

whipped cream (garnish)

1 tsp. apricot jam

Directions: Prepare your tea as usual, adding the apricot jam while still very hot to dissolve it. Pour in your brandy, then top with a tablespoon of whipped cream. Sugar may be added for sweetening if desired.

Magickal Associations: Divination, foresight, sagacity, psychic awareness.

History/Lore: The Chinese regard the apricot tree as one of great prophetic power because it was there that Confucius wrote his commentaries. Additionally, one of the great religious minds of China, Lao-tse, was allegedly born under an apricot tree, already cognizant at birth.

Chapter 15

A Toast to Your Health

"The lord hath created medicines out of the earth; and he that is wise will not abhor them."

—Ecclesiastics

"If you have your health, you have everything."

—All mothers, everywhere

Many modern researchers help us live healthier lives by instructing us on diet and natural approaches to home healthcare. These are not a substitute for professional help. Instead, they are a means to improve those little aches, pains, and common colds in a positive, nonchemical manner. This is why many recipes in this section are general in nature, designed to help the body's natural immune system to function well.

It is all but impossible for the body to operate at its best when spiritual energies are out of sync. Sickness tosses the whole person into an irregular state, meaning that we have to attend body, mind, and spirit to affect well-being. The flexibility of brewing techniques allows us to add magickal vision to the formula while achieving these ends. Older folk remedials commonly added magickal elements, even if they weren't called that. From this foundation we can prepare tonics that ease "what ails us," and support spiritual healing too.

"Witch's brews" for health tend to either taste bad and smell great or vise-versa. In particular, eucalyptus and valerian are two of the worst offenders on both counts. Because of this, you may need to add honey or a common aromatic such as mint for more palatable, pleasing results.

Please remember that not all magickal herbs are edible, nor are all old folk remedies safe or effectual. If your symptoms persist, don't stubbornly ignore contemporary medicine. Always check with a physician about potential negative interactions with current medications too.

Note: This chapter is set up specifically for health-related matters, and all recipes pertain to this on a magickal level too. Any additional magickal applications are so noted.

Nonalcoholic

FEVER BREW

1 tsp. flaxseed
1 cup hot water
2 to 3 slices of lemon, juiced
dash cinnamon
1/2 tsp. honey
1/2 tsp. lemon jam

Directions: Steep the flaxseed in hot water for 15 minutes. Strain and add lemon, jam, cinnamon, and honey. Drink as hot as possible. This also soothes the throat.

Magickal Associations: Vitality, comeliness, prosperity, protection.

History/Lore: Bohemian tradition says if children dance in a flax field once every seven years until maturity they will grow to be strong and beautiful. Flax seed can generally be found in many health food stores.

Alternative: If your stomach can tolerate it, some black pepper or other purgative herb can help cleanse out your system.

> In Africa, hollow lemons are often used as magickal containers for potions, herbs, and other important spell components.

FLU RELIEF

(for Dysentery)

1 egg beaten
1 cup skim milk
1 capful vinegar
dash cinnamon

Directions: Warm the milk slowly over a low flame while stirring in the beaten egg. When fully incorporated, add vinegar and cinnamon. Drink small sips until 1 cup is consumed. Procedure may be repeated in six hours.

Magickal Associations: Success, power, love, protection.

History/Lore: In China, vinegar was sometimes vaporized in hot kettles to disburse negative influences or evil magick. Similarly, cinnamon was often used to purify Eastern temples.

Alternatives: If you also have a lot of gas pain, add a 1/2 tsp. of ground clove to this mixture.

SUMAC PHYSIC

1 generous handful of red stag horn sumac
1 gal. water

Directions: Heat water and steep the sumac for 12 hours. Before straining, squeeze the sumac to get as much flavor out as possible. Strain this liquid and sweeten with honey for a lemony-flavored beverage.

Magickal Associations: Sun energy, conscious awareness.

History/Lore: While this recipe was from Morgana's contemporary kitchen, in the 1900s sumac was used as a gargle for sore throat, tonic for fever, and to ease urinary infections.

Alternatives: Any fruits or herbs you enjoy with lemon could be added to this, especially if high in vitamins or beneficial essences. One good choice might be orange rind.

LADIES' TEA

1 tsp. raspberry leaf
1 tsp. black currant leaf
1 tsp. lemon balm
1 tsp. valerian
1 tsp. chamomile
4 cups boiling water

Directions: This beverage is prepared like a normal tea. While it can be enjoyed cold, for most effectiveness on cramps it is best served warm.

Magickal Associations: Protection from spirits, purification, quiet restfulness.

History/Lore: Especially good for female discomforts, an additional dash of valerian tied near your waist helps attract members of the opposite gender.

Alternatives: Mugwort and wintergreen are both effective for similar complaints. If you add them to the recipe, use 1 teaspoon each and increase the water to 5 1/2 cups.

VITAL WATER

1 Tbs. sage

10 comfrey leaves

1/2 tsp. angelica

dash basil

1/2 tsp. ginger root, diced

1/2 tsp. mint

petals from 2 rose buds

1/2 tsp. rosemary

1 slice orange rind

1 1/2 pts. boiling water

lemon

honey

Directions: Another tea-based beverage, the herbs in this should be allowed to steep for about 25 minutes. After straining you can rewarm the liquid or enjoy it cold.

Magickal Associations: Life, revitalization, balance.

History/Lore: This drink is made from favorite restoratives and tonics of the Middle Ages. Angelica root candied or steeped in vinegar is sometimes used as part of ritual fasts. Additionally, this beverage is excellent protection against colds and negative magick.

Alternatives: Most often, the herbalist of the Middle Ages added some type of spirits to this mixture. The additives (see later this chapter) increased the shelf-life and were thought most beneficial to health. Suggestions for this include whiskey, vodka, or rum.

APPLE TEA

2 to 3 apples sliced

3 cups hot water

1 mint leaf

honey and lemon if desired.

Directions: Steep the apples and mint together in hot water for one hour then strain. This is excellent warm with a stick of cinnamon or chilled over ice.

Magickal Associations: Refreshing love. Dreams that teach wisdom, perspective in relationships.

History/Lore: This recipe is favored in France and Australia to help invalids. Additionally apple is one of the popular ingredients for love potions.

Alternatives: If serving this drink cold, adding some soda water or ginger ale (about 1/2 cup) is refreshing.

COLD TONIC

1/2 gal. boiling water

10 eucalyptus leaves

1/2 tsp. sage

1/2 tsp. rosemary

1/2 tsp. anise

1/2 tsp. thyme

1/2 tsp. valerian

1/2 tsp. comfrey

1/2 tsp. ginger root, bruised

1/2 tsp. yarrow buds

1 tsp. chamomile

5 to 10 fresh mint leaves

lemon rind

orange rind

1 bay leaf

Directions: This mixture is best steeped for one hour then strained. I do not recommend drinking it cold as the eucalyptus is far more effective warm.

Magickal Associations: Easing rough nerves, rest, cleansing, amulet creation, prophesy, calm, understanding.

History/Lore: Tried and true from my own household this keeps well in an air-tight jar in the refrigerator and also eases asthma. Magickally, bay leaves were sometimes used to write spells on and were often employed in the preparation of amulets.

Alternative: Add one clove garlic, if tolerable.

NETTLE NUTRITION

2 cups of well-washed nettles

1/2 inch ginger root, bruised

3 medium potatoes, poked

1 gal. water

brown sugar to taste

Directions: Boil the potatoes for one hour in the water then strain. Add nettles and ginger root, returning the liquid to the stove for an additional hour. Strain again and add sugar to taste. Best served warm.

Magickal Associations: New perspectives, cleansing, protection.

History/Lore: A beverage great for a good energy boost and attitude improvement, this drink is high in minerals. Nettle sometimes slows bleeding when applied to skin and was once worn as an amulet to protect against evil spirits.

Alternatives: Dandelion and comfrey are also high in vitamins and minerals and would only increase the benefit of this beverage. Use one-cup dandelion flowers and 2 tablespoons comfrey to the base.

BEEF TOAST

1 piece of toast, broken
2 oz. lean beef shredded
2 cups of boiling water
salt and pepper to taste

Directions: Sprinkle 1 tsp. of salt on the beef and soak it in cold water for 30 minutes. Next simmer this in 2 cups of water for about two hours, taking care to skim off any fat residue. Strain and add toast pieces with whatever other flavoring you desire.

Magickal Associations: Peace and prosperity.

History/Lore: Good for indigestion and fussy stomachs in general; favored in Scotland and throughout the Victorian era to improve physical strength after long bouts of sickness.

Alternatives: After straining, return the liquid to the stove and add a beaten egg, cooking for about 10 additional minutes before serving with toast. This gives a little extra substance to the drink.

HEARTY GRAIN GRUEL

1 Tbs. oatmeal
1 Tbs. rice
1 Tbs. pearl barley
1 lemon, juiced
12 cups water

Directions: Boil your ingredients together for two hours. Strain and add lemon juice and any sweetening desired.

Magickal Associations: Providence, fruitfulness.

History/Lore: Grain is the life line of the land and long-time symbol of good fortune and blessings. On the physical level, this beverage is good for maintaining health and settling the stomach. It was particularly favored in Celtic regions for this purpose.

Alternatives: This also makes a wonderful soup base if you leave the grains in the water and add some bouillon, a dab of butter, and possibly some vegetables.

BARLEY BREW

4 to 5 figs

1/2 cup raisins

1 cup pearl barley

peel of 1/2 orange

3 cups water

1 slice lemon

Directions: Cook the barley in three cups of water. Strain the resulting liquid on to fruits. Return fruits to the stove, cooking until tender. Squeeze the lemon slice over top of the whole mixture, cool, and strain. Drink only the liquid, preserving the cooked fruit for pie or tarts.

Magickal Associations: Divination, anti-magick protection.

History/Lore: Barley has been used in many types of prophetic efforts and was often recommended for kidney stones. This recipe is especially good for babies with colic or anyone with flu symptoms.

Alternatives: You may combine this beverage with the base for beef tea for a heartier flavored drink.

WARM YOU UP!

2 cups milk

1 sliced onion

1 clove of garlic, minced

1 tsp. butter

1 slice of toast, diced

Directions: Place all ingredients except the toast in your blender, mixing until well incorporated. Warm this over a low flame, add butter, and then pour over toast before drinking. This helps relieve chills.

Magickal Associations: Protection of home, prophetic vision, fundicity.

History/Lore: Often used in cold curatives or to improve an appetite. Magickally, Romans were particularly fond of houseleeks (a type of onion) to protect their residence from fire, violence, and the evil eye.

Alternative: Add a cooked potato for a beverage with the thickness of cream soup.

ARROWROOT ARMISTICE

1 1/2 tsp. arrowroot

1 tsp. fine white sugar

1/2 pt. skim milk

Directions: Mix the arrowroot with a little cold milk and let sit. Boil the remaining milk and pour over the mixture. Return all of this to a small pan to simmer for five minutes. Strain and sweeten, drinking it warm.

Magickal Associations: Courage, especially in relationships

History/Lore: This beverage, known for its calming effect, also acts as lubricant. Sometimes called yarrow, arrowroot when carried by a bride is said to insure seven years of joy and love to the couple.

Alternative: To improve the energies in this beverage specifically for bravery, add one teaspoon of black tea or thyme.

STRAWBERRY LEMONADE

1 slice orange

1 pt. distilled water

1 whole lemon, juiced

2 tsp. strawberry syrup

1 tsp. vanilla extract

Directions: Warm the distilled water and orange slice together, adding the juice of one lemon and flavorings. Serve hot.

Magickal Associations: Luck especially in matters of study or the conscious mind. Increased energy.

History/Lore: Recommended mostly for cold symptoms, all the ingredients in this beverage are ruled by Venus, making this an appropriate beverage to bring renewed health to love as well.

Alternative: Raspberry juice or apple could be added to improve romantic aspects of this drink. Another option is to slowly boil down this beverage until it reaches a syrupy stage, adding a little honey. This makes a good topping for ice cream as well as an effective cough relief.

RICE REMEDY

1 oz. rice, rinsed

1/2 qt. water

1/2 qt. milk

add lemon peel and nutmeg powder

Directions: Macerate rice for three hours in hot water. Move this to the stove, boiling for one hour then straining the liquid into another sauce pan. To this, add milk and boil again, flavoring with lemon and nutmeg.

Magickal Associations: Fidelity in love. New romance, rain magick, fertility

History/Lore: This beverage is wonderful for easing the discomforts of diarrhea.

Alternative: Fennel, a native Mediterranean herb, can be added in the quantity of 1/2 teaspoon. per cup to improve digestion of disagreeable foods.

VEGETABLE CHICKEN BROTH

2 qts. cold water

2 lbs. chicken, skinned

2 diced carrots

2 large onions, sliced

2 potatoes, diced

1 cup chopped cabbage

1 tomato, skinned and diced

1 cup diced celery

2 to 3 sprigs parsley finely diced

2 cloves garlic

1 bay leaf

1 Tbs. lemon juice

1 cup fresh chopped chives

1 tsp. thyme

1 tsp. basil

salt and pepper to taste

Directions: Boil your ingredients together over a low heat for two hours, keeping liquid level constant. Strain off vegetables, but do not discard them. These can be retained for another soup to alleviate wastefulness. Cook the broth for another hour or until liquid is reduced by half. Enjoy in one cup servings.

Magickal Associations: Protection in battles, warnings.

History/Lore: Chicken soup or broth has been considered a kind of panacea to folk healers through the ages. This may have slowly developed because it has a soothing effect on nerves, and, certain superstitions claimed the actions of these birds could foretell trouble or victory.

Alternatives: Add additional chives, if desired, when serving. This recipe happens to make a good base for wonton soup just by adding the noodles and a little soy sauce.

GARLIC WATER

1 qt. water

15 cloves garlic

2 bay leaves

2 sprigs fresh sage

1/2 tsp. thyme

1/2 tsp. rosemary

salt and pepper

2 egg yolks

1/3 cup parmesan and Romano cheese

1/4 olive oil

Directions: Boil water with herbs for 45 minutes, strain. Retain the garlic and press into broth. Meanwhile beat eggs, cheese, and oil slowly together. To the egg mixture, add 1 cup of broth and beat again. Mix this thoroughly into garlic bouillon base over low heat until thick. Serve with bread crumbs or croutons on top.

Magickal Associations: Banishing, protection from malevolent influences.

History/Lore: Deemed a kind of cure-all, a recipe similar to this is a favorite part of the French Yule celebrations. This beverage has a purgative quality.

Alternatives: Add an onion or two to the garlic broth. In this form, the drink can become an appropriate part of magickal oath taking or rites of purification.

Alcoholic

Using alcohol as part of medicinal mixtures is nothing new. During the period of Black Death, typhoid, and other life threatening infirmities, alcoholic bases for beverages were used and sold only for medicinal application. These drinks provided relaxation and a momentary flush of heat, regarded as a sign of renewed vitality.

Medicine and magick worked hand in hand, sometimes unwittingly—even by clergymen. The imagery was abundantly clear to superstitious people. Since then, the role alcoholic beverages took in medicine was not totally forgotten or abandoned. We continue to find cough syrups and homemade tonics made from an alcohol base.

BEER TONIC

1 bottle dark ale

1/2 tsp. yarrow

1/2 tsp. rosemary

1/2 inch bruised ginger

Directions: Place rosemary, yarrow, and ginger in a tea ball or gauze covering and steep in the heated ale. Drink warm with a squeeze of lime or chill and enjoy any time.

Magickal Associations: Constancy, tenacity, courage especially during troublesome cycles.

History/Lore: According to folk medicine, tonics like this one are excellent for maintaining health and to purge stomach or chest ailments. Additionally, on the magickal level the herbs in this mixture grant boldness, strength, and mental agility for those trying times.

Alternatives: If you prefer a lighter tasting beer, feel free to use that instead.

HARD CIDER

Directions: Cider is unique among fermented beverages in that it contains one ingredient. In this case, it is apples. Depending on the type you choose, the amount of cider you have once finished will vary. The best ciders are made from a variety of apples, rich in juice including mackintosh, delicious, granny smith, and crab apples.

To prepare, clean and chop your fruit, putting it through a juicer, blender, or even a food grinder to release the internal juices. Then you will need to do several strainings, pressing with the back of a wooden spoon to express as much liquid as possible from your chosen batch of apples.

Once you have it as clear as possible, place in a glass jar or wooden barrel tightly stopped. Check this twice a week (kept in a cool area) for signs of fermentation. Once it has reached a personally pleasing level of natural carbonation, turn the liquid to a large pot on the stove and warm to just under the boiling point. Cool and store. The cider in this form can be kept longer without risk of turning to vinegar. It may also be spiced and served hot or cold.

Magickal Associations: Continual good health and wisdom. Refreshment, rejuvenation.

History/Lore: While we have all heard the saying about an apple a day, the best season to drink hard cider for well being has always been the harvest. This is probably attributable to the abundance of the fruit during that season. Warmed with spices, this is thought to be a good restorative for energy and a way to ease fevers.

Alternatives: Actually, a cider can be made with almost any pressed fruit with a high acid level such as grapes, pears, and cherries. These fruits sequentially provide magickal energy for fertility, sexual attraction, and love.

MATERNITY CORDIAL

1 tsp. anise
1 Tbs. borage flowers
1 tsp. mugwort
1 Tbs. raspberry leaves
1 cup hot water
2 tsp. ginseng
1 cup white grape juice
1 cup peach brandy (not to be consumed if pregnant)

Directions: Place your herbs in a tea ball and allow them to steep in the hot water for 20 minutes. Chill this water, then add grape juice and brandy over ice.

Magickal Associations: Maternal instincts, Moon Magick, Goddess energy, productivity.

History/Lore: Based on an idea presented in a recipe from the 1700s, this beverage not only encourages feminine fertility, but also the general spirit of motherhood to nurture, care for, and protect those we love.

The grape juice and peach brandy are added to this recipe to balance the male/female energies so important in matters of fertility. However, if using this as a magickal additive to conception rites, I suggest taking only a teaspoon full for symbolic internalization.

Alternatives: Because we think of mothering as a "warm" emotion, you may wish to have this heated. To do this, add the grape juice and brandy to the tea water and warm over a low flame to a comfortable drinking temperature.

As it fills the belly, envision you're the center of your being, likewise filled with warm, compassionate feelings (a pink color is good).

(LIQUOR OF LIFE)

5 bay leaves

1 tsp. chamomile

1 tsp. cardamom

1 tsp. anise seed

1 tsp. angelica

1 inch bruised ginger root

rind of one lemon

1 tsp. nutmeg

1 tsp. fennel seed

1 cinnamon stick

1 tsp. licorice

1/2 tsp. mace

5 whole cloves

1/2 tsp. sage

1/2 ltr. brandy

2 cups boiling water

Directions: Place your herbs together in a fine cloth or large tea ball. Steep the herbs for 30 minutes in the boiling water, then add the liquid only to the brandy. This mixture was often recommended by the tablespoon before bedtime. Another recommended technique for preparation was to suspend the herbs directly in the brandy for several months then strain. This yields a slightly stronger flavored beverage.

Magickal Associations: Long life, well being, improved physical energy.

History/Lore: This recipe is a variation of ones dating from the early 1700s that were thought to assure health and longevity.

Alternatives: Whiskey is an appropriate option for a base in this beverage, being used widely for folk remedials. For those looking to make this without alcohol, you may choose to either prepare the herbs such as a tea using equal amounts of water to the original brandy, or steep the herbs in a warm apple juice (similarly to the Vital Water earlier this chapter).

BEER PURIFIER

1 bottle beer (your choice)
1 lemon juiced
1 cup dandelion leaves and flowers
1 Tbs. sassafras bark
1/2 inch bruised ginger root
1 cup boiling water

Directions: Allow your beer to warm to room temperature. Meanwhile, pour the boiling water over the dandelion leaves and flowers (chopped), bark, and ginger. Leave to steep for 20 minutes then strain, pressing as much liquid from the herbs as possible. Mix this with the beer and lemon juice. Drink in 1 cup-helpings, once a day.

Magickal Associations: Cleansing, pure intentions especially in relationships, purging

History/Lore: Recipes like this were still quite commonly found in cookbooks and texts for housewives at the turn of the century, commonly recommended to cleanse the blood. Sassafras is mentioned by Spanish writers of the 1500s from their explorations of Florida, and became one of the most valuable exports to Europe for both medicine and teas.

Alternatives: If sassafras is not available, another purgative is a little red pepper (about 1 tsp.) sliced and steeped with the other herbs.

WHISKEY TEA

(for coughs and colds)

1 cup hot black tea
3 mint leaves
1 sprig of sage
1 shot whiskey
2 tsp. honey
1 tsp. lemon juice

Directions: Once the tea is prepared, float the sage and mint in the liquid for about five minutes while it cools slightly. Then add your honey, lemon and whiskey. Best if consumed before bed time.

Magickal Associations: Tea is a lucky plant, and one often associated with money, valor, or vitality.

History/Lore: This particular recipe is very similar to those of Victorian origins. Here, I have used the three mint leaves not only for their calming quality but to represent a return to health for body, mind, and spirit.

Alternatives: Other herbs that may be steeped in the tea, (1/4 tsp. each) and which are recommended for coughs include angelica, anise, bay, fennel, and mullein.

WHISKEY TEA II

(for asthma relief)

1 Tbs. pennyroyal

1 tsp. raspberry vinegar

3 whole cloves

1/2 tsp. lavender

1 cup hot water

2 tsp. honey

1 tsp. mullein

Directions: Steep the pennyroyal, cloves, lavender, and mullein in boiling water for 15 minutes then strain. To this mix honey until fully incorporated and then add the raspberry vinegar. Sip after an asthma attack has begun to fade.

Directions: Calming winds, Air Magick, grounding flights of fancy, the vital breath.

History/Lore: Asthma has a spasm-like effect on the lungs sometimes caused by allergies, which is why early recipes often included a vinegar addition to clear the nose and throat. The other herbs are included to help relax the body and stimulate improved blood flow.

BLACKBERRY BROTH

(ease restlessness and flatulence)

1/4 tsp. angelica root

1/4 tsp. dill seed

1/8 tsp. horehound

1/2 tsp. fennel

1/2 cup warmed blackberry wine

1/2 cup hot water

3-4 whole blackberries

Directions: Place your herbs in a tea ball to steep in the half cup of hot water for 20 minutes. To this add your blackberry wine and a few whole berries as a garnish. Honey may be added for sweetening if desired. A good beverage to enjoy before bed.

Magickal Associations: Protection from negative magicks, purification, atonement

History/Lore: Horehound is one of the five bitter herbs of Passover. It was also used predominantly in Europe to cure cases thought caused by a magickal toxin. Hyssop was similarly lauded for cleansing, in the words of David, "Purge me with Hyssop, and I shall be clean."

Alternatives: If you are not fond of blackberries, try mulberry wine or plum brandy, the fruits of which both have protective connotations.

SCHNAPPS TONIC

1 pt. peppermint schnapps

1 tsp. chamomile

3 bay leaves

4 dandelion heads

1/2 cup crushed blackberries

1/2 tsp. golden seal

1/2 tsp. catnip leaves

1/4 tsp. sage

1/2 tsp. tansy

1/2 tsp. yarrow

1 cup honey

Directions: Warm the schnapps over a low flame with honey and blackberries until they are fully mixed in. Meanwhile wrap your herbs in a doubled thickness of gauze or cheesecloth. This bundle will be suspended in the schnapps, once cooled to lukewarm, for three months (sealed tightly). Strain before using. If desired to be used as a lighter beverage, mix with equal amounts of water served hot.

History/Lore: Most all purpose tonics are regarded as anything which can improve energy, physical strength, or provide nourishment in order to bring balance back to the body. This recipe combines the traditional tonic herbs into a syrup-like composition to take in teaspoonfuls either in the morning or at night.

GINSENG-ANGELICA REVITALIZER

1 cup angelica liqueur

1/2 tsp. ginseng

Directions: A marvelously easy physic to prepare, simply warm your liqueur with the ginseng and enjoy. If you like, strain it afterwards and serve over ice during hot weather.

Magickal Associations: Reverse undesired magicks. Earth Magick, mystical pursuits.

History/Lore: Medicinally, Ginseng is used to reduce tension, improve recuperative powers, and enhance overall mental awareness in China. In other lands it is used for everything from impotence to headaches. Angelica has a similar reputation for easing indigestion, lung problems, PMS, and even allergic reactions.

Magickally, Ginseng is still used by certain occult practitioners to improve their talents. The Chinese regarded it as having all the best qualities of Earth in concentrated form. Angelica was a popular remedy against enchantment.

BENEFICIENT BALM BLEND

(digestion, moodiness, colds)

1 1/2 qt. balm leaves

2 gal. water

1 1/2 qts. elderberries, pressed

4 1/2 lbs. sugar

1 1/2 qts. raspberries, pressed

1 pkg. wine yeast

Directions: Place the herbs and fruit in the water in a large pan over medium heat. Press the berries regularly to extract as much juice as possible. After about 30 minutes, add sugar, stirring until dissolved. Continue cooking for another half hour. Turn off heat and cool to lukewarm. Strain well. In a small container, mix yeast with a 1/2 cup of warm water, stirring once. Let sit for 15 minutes, then add to lukewarm fruit juice. Cover the pan with a towel for 24 hours, then strain again into a loosely covered container. Watch the wine for signs that fermentation is finishing (namely a decrease in bubbles). Strain once more, then bottle and rack (see also wines in Chapter 13 and 16). Age eight months.

Magickal Associations: Lifting heavy spirits, amiableness, cheerful countenance.

History/Lore: Arabic tales suggest that balm has the remarkable ability to make an individual more agreeable and easier to love. Beyond this, it was a favored herb for fevers, headache, and cooking, its minty-lemon scent generally improving sad spirits. Elder is mentioned in medicinal texts as early as Egypt, most poplar at the turn of the century for throat infections. Raspberry brings a soothing effect to blend the lot together.

Alternatives: Some recipes call for a slice of lemon or orange added to this mixture, both of which are tasty and healthful.

COLD AND FLU RELIEF

1/2 oz. orange rind

2 whole clove

2 pts. brandy

1 tsp. sage

1/2 oz. peppermint leaf

3 to 4 eucalyptus leaves

2 tsp. cinnamon

1/2 inch bruised ginger root

juice of 1/2 lemon

1 cup honey

Directions: Warm your brandy and honey together until the honey is melted. Add the rest of the herbs and fruit, placing in a closed container for a full fortnight, then strain. Take in quantities of one to two teaspoons as needed. For colds, eucalyptus is recommended; when severe stomach problems accompany, substitute chamomile which is gentler (one tablespoon).

Magickal Associations: Improved prosperity, centering and calming the nerves.

History/Lore: The medieval physician or cunning folk might have labeled this a potent Consumption Water, naming the beverage after the disease it's purported and expected to effect.

ALLERGY FORMULA

1/2 cup maple syrup (real)

1 qt. water

1 inch bruised ginger root

1 pt. ginger liqueur

1/4 cup white vinegar

1 tsp. anise seed

Directions: Warm the water, ginger root, anise and maple syrup together until they are fully blended. Remove ginger slices. To this, add all other ingredients in a glass pitcher, stirring well. Chill.

Magickal Associations: Cleansing, purification, health, vital energies.

History/Lore: Beverages such as this were common among early German settlers to America, especially those who did a lot of hay harvesting, which often left the throat and sinuses raw.

Alternatives: Instead of using ginger liqueur, for a non alcoholic alternative substitute one pint of bergamot tea (such as Earl Grey) which is considered quite effective against bronchial discomfort.

METAMORPHOSIS PUNCH

5 cups sugar or honey

2 lemons sliced

1 1/2 L of water

2 to 3 whole cloves

1 cup wine vinegar

1 pt. mint liqueur

3 Tbs. dried mint

Directions: Bring the sugar and water to boil until the sugar is completely dissolved. To this add vinegar, mint, clove, and lemons. Simmer for 20 minutes. Strain and serve chilled. Mix with liqueur.

Magickal Associations: Refinement, well-being, love, poise, personal change.

History/Lore: A version of an ancient Persian beverage considered to be very healthful, this drink gets its magickal potency from the Greek story of Pluto and Persephone. Persephone, in a moment of jealous rage crushed the nymph Minthe under her foot. Pluto, in sadness, transformed her into one of the most favored herbs of history with a gentle, sweet smell.

Alternative: If vinegar is deleted, this beverage will help settle the stomach, especially if enjoyed after dinner.

Chapter 16

Wondrous Wine
and Wine Coolers

"Here with a loaf of bread, beneath the bough, a flask of wine, a book of verse and thou beside me singing in the wilderness."

—Omar Khayyam

"When they drink this barley wine, they sing and dance!"

—Dio, Athenaeus 1.61

Of all the chapters in this book, this is my favorite. Wine is a simple pleasure, but a divine one. As with meads and melomels, the procedure for wine is fairly simple. There are some hints that can help you become increasingly proficient at the art, however.

First and foremost, consider ingredients. At first, using less costly constituents is sensible. Once you get past that point, allow your budget to stretch a bit and you won't be disappointed by the results. After refining your talents, it stands to reason that better quality components yield more pleasant wines. Also bottled or filtered water seems to improve flavor.

Secondly, take extra care when straining wines. The more sediment you eliminate, the easier it becomes to clarify your beverages (which is one reason why I love making tea wines—less fuss! When trying to separate clearer wine from its sediment after the first fermentation, either siphon it off or pour very carefully so the fruit and dead yeast does not enter the new container. This is also a good time to check flavor and add more sugar for sweeter wines.

Next is care with corking. If you tighten your tops or corks too soon and leave the bottles unattended, they will explode from early fermentation pressure buildup. That is why I recommend the use of a balloon secured with a rubber band, or daily "burping." You may also want to store actively fermenting bottles in a cooler or different container just in case (it saves a lot of clean up time).

Finally comes a process called racking, which is somewhat connected to straining. After the second fermentation, the wine rests in its final container. Lay these so they tilt slightly downward, keeping the corks damp. Initially every month a certain amount of sediment will appear in the bottle. Because of this, many brewers like to pour off the clear wine, rinse the containers and rebottle on a regular basis.

If you choose this method, keep one spare bottle of each batch of wine to refill any air spaces left after siphoning and rebottling. As you follow this procedure, the need to rack the wine decreases and your wine will clarify to look closer to store-bought blends.

BASIC WINE

Because the procedure for wine making is pretty standard, instead of including a lot of repetitious directions in this chapter, this recipe will serve as a foundation for all those which follow. Any variations on this, distinct to a particular recipe will be noted below. All proportions are for one gallon yields. Recipes may be halved or doubled.

1 to 2 lbs. fruit

spices to taste

1 12 oz. can frozen juice

2 to 3 lbs. sugar

1 gal. water

slice of lemon or orange

1 tea bag

1/3 pkg. wine yeast

Directions: If using spices, place these first in your water and simmer for 30 minutes until a tea-like substance is formed. For spicier drinks, leave the herbs in the water adding fruit, juice, tea bag, lemon/orange, and sugar. Bring to a low rolling boil for fifteen minutes, then reduce heat for another fifteen minutes. Cool to lukewarm. Meanwhile in a small separate container dissolve the wine yeast in 1/4 cup warm (not hot) water. Let this sit for a minimum of 20 minutes to work before stirring it into the cooled juices.

Leave the entire blend in your pan (preferably not aluminum) overnight with a heavy cloth or dish towel over top. In the morning, strain the fruit (and herbs if they were left in) out of the juices and let sit covered in a warm area for another twenty four hours. Strain again and move to a loosely covered glass container for one month. As fermentation slows, activity in the container will decrease (less bubbles) and you can move the beverage into smaller bottles for racking. Strain or siphon the wine into your chosen containers to further clarify it, corking loosely for another two to three weeks. If the corks pop out frequently, you know it is too soon for final capping.

All wines should be stored in a dark, cool place. Depending on how dry you like your beverages, eight months to three years aging time produces tasty wines. You will have to experiment to find exactly when you are content with the flavor. At this point, to stop fermentation you may either refrigerate your wine, or bring it to a very brief, low rolling boil, then bottle again in air tight containers. I usually age wine for about eight months unless a recipe says otherwise. This creates a sweet, but not too heavy-bodied beverage.

Hints: At first, match your ingredients by flavor such as apples, apple juice and apple tea. Apples and grapes are two excellent fruits to start with, almost always yielding positive results. Later, once you feel more certain of the procedure, try mixing and matching your fruits and juices as exhibited in several recipes below.

Magickal Associations: Changes with fruits and herbs used.

History/Lore: Wine in general is considered the beverage of the Gods. It is a type of ambrosia, being used in magickally and in religion for everything from offerings and libations to oath taking and oracles.

PINK GRAPEFRUIT-STRAWBERRY SURPRISE

2 qts. fresh strawberries

8 cups sugar

4 pink grapefruit (large)

1 slice lemon

1 lb. seedless raisins

1/3 pkg. wine yeast

1 black tea bag

Directions: Juice your grapefruit, extracting as much liquid as possible. Place this in a large container with raisins and water, then leave overnight in a warm area.

Move this kettle to the stove, adding strawberries, the tea bag, sugar, and lemon. Follow basic cooking recipe as given above except that you should allow cloth-covered fermentation for six days before straining off berries and raisins. This will allow a fuller flavored wine.

After first fermentation, wine should be allowed to set for four months before another straining, then aged an additional six months before serving.

Magickal Associations: Kinship, leisure, positive attitudes.

History/Lore: While strawberries are a traditional love fruit, the light pink coloration of this wine turns its energy more towards matters of friendship and simple pleasures.

Alternative: For a wine with cleansing qualities, try opting for 1 lb. of fresh or canned pineapple in place of the berries.

MAPLE WINE

1 gal. apple cider or juice

1 apple tea bag

4 cups real maple syrup

1/4 tsp. orange rind

1 cinnamon stick (optional)

1/3 package yeast

Directions: You can use the basic directions given at the beginning of this chapter for maple wine, except that in this instance, the syrup is your sugar substitute. Open air fermentation with a towel takes place for 10 days before straining. After this, a loosely covered container will be needed for four to five months until wine is clear. Then bottle with good corks or tightened tops.

Magickal Associations: Renewed life and energy, health and sweet diversions.

History/Lore: In the spring, tree sap begins to move freely again through the trees bringing them essential nutrients to bear leaves and come out of their sleep. Cider and apple juice blend nicely with this energy, being strongly associated with well-being.

Alternatives: You can try other fruit juices or simple herbs in this recipe which may go well with the maple flavor. Strawberries are one good choice.

Mulberry Wine

1 gal. water
1/2 lemon, sliced
3 lbs. sugar
1/3 pkg. yeast
5 lbs. mulberries
1/2-inch slice bruised ginger root

Directions: Place your mulberries with the water and mash them, leaving to set over night. Follow the basic recipe, allowing open air fermentation for one week, followed by a straining, then another week of open air working. Pour into glass containers to let sit for three more weeks, then strain again into final containers. This should age two years for best flavor.

Magickal Associations: Remembrance, honor, memorials.

History/Lore: Shakespeare gives us some food for thought when in *A Midsummer's Nights Dream* Thisbe and Pyramus die tragically beneath the mulberry tree. Until this time, the berries of the tree were believed white. The innocent blood of this couple stained them a purplish color forever. The Chinese hold this berry in such fervent regard as to believe it can eliminate the need for food and eventually transform the consumer into a being of light!

Note: Mulberries are sometimes difficult to find. Try country markets and old rural farm regions if they are not readily available locally.

BLUEBERRY REPOSE

5 qts. blueberries

1 slice orange

1 gal. water

2 1/2 lbs. sugar

1 fruit tea bag

1/3 pkg. yeast

Directions: Wash your blueberries thoroughly, then mash them in a large container. In another pan, boil the water then pour it over the berries to sit for 24 hours. Strain this juice back into your cooking pot, pressing to extract as much of the berry nectar as possible. Follow as with basic recipe, allowing open fermentation for 15 days then strain thoroughly. Move to a secondary container with loose corking until liquid is a bright, bluish red hue, then refine again and bottle for aging.

Magickal Associations: Happiness, peacefulness, contemplation.

History/Lore: It seems many things with blue coloration are associated with joy and harmony. When we see a blue sky, our hearts rejoice; the flower bluebell is considered lucky, and of course there is the famous "blue bird of happiness."

CURRANT VITALITY

3 1/2 lbs. currants (red)

3 lbs. sugar

1 raspberry tea bag

1/4 lb. raisins

1/4 orange sliced

1/3 pkg. yeast

1 gal. water

Directions: Place your cleaned currants in a large bucket with orange slices. Heat half of the water to boiling and pour it over the berries. While hot, crush the fruit then leave the mixture to set covered for two days. Strain thoroughly. Move the currant juice to the stove adding remaining water and sugar. Bring to a simmer stirring constantly until the sugar is dissolved. Follow as with basic recipe, allowing four days of open air fermentation. When you strain this mixture again for bottling, place three raisins in the bottom of each vessel then age.

Magickal Associations: Energy, bounty, courage, fire magick.

History/Lore: This wine turns a beautiful bright red color reminiscent of life's blood making it an excellent vehicle to internalize that vital energy.

Alternatives: Reduce your currants by half and add an equal commodity of raspberries for an abundance of love.

CHERRY-ALMOND DELIGHT

1 12-oz can frozen cherry juice
1 slice orange
1 lb. pitted cherries
1 tea bag
6 cups apricot nectar
1 1/2 gal. water
2 1/2 Tbs. sugar
1/3 pkg. yeast
1/2 tsp. almond extract

Directions: Follow basic recipe allowing a two day open air fermentation before straining off fruit. Please note that cherries exhibit a slow, steady fermentation.

Magickal Associations: Productivity, love magick, sexual equilibrium and harmony.

History/Lore: As early as 8 B.C. herbalists in the region of Assyria were acclaiming the cherry for its wonderful smell and value to health. Magickally, cherries, apricots, and almonds are all associated with the energy of love and romance.

Alternative: Three pounds of strawberries may be substituted for the cherries, yielding a marvelous wine with similar magickal results. However, please note that strawberries are *very* active fermenters and extra caution will have to be taken with excess pressure in your aging containers.

HAPPINESS WINE

3 qts. strawberries
1/4 inch ginger root
3 large seedless oranges

316 Kitchen Witch's Guide to Brews and Potions

1 gal. water

3 lbs. sugar

1/3 pkg. yeast

Directions: Hull your strawberries and peel all but one of the oranges. Slice the strawberries and oranges into your brew pot, then follow basic recipe. Extra straining may be required.

Magickal Associations: Revitalization, health, happiness.

History/Lore: In the East, the orange is an emblem of satisfaction and pleasure. The strawberry is sacred to Freya, the Norse Goddess of love and beauty.

Alternatives: Other berries are tasty substitutes for the strawberries here, and as the found bounty of the earth they offer magickal energies for prosperity and joy.

POTION OF LOVE

6 small apples, sliced

1 gal. water

3 cups strawberries

1/8 tsp. ginger

2 oranges

1/8 tsp. cinnamon

2 small slices lemon peel

2 1/2 lbs. sugar

3 cups raspberries

1/3 package yeast

Directions: Find deep red apples for this recipe and leave the skins on. These combined with the berries yields a deep red color to encourage love. Follow basic recipe, removing oranges, and lemon peel after liquid has cooled to lukewarm, then continue as directed.

Magickal Associations: Spirited romance, dedication, fervor, compassion, sagacity.

History/Lore: All the herbs and fruits of this recipe have been chosen for their long standing association with love. The number of slices of fruit were chosen to represent partnership (2), the union of two people (3), and devotion to the relationship(6).

PLEASING PEACHES

12 large peaches

1 tsp. vanilla

1 apple tea bag

1 gal. water

1 slice of orange

2 1/2 lbs. sugar

1/3 pkg. yeast

Directions: Peel the peaches, removing the pits, then slice them into your pot. Follow as with basic recipe, however if you find the peach flavor is not strong enough try to find some peach nectar at a health food store to add for improved taste. This can be mixed in during the initial cooking process, but will require extra straining after open fermentation.

Magickal Associations: Wisdom, discernment, good judgment, protection, and long life

History/Lore: In China, the peach is a potent symbol appearing frequently in their arts to represent matrimony and longevity. Its blossoms announce the arrival of spring, and peach handled brooms are used to sweep away undesired magick in the land.

Alternatives: Because this is a very simple recipe, almost any fruit may be substituted to better accentuate your magickal goals.

PLUM PASSION

1 gal. spring water
15 good-sized plums
1 strand saffron
3 lbs. sugar
1 tsp rose water
1/3 pkg. sparkling yeast

Directions: Bring your water to a low rolling boil while plums are being sliced and all pits are removed. Please note that your fruit should be sweet and ripe. The plums need to simmer in the water for a half hour until the liquid turns very red. Now add your sugar, saffron, and rosewater, following the basic recipe.

Watch your wine closely. When it begins to get tart, return the entire batch to the stove adding more plums and sugar until the taste is slightly sweeter than you might like. Age again, and repeat this process one more time for an almost liqueur-like wine. At this point, sweeten to personal taste, boil, strain, and rebottle for gift giving or your own enjoyment.

Magickal Associations: Long life, kinship, companionship.

History/Lore: In Eastern lands, plums are regarded as an emblem of friendship. It also represents immortality because it is the first tree to begin to show signs of life in spring.

Alternatives: A combination of plum and apple is very refreshing. Magickally the two blend nicely for good, overall well-being and wisdom in relationship.

AMENDMENT WINE

1 lb. sweet almonds
2 lbs. sugar
1 tsp. cinnamon

1 pt. cherry juice

2 tsp. almond extract

1 gal. water

1/2 oz orange blossom water (opt.)

1/3 pkg. yeast

pinch of lemon rind

Directions: Finely crush the sweet almonds. Meanwhile, bring one half of your water to boil, then pour this over the almonds. Let the nuts soak for 48 hours, then move to the stove and follow basic recipe.

Magickal Associations: Restoring relationships, reconciliation, forgiveness.

History/Lore: This recipe has its origins in Russia, where like many European lands, orange water symbolizes faithfulness. Almond is employed with this for rejuvenate energy.

FINNISH FANTASY

2 small lemons

1 gal. water

2 medium oranges

1/4 tsp. yeast

1 cup raisins

2 cups brown sugar

Directions: Peel the fruit, setting aside the rind. Using a fine knife or fork, remove as much of the white membrane as you can from both the fruit and rind. Slice the lemons and limes into a large bowl with the sugar and cleaned fruit skins. Pour the boiling water over it, allowing to cool to lukewarm. Next, add your yeast as directed in general recipe allowing open air fermentation for 24 hours. Finally, place your raisins in the bottom of a bottle and pour the liquid into it, capping tightly. Continue to allow the beverage to ferment at room temperature until the raisins move to the top of the bottle then refrigerate for use. Please note that this wine has the extra advantage of a very mild alcohol content.

Magickal Associations: Vision, predictions, oracular power.

History/Lore: In Finland wines like this one are called Sima. The citrus fruits add precision to your magickal efforts, and raisins are thought to help encourage psychic dreams.

(TEA WINE)

20 Earl Grey tea bags

1 tsp. lemon juice

1 orange sliced

2 lbs. sugar

1/2 inch ginger root bruised

1 gal. water

1/3 pkg. wine yeast

Directions: Steep the tea bags in the boiled water overnight. Remove and press out any liquid you can. Place this container back on the stove adding the remaining ingredients except yeast. Remove citrus fruit once the tea is cooled to lukewarm then follow basic recipe. This yields a dry wine with a flavor similar to sun tea.

Magickal Associations: Friendly conversation, relaxation, social gatherings.

History/Lore: One legend has it that the Emperor She Nug (also known as a great healer) invented hot tea when some nearby leaves accidentally fell into a pot of water he was boiling for consumption around 2700 B.C.

Alternative: After your initial straining of this beverage, place in a glass container with a screw top. Leave the top loose for several days while the wine works (bubbles will appear in 1/4 inch thickness on top of the liquid). When the bubbles almost disappear, turn the top tightly and leave for 24 hours then refrigerate. This yields almost a soda-pop-like wine with very little alcohol.

SLAVIC BREAD WINE

1/2 lb. dark rye bread
1/2 lb. buckwheat meal
2 large apples
1 gal. water
1/2 cup raisins
3 Tbs. dry active yeast
2 cups brown sugar
1/2 cup minced meat

Directions: Slice and toast rye bread then set aside. Meanwhile, boil the water in a large pot with apples which have been peeled and diced for 30 minutes. Remove this from the heat adding toasted rye pieces and barley which need to soak for four hours. Strain thoroughly. Dissolve your yeast in warm water, adding this to the juice along with minced meat. Follow as with basic recipe, pouring into a gallon jug with raisins and setting in a cool area to ferment for one week. Strain again and chill for use.

Magickal Associations: Good wishes, comfort of hearth and home, lifting burdens.

History/Lore: Known by the local name of Kvass, this wine's title literally translates to mean "leaven." Because Kvass is only mildly alcoholic, it was often part of the meal table and considered quite healthy.

Alternative: Raspberries were sometimes substituted for apples using 2 cups of fresh fruit. Magickally this would encourage love and joy.

TROPICAL TEMPTATION

16 oz. pineapple juice
1 gal. water
2 cups coconut
3 lbs. sugar
1 8 oz. can mandarin oranges
1/3 pkg. yeast
1 large ripe banana
2 cups papaya juice
5 kiwi fruit, peeled and diced

Directions: Follow basic directions, making sure to boil this beverage before cooling for yeast. The boiling process helps to incorporate the different weighted fruit juices. Shake daily during fermentation and strain well.

Magickal Associations: Repose, luxurious retreat, safety from the elements.

History/Lore: The fruits of warm regions offer a refreshing change from apples and grapes. In Honduran legend, it was the banana leaf that covered Adam and Eve, not fig or apple. Pineapple is the fruit of welcome, and coconut shells figure predominantly in protective magick.

WINE COOLERS

To make any of your wines into a "cooler" simply mix equal portions of wine to soda water, or ginger ale and add a few fresh pieces of fruit as a garnish. If you prefer a fruitier flavored cooler, mix one part wine with one part soda and one part matching fruit juice.

Common Ingredients, Elemental Correspondences, Magickal Associations, and Uses in Brewing

> *"...read a mystic meaning which only the rapt and parting soul may know."*
> —James G. Blaine

Ale and Beer: Fire; offerings and purification. Sometimes used as a base for punches or spiced beverages. Sacred to Tenemit, Isis, and Hathor (Egypt); Shoney (Scotland), and Kremana (Slavonic).

Allspice: Fire; prosperity, good fortune, and health. Use somewhat sparingly as it can have a "hot" taste.

Almond: Air; wisdom, financial matters, well-being. Extract makes an interesting addition to fruit beverages. Sacred to Artemis in Greece, Chandra in India, and Ptah in Egypt.

Anise: Air; safety, vitality, cleansing. A pungent herb that can take over the flavor of a beverage. Add in small quantities until achieving the desired flavor.

Apple: Water; discernment, prudence, love, the soul. Apples are a steady, dependable fruit for fermented beverages. They help to balance flavor without overwhelming it. Sacred to Induna of Norse traditions, Venus and Apollo in Rome, and Zeus in Greece. Apple juice makes an interesting alternative base for beer.

Banana: Air; the masculine element (specifically sexual), commitment, love, and protection. Not the easiest fruit to get to ferment properly, it is very heavy and often separates out of wines. Sacred to Kanaloa (Hawaii).

Bay: Fire; intuition, vigor, protection. One bay leaf can be added to almost any drink without noticeable changes in flavor. Bay is a nice addition to mulled beverages. Sacred to Eros and Adonis in Greece and Buddha in India.

Birch: Water; cleansing, earth magick, banishing. Birch twigs are most often used in birch beer, but also make an interesting augmentation to other creative efforts. Sacred to Thor.

Carrot: Fire; sexuality, insight, grounding. Carrot juice is best suited to nonalcoholic beverages and is great for personal energy.

Celery: Fire; mental keenness, weight loss, desire. If you wish, celery leaf can be substitute with almost no change in flavor.

Cherry: Water; psychic insight, love, whimsy. Cherries ferment slowly and are exceptionally excellent when blended with vanilla bean.

Cinnamon: Fire; spiritual pursuits, potency, victory. Another strong aromatic with intense flavor. Unless you really enjoy the taste of cinnamon, it needs to be added in slight amounts. Stick cinnamon recommended. Sacred to the alters of Aphrodite (Greece) and Venus (Rome).

Citron: Fire; safety and power, cleansing. Lemon-like fruit, but larger. Can be used in place of lemon in any recipe. Sacred to Ge (Egypt) and Zeus and Hera (Greece).

Clove: Fire; protection, love, prosperity. Only a few whole cloves are needed in any beverage to get enough tang to be noticeable.

Currants: Fire (red currants) or water (juice), abundance. Currant wine is fabulous if you have the patience to clean all the leaves and branches of this bush.

Daisy: Water; simplicity, prophesy, youthful energy. This flower most often appears as part of spring wines. Sacred flower to Freya.

Dandelion: Air; wishes, sensitivity to spirits, divination. A pesky weed which, true to nature's sense of humor, can be made into wine, coffee, and salads. Sacred to Hecate and Theseus (Greek).

Date: Air; spirituality, strength, vitality. Dates are rather heavy in taste and are best used for liqueurs or purgative juices. Sacred to Ea and Anu (Babylonian), Artemis (Greek), and Isis (Egypt).

Elder: Water; peace, wholeness, safety, healing. Elderflower wine is a favorite spring creation especially for magick Circles. Sacred to Venus.

Fennel: Fire; purification, protection from evil, physical well-being. Caution again here on amount used—strong taste. Sacred to Prometheus (Greek).

Fig: Fire; potency, love charms, fundicity. Similar in texture and body to dates. Sacred to Amun Ra and Isis (Egypt), Brahma (Hindu), and Juno (Greece).

Ginger: Fire; success, increasing power, money, romance. Ginger adds a crisp boost to most beverages if used with prudence. Ginger root is much better than powder.

Grains: Earth; prosperity, good fortune, abundance. Grains are featured as part of health drinks or beer. Barley specifically is Sacred to Demeter (Greece), Taliesin (Welsh), and Vishnu (Hindu).

Grape: Water; the conscious mind, celebration, fruitfulness. The acclaimed base ingredient for most wines also makes a lovely addition to many other juices. The favored fruit of Bacchus (Rome) and Hathor (Egypt).

Honey: Air; purification, well-being, happiness, discernment. A prime ingredient in mead, honey is an excellent choice of sweeteners for almost any beverage. Sacred to Min (Egypt), Ea (Babylonia), Artemis (Greek), and Kama (India) among others.

Hops: Rest and peacefulness, health. A main constituent in beers, I tend to add hops judiciously or their flavor becomes overwhelming.

Kiwi: Water; leisure, young love. You need a fair amount of kiwi fruit to produce a strong flavor in any brewing, but it is well worth the effort for its mixed berry-like flavor.

Lavender: Air; restfulness, joy, peace, purity. A little French lavender in any beverage lifts the bouquet without overpowering the taste.

Lemon: Water; freshness, kinship, longevity. A fruit that adds a slight tang to everything, it also affords a lovely fragrance when blended sagaciously. An appropriate offering on the Buddhist altar to Jambhala.

Mango: Fire; passion and romance. An orangey under taste but richer, the weight of mango juice makes it difficult to mix with other fruits. Sacred to Buddha.

Maple Syrup: Air; sweet things in life, health, love. Maple syrup is an interesting taste sensation when used as an alternative to sugar or honey in wines, meads, and ales.

Marjoram: Air; happiness, safety, bounty, well-being. Best when used in melomels, metheglyn and tea. Sacred to Venus (Gk), and Ilmarinen (Finish).

Milk: Water; the Goddess aspect, maternal nature, lunar energy. Honored among Hathor, Isis and Min (Egypt), Zeus (Greek), and Ilmarinen (Finland). Use carefully to avoid spoilage.

Mint: Air; revitalization, lust, adventure, safety, money. A subtle herb when added to fermented brews in whole, fresh leaves (three to four at a time). Can be used plain for iced or hot tea too. Sacred to Pluto (Rome).

Mulberry: Air; sagacity, practicality, psychic awareness, inventive energy. One of the first berries used readily in wine and still an excellent choice. Sacred to Minerva (Rome).

Nutmeg: Fire; good fortune, fidelity, fitness. Good all-around mild tasting herb.

Orange: Fire; love, luck, prosperity, health. Orange is an integral part of many fermented beverages in small amounts and is a wonderful morning juice, addition to coffee, and so on. At one time oranges were thought to prevent drunkenness, which may explain why slices still appear in many mixed drinks.

Passionfruit: Water; love, peace and friendship. Another heavy tropical fruit, is best mixed with other heavy liquids notably mango and banana.

Peach: Water; long life, fertility, good wishes. Peach is a light fruit which can be used alone or as an accent to other fruits and herbs. Sacred to Hsi Wang Ma (China).

Pear: Water; passion, zest, love. Pear juice is subtle enough to be mingled with multiple other ingredients. Its weight, however is a little "thick" and is best when diluted some. Sacred to Athene (Greece).

Pineapple: Fire; luck, money, commitment, dedication, protection. The cutting taste of pineapple makes it a good pallet cleanser. Its citric content helps it to mix well with other fruits.

Plum: Water; adoration, respect, protection. Makes a wonderful liqueur or sparkling wine with an oriental flair.

Pomegranate: Fire; creativity, invention, prosperity. While the juice is difficult to extract, it is well worth the time. Makes a wonderful, deep red wine or mead. Sacred to Dionysus (Greek), Persephone (Phoenician), Ceres (Rome).

Quince: Earth; love, protection, happiness and fulfillment. A pear-like fruit with similar taste and body. This makes a nice blending fruit as it doesn't overcome other flavors. Sacred to Venus (Rome).

Raspberry: Water; safety and love. Raspberries ferment quickly and always provide hearty, full-flavor to beverages.

Rhubarb: Earth; protection, faithfulness, devotion, health. A rather tart addition, rhubarb can balance out sweeter drinks.

Rose: Water; intuitive senses, love, divination, well-being. Rose water is one means of smoothing out the flavor of a beverage. Roses in quantity lend an strong aroma and lovely coloring to your brew. Sacred to Venus (Rome).

Rosemary: Fire; mental acuity, cleansing, rest, youthful vigor, memory. Use in minimal quantities, according to personal taste. Likewise sacred to Venus.

Saffron: Fire; weather magick, prosperity, joy and psychic awareness. Added in small amounts, saffron helps smooth out the body of a beverage. Appeared as an offering in the temples to Eos (Greece), Amun Ra (Egypt), and Brahma (Hindu).

Sage: Air; panacea of health, wisdom. Best used in metheglyn and other fitness-related drinkables. A favored herb by Zeus (Greece) and his Roman counterpart Jupiter.

Strawberry: Water; light-hearted love and joy, energy of summer. Strawberry is a very active fermenter with lovely flavor and scent. Sacred to Freya (Norse/Teutonic).

Sugar: Earth; dispel evil, sweeten ill-disposition. Sugar is the key ingredient to most alcoholic beverages, but not recommended for those with weight problems or sugar imbalances. Sacred to Kane (Hawaii).

Tea: Fire; wealth, courage, strength, vitality, health, rest. Tea is a good substitute for ginger root or other barks/roots for tannic acid. Herb teas provide additional flavor.

Thyme: Water; bravery, fortitude, purification, awareness. Another herb excellent for metheglyns and teas. An honored herb among the Faery folk.

Vanilla: Water; mental awareness, love, productivity, zeal. I like a little vanilla bean or extract in almost all my brews.

Watermelon: Water; love, and heath. Melons in general are tricky to use for brewing being very susceptible to temperature changes. Probably best used to flavor grain spirits. Sacred to Set (Egypt).

Wine: Fire; observances and offerings. Used as a base for Horilka and certain spiced punch bowls. Sacred to Gestin (Sumeria), Ishtar (Mesopotamia), Osiris and Isis (Egypt), Bacchus (Rome).

Yogurt: Water; spirituality, awareness, dietary focus. Yogurt is employed in nonalcoholic drinks frequently for health and weight loss.

Possible Brewing Deities

"These things surely lie on the knees of the Gods."

—Homer

Reading the myths and legends of many cultures is an enriching experience. In the process, you get a clearer understanding of how diverse our world has been throughout history, and insight into why we are, who we are. Among these legends, many Divine images appear, and reappear, inspiring humanity towards better living.

Earlier in this book, I briefly mentioned calling on a Divine presence to bless magickal brewing efforts. The obvious question for most Wiccans and Pagans is which visage of God and Goddess to choose? Ultimately, we could look to one who rules over a specific attribute or Element, such as Thor for weather related beverages used in libations, or Athena for elixirs of romance. Beyond this, we can also consider the gods and goddesses who have somehow been associated with a specific beverage, fruit, spice, vegetable, or grain according to our chosen ingredients (see Appendix A).

Either of these approaches is perfectly good. Just decide which one makes the most sense to and works the best for you.

Below are some possible gods, goddesses, heroes, heroines, and even saints to choose from including their country of origin and spheres of influence. This list could be much longer, but I have limited myself to some of the more interesting and assorted options here. For additional ideas, look at fruits or spices sacred to your patron deities and check resource books like *The Witches God*, and *The Witches Goddess* (Janet and Stewart Farrar).

Apollo: As a god of science, music, and poetry, Apollo is sometimes associated with mead. His "science" aspect combined with art make him a good choice to call on to hone your skills in general brewing efforts.

Ahurani: Persian; goddess of water.

Anat: Canaanite; fertility goddess who is appropriate for any milk based beverage.

Aphrodite: Greek; goddess of love. Any beverage with roses, clover, sweet aromas or apples.

Athena: Greek; warrior goddess. Any beverage with coconut. In Rome, known as Minerva.

Baldur: Norse; god of sacred wells and light. Good for non alcoholic beverages which are going to be used for magick.

Binah: Hebrew; the supernatural Mother also known as "She Who Nourishes." Her cabalistic symbol is the cup.

Blodeuwedd: Welsh; known as "flower face," any flower based drinks especially those with broom or meadowsweet.

Bragi: Norse; keeper of the mead of inspiration, god of eloquence and wisdom.

Buddhi: Tibetan; Goddess of achievement. Ask for her aid in learning your art(s).

Carmenta: Roman; inventor of arts and sciences, similar in function to Buddhi.

Ceres: Roman; Goddess of agriculture. Appropriate for most beverages, but beer especially.

Cerridwen: Welsh; goddess of the cauldron and grain.

Chicomecoatz: Aztec; goddess of maize and rural abundance; good for corn-based drinks and harvest festival beverages.

Cormus: Greek; god of laughter and mirth, good for celebratory brewing efforts.

Dionysus: Greek; god of wine and mead. In Rome known as Bacchus or Liber and has similar personifications in almost every culture.

Esculapius: Greek; god of physic and all health beverages.

Euphrosyne: Greek; muse who rejoices the heart.

Frigg: Norse; personification of earth, especially appropriate for beverages of libation.

Gambrinus: Germanic; dubbed the inventor of beer and patron saint of beer and brewers in this country.

Ganemede: The cup bearer to Jupiter, good for hospitality.

Gibil: Babylonian; god of arbitration, especially good for beverages prepared for oath cups or peace cups.

Gunnloed: Teutonic; god of mead.

Hesperides: Greek; three sisters with golden apples in their magick garden.

Hygeia: Greek; goddess of health.

I: Chinese; god of archery who possesses the drink of immortality.

Idun: Norse; keeper of apples of immortality.

Isis: Egyptian; goddess whose sacred fruits include figs and dates and whose offerings often consisted of beer, milk, and wine.

Ivenopae: Indonesian; mother of rice, good to bless saki. Also consider **Inari** from Japan or **Gauri** from India as alternatives.

Kanaloa: Hawaii; goddess whose sacred fruit is the banana.

Lares: Roman; home and hearth god.

Momus: Greek; god of raillery.

Nikkal: Canaanite; goddess of first fruits good for beverages to be used in offerings.

Oegir: Norse; beer brewer of Asgard.

Omacatl: Aztec; god of delight and celebration.

Osiris: Egyptian; god of cereals and common people especially appropriate for beer.

Penates: Roman; home and hearth god

Pomona: Roman; goddess of fruits and autumn. All fruit based beverages or harvest drinks.

Shoney: Scotland; god of Ale. Mirrored in Egypt by Tenemit.

Thor: Norse; red fruited drinks.

Vertumnus: Roman; god of orchards.

Wang Mu: China; goddess who was served the peaches of immortality.

Bibliography

Arnold, John P. *Origin and History of Beer and Brewing*. Chicago: Wahl-Henius Institute of Fermentology, 1911.

Aylett, Mary. *Country Wines*. London: Odhams, 1953.

Baker, Margaret. *Folklore & Customs of Rural England*. Totowa, NJ: Rowman & Littlefield, 1974.

Bartlett, John. *Familiar Quotations*. Boston: Little Brown & Co.,1938.

Beliefs, Behaviors and Alcoholic Beverages. Mac Marshall, Editor, University of Michigan Press, 1979.

Belt, T. Edwin. *Vegetable, Herb & Cerial Wines*. London: Mills & Boon LTD, 1971.

―――――. *Flower, Leaf & Sap Wines*. London: Mills & Boon LTD, 1971.

Beyerl, Paul. *Master Book of Herbalism*. Custer, Ariz.: Phoenix Publishing, 1984.

Black, William George. *Folk Medicine*. New York: Burt Franklin, 1883.

Broth, Patricia and Don. *Food in Antiquity*. New York: Frederick A. Praeger, 1969.

Chase, A.W. M.D. *Receipt Book & Household Physician*. Detroit: F.B. Dickerson Company, 1908.

Chase, Edithe L. and French, W.E.P. *Waes Hale*. New York: Grafton Press, 1903.

Chow, Kit and Kramer, Ione. *All the Tea in China*. San Francisco, Calif.: China Books and Periodicals, 1990.

Clarkson, Rosetta. *Green Enchantment*. New York: McMillian Publishing, 1940.

Clifton, C. *Edible Flowers*. New York: McGraw-Hill, 1976.

Complete Anachronist Guide to Brewing. Milpitas, Calif.: Society for Creative Anactronsim, 1983.

Culpepper, Nicholas. *Complete Herbal and English Physician*. Glenwood, Ill.: Meyerbooks, 1991.

Cunningham, Scott. *Encyclopedia of Magical Herbs*. St. Paul: Llewellyn Publications, 1988.

————: *The Magic in Food*. St. Paul, Minn.: LlewellynPublications, 1991.

————; *The Magic of Incense, Oils and Brews*. St. Paul, Minn.: Llewellyn Publications, 1988.

Davids, Kenneth. *Coffee*. San Francisco, Calif.: 101 Produc tions, 1976.

Digby, Kenelm. *The Closet Opened*. Little Britain, London: E.L.T. Brome, 1696.

Doorn, Joyce V. *Making your own Liquors*. San Leandro, Calif.: Prism Press, 1977.

Elspan, Ceres. *Herbs to Help you Sleep*. Boulder, Colo.: Shambhala Press, 1980.

Encyclopedia of Creative Cooking; Charlotte Turgeon Editor. New York: Weathervane Press, 1982.

Every Day Life through the Ages. London: Readers Digest Association, Berkley Square, 1992.

Foster, Carol. *Cooking with Coffee*. New York: Fireside Books, 1992.

Fox, William MD. *Family Botanic Guide*. Sheffield, Ill.: William Fox and Sons, 1907.

Freeman, Margaret. *Herbs for the Medieval Household for cooking, Healing and Divers Uses*. New York: Metropolitan Museum of Art, 1943.

Freid, Mimi. *Liquors for Gifts*. Charlotte, N.C.: Garden Way Publishing, 1988.

French, R.K. *The History and Virtues of Cyder*. New York: St. Martin's Press, 1982.

Gayre, Robert. *Brewing Mead*. Boulder, Colo.: Brewers Publ ications, 1986.

Gordon, Lesley. *Green Magic*. New York: Viking Press, 1977.

Haggard, Howard W. M.D. *Mystery, Magic and Medicine*. Garden City, N.Y.: Doubleday & Co., 1933.

Hale, William Harlan. *Horizon Cookbook & Illustrated History of Eating and Drinking*. New York: Ameri can Heritage, 1968.

Hall, Manly. *Secret Teachings of All Ages*. Los Angeles, Calif.: Philosophical Research Society, 1977.

Hardwick, Homer. *Winemaking at Home*. New York: Wilfred Funk, 1954.

Hechtlinger, Adelaide. *The Seasonal Hearth*. New York: Overlook Press, 1986.

Hiss, Emil. *Standard Manual of Soda & Other Beverages*. Chicago: GP Englehand & Co, 1897.

Hobson, Phyllis. *Wine, Beer & Softdrinks*. Charlotte: Garden Way Publishing.

Honey, Babs. *Drinks for All Seasons*. Wakefield: E.P. Publishing Ltd, 1982.

Hopkins, Albert A. *Home Made Beverages*. Chicago: North Chicago Printing, 1918.

Hosletters US Almanac. Pittsburgh, Pa.; Hosletter Co, 1897.

Hunter, Beatrice. *Fermented Foods and Beverages*. New Canaan, Conn.: Keats Publishing,1973.

Hutchinson, Ruth and Adams, Ruth. *Every Day's a Holiday*. New York: Harper & Brothers, 1951.

Jagendorf, M.A. *Folk Wines, Cordials & Brandies*. New York: Vanguard Press, 1963.

Kieckhefer, Richard. *Magic in the Middle Ages*. Melbourne: Cambrige University Press, 1989.

Long, Cheryl. *Classic Liqueurs*. Lake Oswego: Culinary Arts, 1990.

Lorie, Peter. *Superstitions*. New York: Simon & Schuster, 1992.

Lowe, Carl. *Juice Power*. New York: Berkley Books, 1992.

Luce, Henry R. *Beverages*. Alexandria, Va.: Time Life Books, 1982.

MacNicol, Mary. *Flower Cookery*. New York: Fleet Press,1967.

Magnall, Richmal. *Historical and Miscellaneous Questions*. London: Longman, Brown, Green and Longman, 1850.

Mares, William. *Making Beer*. New York: Alfred A. Knopf Co., 1992.

Murray, Keith. *Ancient Rites & Ceremonies*. Toronto: Tudor Press, 1980.

Murray, Michael T. *The Healing Power of Herbs*. Rocklin: Prima Publishing, 1992.

Olney, Bruce. *Liqueurs, Aperitifs and Fortified Wines*. London: Mills & Boon LTD, 1972.

Opie, Iona and Tatem, Moria. *Dictionary of Superstitions*. New York: Oxford University Press, 1989.

Palaiseul, Jean. *Grandmother's Secrets*. New York: G.P. Putnam's Sons, 1974.

Paulsen, Kathryn. *The Complete Book of Magic &
WitchCraft*. New York: Signet Books, 1970.

Plat, Hugh. *Delights for Ladies*. London: Humfrey
Lownes, 1602.

Ryall, Rhiannon. *West Country Wicca*. Custer, Ariz.: Phoe
nix Publishing, 1989.

Schapira, Joel, David and Karl. *The Book of Coffee and
Tea*. New York: St. Martins Press, 1906.

Singer, Charles J. *Early English Magic and Medicine.*
London: British Academy, 1920.

Skinner, Charles M. *Myths and Legends of Flowers, Trees,
Fruits and Plants*. Philadelphia, Pa.: Lippincott, 1925.

Tchudi, Stephen N. *Soda Poppery*. New York: Charles
Scribner Sons, 1942.

Telesco, Patricia. *Folkways*. St. Paul, Minn.:
Llewellyn Publications, 1994.

————. *A Victorian Flower Oracle*. St. Paul, Minn.:
Llewellyn Publications, 1994.

————. *A Victorian Grimoire*. St. Paul, Minn.:
Llewellyn Publications, 1992.

Tillona, P. *Feast of Flowers*. New York: Funk & Wagnall,
1969.

Turner, B.C.A.. *Fruit Wines*. London: Mills & Boon LTD,
1973.

Urdag, Geore. *The Squib Ancient Pharmacy*. New York:
Squibb and Sons, 1940.

Walker, Barbara. *Women's Dictionary of Sacred Symbols
and Objects*. San Francisco, Calif.: Harper Row, 1988.

Webster's Universal Unabridged Dictionary. New York:
World Syndicate Publishing, 1937.

Wheelwrite, Edith Grey. *Medicinal Plant and their
History*. New York: Dover Publications, 1974.

Whiteside, Lorraine. *Fresh Fruit Drinks*. New York: Thorsons Publishers, 1984.

Williams, Judith. *Judes Home Herbal*. St. Paul, Minn.: Llewellyn Publications, 1992.

Woodward, Nancy Hyden. *Teas of the World*. New York: Macmillan Publishing Company, 1980.

Younger, William. *Gods, Men & Wine*. Cleveland, Ohio: World Publishing, 1966.

Index

About the Author

Patricia Telesco, a.k.a. Marian Singer, is the mother of three, wife, chief human to five pets, and a full-time professional author with numerous books on the market. These include the best selling *Goddess in my Pocket (Harper SanFrancisco, 1998)*, *How to be a Wicked Witch (Fireside, 2001)*, *Kitchen Witch's Cookbook (Llewellyn Publications, 1998)*, *Charmed Life (New Page Books, 2001)* and other diverse titles, each of which represents a different area of spiritual interest for her and her readers.

Trish travels minimally twice a month to give lectures and workshops around the country. She (or her writing) has appeared on several television segments including *Sightings* on mulicultural divination systems and *National Geographic Today—Solstice Celebrations*. Additionally, Trish hosts metaphysical cruises (*www.pagantravel.net*), and maintains a strong, visible presence in metaphysical journals and on the internet through popular sites such as *www.witchvox.com*, her interactive home page located at *www.loresinger.com*, and Yahoo club *www.groups.yahoo.com/groups/folkmagicwithtrishtelesco*, and various appearances on Internet chats and BBS boards.

Trish considers herself a down-to-earth Kitchen Witch whose love of folklore and worldwide customs flavor every word she writes. Her passions include gourmet cooking and gardening, and her strongest ethical guidelines are honor, respect, and gratitude in all things.

Notes